RUSSELL'S STANDARD FASHIONS

1915–1919

EDITED BY

Phillip Livoni

DOVER PUBLICATIONS, INC.

Mineola, New York

ACKNOWLEDGMENTS

I am most grateful to Helena Allen for her love of the English language and for her generosity in sharing her time and expertise with me. Special thanks go to Satch LaValley for his kindhearted and unselfish loan of primary resource materials and his shared passion for historic costumes. My deepest appreciation goes to my wife, Linda, for her unparalleled support and encouragement.

Bibliographical Note

Russell's Standard Fashions, 1915–1919 is a new work, first published by Dover Publications, Inc., in 1996.

Library of Congress Cataloging-in-Publication Data

Russell's Standard Fashions, 1915–1919 / edited by Phil Livoni.
      p.   cm.
  A republication of the catalog of the Standard Fashion Company's dressmaking patterns originally published 1915–1919 by Russell's Department Store.
  Includes bibliographical references.
  ISBN 0-486-29122-7 (pbk.)
  1. Dressmaking—United States—Patterns—History—20th century. 2. Costume—United States—History—20th century. 3. Fashion—United States—History—20th Century. I. Livoni, Phil. II. Russell's Department Store (Pomona, Calif.) III. Standard Fashion Company.
TT556.R87 1996
746.9'2'097309041—dc20   96-10939
                                                          CIP

Manufactured in the United States of America
Dover Publications, Inc., 31 East 2nd Street, Mineola, N.Y. 11501

RUSSELL'S STANDARD FASHIONS

The Period

The decade of the 1910s is one of the most difficult, yet fascinating, periods for fashion historians to understand. Fashion seldom deviates from the constant, paced ebb and flow of stylistic change. Because of the enormous upheaval created by the Great War (1914–18), this natural flow was stopped abruptly. Paris was the central and vital source for fashion news and inspiration, and for a short period at the outbreak of the war the famous couture houses closed their doors. Though the French textile industry was soon back on its feet, it necessarily took back seat to the nation's focus on its German border. In the turmoil, fashion styles changed with unprecedented speed. It is precisely this transition of monumental change that is so difficult to document. This republication of *Standard Fashions* chronicles the period from November 1915 to January 1919, making it possible to trace fashion's quickened pace through the war years.

The Standard Fashion Company began making paper dressmaking patterns in the 1890s. Their popular publication *Standard Quarterly* advertised the latest patterns, providing nationwide access to Paris fashions. It also published a monthly catalogue, *Standard Fashions,* which could be imprinted with the name of the store distributing it. It is a selection of pages from *Standard Fashions* as distributed by Russell's (see below) that forms the basis of this volume. The patterns in *Standard Fashions* parallel those of such leading periodicals as *The Ladies' Home Journal, The Delineator, Woman's Home Companion, Pictorial Review* and *McCall's,* all of which trailed the trendier *Harper's Bazar* pattern styles by approximately three months and *Vogue* patterns by at least six months to a year. This close similarity confirms that *Standard Fashions* represented what American women *really* wore. The company also published a monthly pattern magazine, *The Designer,* for 75 cents yearly. An advertisement in *The Ladies' Home Journal* in November 1916 consists of a beautifully illustrated spread reminding readers that "Standard Patterns are on sale at the best stores everywhere."

One of those stores was Russell's in Pomona, California, 32 miles east of Los Angeles. This booming southern California town was founded in 1875 when the railroads first came through. In 1916, the population of Pomona was 15,785. The Chamber of Commerce boasted they had "the largest section of orange and lemon groves in Southern California, four banks, two live [sic] daily newspapers, 5,000 telephones, 25 churches, and no saloons." The Chamber attempted to assuage even the remotest of fears as they concluded, "No fleas; no vermin; no mosquitos; no malaria." Russell's announced in both local papers on February 12, 1915, "People of Pomona Valley, we will open our doors for business on Friday morning." They assured "Lowest possible prices, quality considered." In November 1915, Russell's sent out its first *Standard Fashions* catalogue with the following endorsement: "We always consider long and carefully before adopting or endorsing any particular line of merchandise, a fact which adds weight to our decision to sell Standard Patterns, and to our unqualified endorsement of them." They listed the reasons that influenced them as advanced style and variety, correct measurements, superiority of fit, simplicity of construction, economy of materials and their practical styles. They concluded with an invitation to "visit our Pattern Department at the earliest possible date in order to acquaint yourself with the remarkable possibilities of Standard Patterns."

The typical woman who patronized Russell's Department Store during the mid-teens was decidedly different from the woman of the 1990s and lived in an entirely different society. One of the most accurate means of gaining a clear picture of the woman who wore the clothes illustrated in this book is by studying her image as it was reflected by the articles that appeared in the many ladies' magazines of the period.

A sampling of the topics includes: literary reviews and promotions, historical features, music techniques, the whole realm of the culinary arts, Bible stories, birth control, travel, America's unending fascination with European royalty, and suffrage news. "Regulation of the household" was high on the list of priorities. How successfully a woman decorated her home, maintained her household budget, managed her servant(s), canned her homegrown fruits and vegetables, provided sanitary and fresh linens and clothing for her family, nurtured her children and built their intellectual and spiritual character were the measure of her importance to society. A large portion of the articles were essays devoted to child rearing, such as, "Teach Your Child the Value of Money" and "Managing Boys." Among other articles, advanced topics such as ecology appeared. One was entitled, "The Fast-Dwindling Timber Supply" (logging was the nation's fourth largest industry), claiming that the United States' lumber supply would be entirely depleted by the 1930s.[1]

Matters of etiquette were gravely important. In the days of class democratization and mail-order catalogues, when everyone had nearly equal opportunity to dress alike and class distinction was on the decline, one firmly planted bastion of old society was proper etiquette. One must know the way to "call" properly, the difference between an oyster fork and an olive fork, whether to take a lady's hand gloved or ungloved, the difference between dressing for a formal luncheon versus an informal luncheon, the proper stages of mourning, and innumerable other things.

Sports articles were a regular feature. There were usually great societal wars waged through the decades as women broke into the world of sports that had always belonged to men. Women's involvement in sports began in the 1860s with the exhilarating games of croquet and archery. The next great attempts were roller-skating and ice-skating in the 1870s, followed by tennis in the 1880s, played in tightly basqued and bustled full-length dresses. In the 1880s women took to hunting. Though the first bicycling began in the 1860s, persistent female cyclists did not come into their own until the tricycling craze hit in the 1880s. Woman had conquered bicycling by the mid-1890s. Women were finally admitted on the golf links in the 1890s. Swimming and canoeing followed in the first decade of the twentieth century. These activities soon developed new modes of specialty clothing, often borrowing motifs and styling details from established male sports clothing.

Newly developing technologies often challenged the reader to assimilate them into their lives. Though the automobile was hardly new (not with Henry Ford selling more than five million to the American public between 1910 and 1915), this was, however, the period when it became accepted that women drove as frequently as men. Articles regularly poured forth with information ranging from the correct dress for "motoring" (and how to make it), the desirable features and costs of buying an "auto" and even how to maintain it.

The many facets of handiwork and fashion took up probably the single largest section of ladies' periodicals. Detailed instructions taught women how to adorn all manners of runners, tablecloths, doilies and items of clothing with padded-stitch embroidery, cut-work, bobbin laces, needle laces, Battenburg-lace and tape-lace insertions, crochet and knit laces, silk appliqué and innumerable other forms of fine handiwork. Several regular columns expounded on the exacting skills of making one's own tailored suits. Two hundred years earlier, American women had learned handiwork skills more as a matter of survival, spinning their own yarns and threads and weaving their own cloth. By the turn of the twentieth century, long after the effects of the Industrial Revolution produced endless supplies of quality fabrics, handiwork skills were still essential for the woman who wished to have society's nod of approval. The magazines churned out article after article on "Filet Crochet for Underwear," "Embroideries for Little Folks," "Chic Hats Gay with Ribbon and Wings," "All that is New and Smart in Lingerie and Negligees," "Six Hats from 10-cent Foundations," "Fashion for Elderly Women [over 50]" and the ever-present discussion of "The Latest Sleeve."

Although America did not declare war until April 6, 1917, the European front had been foremost on the minds of Americans since the war began in 1914. The journals charged their fellow women, "Every American woman is in business to-day. She is a partner in the greatest business enterprise which the nation has ever undertaken: the business of waging war for democracy."[2] A more sobering article stated, "We have had our time for the dance and the dinner and the pretty frock. But that time is over."[3]

As the nation became more and more involved in the war, and as more men were shipped overseas, women were advised they might need to fill the nation's employment slots that men had filled before the war. Bold headlines in *Pictorial Review,* December 1918, announced, "Bigger Salaries for Women . . . Besides the normal demand, places left by men gone to the war have opened thousands of splendid business positions for which women can easily qualify."[4] Articles appeared with photographs of women transplanted into traditionally male jobs. There were women working in munitions factories, driving heavy farm equipment or taxicabs, wearing postal uniforms, and opening barber shops. No gender wars were fought this time as women stepped into men's shoes. It was done with extreme gravity and devotion to country and God. It is doubtful that before the war anyone could conceive of the impact these new occupations would have on women's clothing. As women joined new professions with new responsibilities and corresponding new activities, their clothing adapted. Skirts were actually occasionally bifurcated into long, loose-fitting trousers. These were simple garments, simply trimmed. During the war women were continuously advised to be economical and practical. "Do not misread the word Economy. It does not mean do not buy or do not make clothes, but make and buy sensible ones."[5] The American woman was expected to conserve as even the government "had asked the leading dressmakers to use as little wool as possible in their new spring clothes, to save labor, . . . and to do away with luxurious trimmings and brilliant colors, which are not in harmony with war times."[6]

Standard Fashions clearly documents the fact that women applied the simplicity and practicality they were encouraged to adopt. The earlier fashion plates—1915 and 1916—display the sunset of Edwardian froufrou. The final plates of 1919 demonstrate a markedly relaxed silhouette. A quick comparison of waistlines during this period reveals the loosening and/or discarding of the obligatory corset. Women, literally and figuratively, needed more freedom of movement to function in their new roles.

The Fashions

Foundation garments change as rapidly as outer garments and are, in fact, what support the "latest" silhouette. The term "brassiere" first appeared in 1907. Yet the concept was still novel in 1915. Previously, corsets not only nipped in, lengthened, shortened, raised, or lowered the waist, but also supported the bust. In the early teens, corsets had quite long skirts narrowing the hips more than reducing the waist. For the first time in a century, the top of the corset shortened, and there was need for a new garment to take its place to support the bust. Figure 8558, page 5, describes a pattern for a "ladies' brassiere or corset cover." This garment would function as a corset cover when worn over a traditional bust-supporting corset or could double as a brassiere or "bandeau" when worn under the newer low-topped corsets.

A variety of necklines was offered during the teens. In 1909, the high Edwardian collars began coming down for ladies' day wear. Between 1911 and 1921 ladies' dresses and blouses could have high collars in varying styles, although open rounded and V necklines increased in popularity throughout the decade. Sailor collars and convertible collars were also quite trendy (pp. 22, 67, 100, 144).

In 1910, the fashionable silhouette was straight and slender—no fullness in the sleeves or the ankle-length skirts. Waistlines had begun rising in 1907, becoming the Empire waistline of the first half of the 1910s. This pencil-slim silhouette at the beginning of the teens began changing in late 1913 with an emphasis on fullness at the knee level. There was no end to the creative manner in which pleats, drapes, puffs and tucks were used to achieve the latest hobble-skirt look. Another version had a long, straight underskirt with a flared, knee-length overskirt. This became the most popular way to create the desired silhouette. By late 1915, the overskirt had flared significantly and lengthened to just above the ankle. Most dresses dropped the slim underskirt entirely, making the transition to the new hourglass silhouette (p. 15).

The width of the new skirts blossomed throughout 1916. In November 1915, hem widths were already 1¾ to 2¼ yards in circumference. By mid-1916 they were peaking at 3 to 3¾ yards. Fashion editors in the spring of 1916 proclaimed: "We had bouffant fashions this past fall. Now for spring, just add buoyant to the bouffant, and you'll get the effect of the new fashions in a nutshell."[7] Creative versions of these full skirts included additional overskirts and flying panels in sundry cuts and shapes, each with its own catchy name. The Russell catalogues illustrate numerous "apron tunics" and "side tunics" which were "used freely to increase the pretty, full effect of skirts"[8] (fig. 8728, p. 22; fig. 8714/15, p. 25).

It had been a decade since there was any appreciable fullness in skirts. And although it was not uncommon for Edwardian skirts of 1905 to have hemlines of eight yards, the silhouette was nevertheless form-fitting over the hips. The mid-teens dirndl-type skirts conjured up many historical fashion images, and fashion arbiters freely alluded to them. There were frequent references to the period from the 1830s to the 1880s. "The new fashions [feature] the swaying effect of the old-time hoop and the audacity of the old-time bustle."[9] Several ladies' magazines ran articles illustrating the revived bustle, which looked like figure 8708/09, page 23, and figure 1261, page 102. Another way to obtain the expansive silhouette was the use of eighteenth-century "bouffant Watteau draperies at each side"[10] (fig. 8593, p. 24; fig. 8711, p. 25; fig. 9046/47, p. 37).

Tailored suits were a staple of every woman's wardrobe. In addition to being practical for work and travel, they were usually cut conservatively and could be worn for years without falling out of style. One article discussing the latest suits stated, "As it happens every year, spring fashions of 1916 show certain new features which make the season's clothes distinctive.... Most noteworthy among them are—in the tailored suit—the semi-fitted jacket with the rippling godet sides."[11] This description matches the jacket shown in figure 8722, page 23. Another notable feature of the suits of 1916 was the nearly scandalous short hemline that caused much discussion. Many eyebrows were raised as suits were worn with hemlines as high as eight inches above the ground![12] Convertible collars were popular on coats and suits. In the spring of 1916, *Woman's Home Companion* illustrated a coat similar to the ones on page 91, with one of these versatile new collars. It could be worn open forming a V neck, closed at the base of the neck, or worn very high forming the new "chin-chin" collar.[13]

Skirts began deflating in the spring of 1917. Oversized, stand-away pockets became a focal point as a vestige to the previous voluminous skirts (p. 81). Also, the "barrel" skirt became popular. In August 1917, *Vogue* stated, "The 'barrel' silhouette, which was so extensively shown in the spring, is still seen this season, though in moderation."[14] The barrel skirt was accomplished by slightly lengthening the top sides of the still full skirt, thereby caving the flared portion in (fig. 9563/64, p. 69; figs. 9578 and 9566, p. 70). A second way to reduce skirt width was to gather a skirt hem to a narrow or wide band of fabric, often contrasting in color (figs. 9566 and 9558/59, p. 68; fig. 9863, p. 81). Yet another clever method to slim the silhouette was to gather the hem onto a shorter narrow underskirt, thereby producing the Turkish hem (figs. 9601-A and 9593/94, p. 75). Fashion critics applauded the simplicity of the newer dresses as they were "easy to get into," "sensible" and yet "stylish." With the problem of how to achieve the latest skirt silhouette solved, the question immediately turned to the bothersome issue of where to place the waistline.

"The problem of where to place the elusive waist-line appears to be successfully settled, for the time being at least, . . . [at the] normal waist-line." So suggested *Harper's Bazar* in 1916, rather prematurely.[15] Actually, for several years during the mid-teens, Fashion was clearly *undecided* about the placement of the waistline. For the first time in fashion history, Empire waistlines, natural waistlines and dropped waistlines coexisted side by side, making it one of the more difficult periods for fashion historians to document. One of the safest options was the use of the "girdle," a loosely draped, wide, sash-like belt gathered across the midriff. The upper edge rested just below the bust, saluting the established Empire waistline; the slightly fitted middle portion defined the natural waist-line; the bottom edge forecast the increasingly popular dropped waist that would entirely dominate by 1921 (fig. 9253/54, p. 46; figs. 9412 and 9253, p. 59; fig. 9566, p. 68; fig. 9861, p. 78).

High waistlines inevitably engendered images of the Empire style, created at the beginning of the nineteenth century during Napoleon's reign. *Standard Fashion* made frequent reference to this period, especially as the silhouette slimmed in 1917 and 1918. Empire dresses were extremely simple designs with plain, long skirts lightly gathered at an uncommonly high waistline (figs. 9226 and 9247, p. 46; fig. 9226, p. 47; fig. 9278, p. 54; fig. 9262, p. 56; both figs. 1055, p. 96; fig. 1277-A, p. 107). Empire coats had the same design lines, some with Regency capes (fig. 9153, p. 37; fig. 9153, p. 40; fig. 1505, p. 122). Another remake from the period was the redingote. Fashionable for women from the 1780s on, it was originally adapted from the man's greatcoat which was used throughout the eighteenth century. It was a long-sleeved, fitted coat, often double-breasted. The skirt portion was open from the center front down and was sewn to a high waistline (fig. 9295, p. 50; figs. 9315 and 9295, p. 58; fig. 9423, p. 60).

Several areas of clothing promoted the dropped-waist look. The vast majority of jackets and coats featured in *Standard Fashions* depict a notably loose, lowered waistline accentuated by a deep belt or knotted sash (pp. 21, 65, 91). Children's clothing also advanced the comfortable new waistline. Several costume historians attribute this source as the chief inspiration for the long-waisted style. For the previous three decades, children's clothing had been marked by loose-fitting, often drop-waisted, garments that allowed for greater mobility. All the pages in these catalogues illustrating children's clothing—boys' or girls'—feature such garments (pp. 20, 66, 138).

The loosely fitted and longer-waisted Russian blouse was commonly used for sports clothing around 1910. It gained in popularity as the decade progressed, even becoming favorable for afternoon wear.[16] *McCall's* Paris correspondent eagerly reported to American readers, "I must tell you about the great vogue for the Russian, or slip-on blouses. They are sometimes called basque-blouses, too. Their name is legion, their variety endless, and above all, they are thoroughly fascinating. All of them are characterized by peplums worn over the skirt, some finely pleated and others gathered. They are worn with separate skirts of satin and velvet . . . and are of sheerest materials, except when used for sports."[17] The craze soon led to "Russian" dresses and "Russian" coats, too (fig. 9076, p. 36; fig. 9239, p. 41; figs. 9274 and 9269, p. 51; fig. 9269, p. 54; fig. 9382, p. 65). By 1918, these blouses had become so common in women's wardrobes that they were no longer referred to as Russian blouses by the pattern companies, but simply ladies' blouses.

As women reveled in this refreshingly comfortable new style, designers searched through fashion history to the Middle Ages. The Moyen Age (as it is called in French) was a period when the majority of ladies' wear consisted of simple, long unfitted robes with sashes belted around the waist. When *Standard Fashions* first mentioned the "Moyen-Age" style, it was referring to the least-fitted, low-waisted dresses and coats that it produced (fig. 8089, p. 7; fig. 9307, p. 52). By late 1917 through the end of the decade, "Moyen-Age" referred to dresses that were truly unwaisted, chemise-style garments which were slightly belted and "loose enough to slip over the head" (fig. 1020, p. 92; fig. 1398, p. 112; fig. 1398, p. 116). The catchiness of this new phrase wore off, but the freedom of movement and comfort women experienced were here to stay. The Moyen-Age–style dresses increased in popularity to become the chemise dress of the 1920s. In 1918 and 1919 they were referred to as "slip-on" dresses (fig. 1417, p. 113; fig. 1555, p. 133; fig. 1549, p. 134; figs. 1764 and 1780, p. 142; fig. 1783, p. 143; figs. 1352 and 1657, p. 147).

In the latter half of 1917, *Vogue* accurately predicted, "We have worn the straight frock for months, and we shall doubtless wear it for months to come. The pocket has disappeared from the latest version of the straight frock, and now the rumor is that the belt is to follow the pocket into oblivion."[18] *Vogue* was, of course, absolutely right. The last stage in the transition towards the unfitted "straight frock" was the addition of unfitted, flowing panels to the already popular slip-on dresses. In December 1918, *Pictorial Review* featured several "panel blouses."[19] They were ever so slightly fitted bodices with swinging fabric panels attached to the dropped waist. They could be positioned at the sides, front or back (fig. 1721, p. 142; fig. 1789, p. 146). Also pictured are several versions of the "apron panel dresses to be slipped over the head," which incorporated unbelted flying panels onto a loosely fitted underdress, allowing narrow glimpses of the lightly defined waistline between the panels (figs. 1783 and 1787, p. 143; fig. 1750, p. 144).

Defined waistlines had been one of the key elements of the nineteenth-century woman's definition of femininity. In fact, for the previous century, women not only accented their waistlines, but they happily delineated them further by corseting them to remove additional inches of circumference. Any restriction of movement or discomfort was overwhelmingly outweighed by the satisfaction they gained as they fit neatly into their contemporary definition of "womanhood." The early-twentieth-century American woman lived in a different world with entirely different demands. Leaving all vestiges of Victorian prudery behind, she no longer derived her sense of security from her tightly cinched waistline but cheerfully reveled in each and every new freedom she earned.

Notes

1. *Ladies' Home Journal,* October 1908, p. 45.
2. *Ladies' Home Journal,* February 1918, p. 34.
3. *Ladies' Home Journal,* June 1917, p. 7.
4. *Pictorial Review,* December 1918, p. 86.
5. *Ladies' Home Journal,* February 1918, p. 101.
6. Ibid.
7. *Woman's Home Companion,* March 1916, p. 52.
8. *Russell's,* February 1916, p. 3.
9. *Woman's Home Companion,* March 1916, p. 52.
10. Ibid., p. 71.
11. Ibid., p. 56.
12. Ibid., p. 52.
13. Ibid., p. 46.
14. *Vogue,* August 15, 1917, p. 68.
15. *Harper's Bazar,* March 1916, p. 82.
16. *Woman's Home Companion,* August 1916, p. 26. Describes the Russian blouse as "Quite the newest fad this summer. It is fitted at a low waistline with an outside belt."
17. *McCall's,* January 1917, p. 29.
18. *Vogue,* August 1917, p. 37.
19. *Pictorial Review,* December 1918, pp. 72–75.

A SEASON OF SMART ONE-PIECE FROCKS,

Guimpe—8284   Overblouse—8524
Skirt—8162

Blouse—8525
Skirt—8526

Blouse—8511
Skirt—8512

8518

8284—8524—8162

8525—26

8518

8511—12

8552

8552

8511—LADIES' BLOUSE. 7 sizes, 32 to 44 inches bust. **8512**—LADIES' SKIRT. Lower edge with plaits drawn out about 3 yards. 7 sizes, 22 to 34 waist, to 36 to 49½ hip. As on figure, the medium size requires 2¼ yards of 40-inch crêpe de Chine for blouse, with ⅜ yard of 27-inch contrasting crêpe de Chine for pipings, ⅝ yard of 18-inch net for standing collar and to face chemisette, and 3¾ yards of 44-inch novelty cloth will be required for skirt. PRICE, **15** CENTS EACH.

8552—LADIES' DRESS: High or Open Neck; Long or Short One-Seam Sleeves; Bolero; Dart-Fitted Lining; High Waistline; Two-Piece Shirred Skirt; Clearing or Shorter Length. For the Braiding design illustrated on figure use Standard transfer pattern 10301. Lower edge about 2¼ yards. The pattern is cut in 7 sizes from 32 to 44 inches bust measure. As illustrated on figure, the medium size will require 5⅛ yards of 36-inch satin, with ¾ yard of 18-inch lace for chemisette. PRICE, **15** CENTS.

8524—LADIES' OVERBLOUSE. 8 sizes, 32 to 46 bust. **8284**—LADIES' GUIMPE. 9 sizes, 32 to 48 bust. **8162**—LADIES' SKIRT. Lower edge about 2½ yards. 9 sizes, 22 to 38 waist, to 36 to 54 hip. As on figure, the medium size requires 2¼ yards of 36-inch plain taffeta, with ¾ yard of 24-inch white silk, 1½ yards of 40-inch lace, and 3⅜ yards of 36-inch striped taffeta for skirt. PRICE, **15** CTS. EACH.

8525—LADIES' BLOUSE. 7 sizes, 32 to 44 inches bust. **8526**—LADIES' FOUR-PIECE PLAITED SKIRT. Lower edge with plaits drawn out about 3½ yards. 9 sizes, 22 to 38 inches waist, to 36 to 54 inches hip. As on figure, the medium size requires 6 yards of 44-inch gabardine, with ⅝ yard of 36-inch satin for collar, cuffs and vest, and ⅝ yard of 18-inch net will be needed for chemisette. PRICE, **15** CTS. EACH.

8518—LADIES' PRINCESS DRESS: Back Extending Over the Shoulders to Form a Yoke; Closed to the Neck or Rolled Open; Long Dart-Fitted or Short Sleeves; Lower edge about 2¼ yards. 6 sizes, 32 to 42 inches bust measure. As illustrated on figure, the medium size will require 5¼ yards of 36-inch material, with ½ yard of 20-inch contrasting material for collar and 2⅜ yards of fur banding. **15** CTS.

LATEST DESIGNS

In the new designs, blouses, for the most part, are tucked or gathered, yet they find strong rivals in the fitted bodices, some types of which appear with draped over-blouses. Tailored skirts show no end of fancy outlines in the pockets and belts which they feature.

Blouse **8535**
Skirt **8536**

Bodice **8549**
Skirt **8550**

Blouse **8539**
Skirt **8540**

Blouse **8544**
Skirt **8545**

Blouse **8520**
Skirt **8521**

8535—LADIES' BLOUSE: Closed to the Neck or Rolled Open; Long or Short One-Seam Sleeves. (May be Attached to a Skirt or Worn Separately.) The pattern is cut in 8 sizes from 32 to 46 inches bust measure. **8536**—LADIES' FIVE-GORED SKIRT: Slightly High Waistline; Jumper, Pockets and Belt which may be Omitted; Clearing or Shorter Length. Lower edge with plaits drawn out about 2¾ yards. The pattern is cut in 9 sizes from 22 to 38 inches waist measure, corresponding to 36 to 54 inches hip measure. As illustrated on figure, the medium size will require 2 yards of 40-inch crêpe de Chine for blouse with 3 yards of 44-inch cheviot for skirt, and 5⅓ yards of braid to trim. A dainty tucked blouse and tailored skirt. **15 CTS. EACH.**

8549—LADIES' BODICE: Draped Over-blouse, Closed at the Left Side; Dart-Fitted Lining in High or Open Neck and with Long Dart-Fitted or Short Sleeves. 7 sizes, 32 to 44 inches bust measure. **8550**—LADIES' TWO-PIECE SKIRT: Slightly High Waistline; Four-Piece Belt in High Waistline and Suspenders which may be Omitted; Clearing or Shorter Length. Lower edge about 3 yards. 5 sizes from 22 to 30 inches waist measure, corresponding to 36 to 44½ inches hip measure. As illustrated on figure, the medium size will require 4⅜ yards of 40-inch satin, 1⅜ yards of 36-inch crêpe for sleeves, collar and to face lining ⅝ yards of 18-inch all-over lace, and ¾ yard of 36-inch lining. **15 CENTS EACH.**

8539—LADIES' BLOUSE: Closed to the Neck or Rolled Open. (May be Attached to a Skirt or Worn Separately.) 8 sizes, 32 to 46 inches bust measure. **8540**—LADIES' THREE OR FOUR PIECE SKIRT: Slightly High or Regulation Waistline; (May be Attached to a Blouse or Worn Separately.) Lower edge about 2¾ yards. 9 sizes, 22 to 38 inches waist measure, corresponding to 36 to 54 inches hip measure. As illustrated on figure, the medium size will require 1⅞ yards of 40-inch crêpe for blouse, and 2⅓ yards of 50-inch cloth for skirt. PRICE, **15 CENTS EACH.**

8544—LADIES' BLOUSE: High or Open Neck; Long One-Seam Gathered Sleeves or Short Sleeves. 7 sizes, 32 to 44 inches bust measure. **8545**—LA-DIES' EIGHT-GORED SKIRT: Slightly High Waistline, with Three-Piece Yoke-Belt or Regulation Waistline. Lower edge with plaits drawn out about 2¾ yards. 9 sizes, 22 to 38 inches waist measure, corresponding to 36 to 54 inches hip measure. As illustrated on figure, the medium size will require 1¼ yards of 50-inch chiffon cloth with 2 yards of 9-inch lace flouncing and 2¼ yards of 54-inch gabardine. **15 CTS. EACH.**

8520—LADIES' BLOUSE: Long Dart-Fitted or Short Sleeves; Three-Piece Peplum. 9 sizes, 32 to 48 inches bust measure. **8521**—LADIES' THREE-PIECE SKIRT: One-Piece Straight Plaited Section at Each Side. Lower edge with plaits drawn out about 3⅓ yards. 7 sizes, 22 to 34 inches waist measure, corresponding to 36 to 49½ inches hip measure. As illustrated on figure, the medium size will require 6½ yards of 36-inch faille, with ⅞ yard of 36-inch satin for collar, belt and cuffs, 4½ yards of silk braid and ⅞ yard of 18-inch all-over lace. PRICE, **15 CENTS EACH.**

8535—36

8549—50

8539—40

8544—45

8520—21

SMART NEW MODELS

A great deal of interest is being shown in the smart, one-piece dress known as the redingote. It hangs directly from the shoulders or from a yoke, and is belted loosely at the waistline in one of the favored designs. This is one of the most popular styles this season.

8509

8562-63

8509

8530-31

8559

8515-16

8509

Blouse—8562 Skirt—8563

8559

Bodice—8530 Skirt—8531

Blouse—8515
Skirt—8516

8509—LADIES' DRESS : High or Open Neck; Long Sleeves in Two Styles at the Wrist or Short Puff Sleeves; One-Piece Straight Skirt Gathered or Gauged at the Waistline; Clearing or Shorter Length. Lower edge about 3½ yards. The pattern is cut in 5 sizes from 32 to 40 inches bust measure. As illustrated on figure, the 36-inch size will require 6 yards of 40-inch voile, with ¾ yard of 36-inch white organdy and 1½ yards of black ribbon for tie. One of the new quaint styles is this design with its fitted bodice, gathered skirt and large cape collar. PRICE, **15** CENTS.

8562—LADIES' BLOUSE: Closed to the Neck or Rolled Open; Long or Short One-Seam Sleeves. 7 sizes, 32 to 44 inches bust. **8563—LADIES' SIX-PIECE BOX-PLAITED SKIRT:** Slightly High Waistline; Plaits Stitched to Yoke or Flounce Depth; Belt which may be Omitted; Clearing or Shorter Length. Lower edge with plaits drawn out about 2⅞ yards. 8 sizes, 22 to 36 inches waist to 36 to 52 inches hip. As illustrated on figure, the medium size will require 2 yards of 36-inch taffeta for blouse, with 3⅜ yards of 44-inch checked suiting for skirt. PRICE, **15** CENTS EACH.

8530 — LADIES' DRAPED BODICE: Long Dart Fitted or Short Sleeves; Dart-Fitted Lining; One-Piece Peplum. 6 sizes, 32 to 42 inches bust. **8531 — LADIES' SKIRT:** Two or Three Piece Upper Part; Two or Three Piece Circular Lower Part. Lower edge about 3 yards. 7 sizes, 22 to 34 inches waist, to 36 to 49½ inches hip. As illustrated on figure, the medium size will require 5 yards of 36-inch taffeta, with ½ yard of 36-inch striped silk for vest, ⅝ yard of 18-inch all-over for vest and collar and ⅞ yards of 36-inch lining material. PRICE, **15** CENTS EACH.

8559—LADIES' DRESS: Blouse in One with Skirt or Tunic; Back Extending Over the Shoulders to Form a Yoke; Closed to the Neck or Rolled Open; Long or Three-Quarter Length Dart-Fitted Sleeves with or without the Puff; Separate Two-Piece Foundation Skirt; Clearing or Shorter Length. Lower edge of foundation skirt about 1¾ yards. Lower edge of skirt about 2⅜ yards. The pattern is cut in 6 sizes from 32 to 42 inches bust measure. As illustrated on figure, the 36-inch size will require 4¼ yards of 50-inch material, with ½ yard of 36-inch checked silk for collar and belt. This smart dress known as the redingote, will be excellent in serge, gabardine, broadcloth, wool poplin, faille, taffeta or satin. PRICE, **15** CENTS.

8515—LADIES' BLOUSE: Closed to Neck or Rolled Open; Long or Short One-Seam Sleeves. The pattern is cut in 9 sizes from 32 to 48 inches bust measure. **8516—LADIES' SKIRT:** Slightly High or Regulation Waistline; Two-Piece Yoke; Six-Piece Box-Plaited Lower Part Attached Under a Tuck Edge; Clearing or Shorter Length. Lower edge with plaits drawn out about 3 yards. The pattern is cut in 7 sizes from 22 to 34 inches waist measure, corresponding to 36 to 49½ inches hip measure. As illustrated on figure, the medium size will require 2 yards of 36-inch silk for blouse, with ¾ yard of 36-inch contrasting silk for collar, tie and pipings and 3⅜ yards of 50-inch broadcloth for skirt. PRICE, **15** CENTS EACH.

Guimpe—8438
Skirt—8536

8523

Blouse—8520
Skirt—8526

8255

8515

8535

INDIVIDUAL STYLES FOR LARGE FIGURES

8438—LADIES' GUIMPE: Long **Dart-Fitted** or Flowing Sleeves. 9 sizes, **32 to 48** inches bust. **8536**—LADIES' FIVE-GORED SKIRT. Lower edge with plaits drawn out about 3 yards. 9 sizes, 22 to 38 inches waist to 36 to 54 inches hip. As on figure the 44-inch bust and 34-inch waist size requires 3½ yards of 27-inch silk for blouse and 3¼ yards of 54-inch cloth for over-blouse and skirt. **15 CENTS EACH.**

8523—LADIES' COAT: 52-Inch Length at the Back or 45 Inch Length at the Back; Three-Piece Lower Part Attached Under a Tuck Edge. 8 sizes, 32 to 46 inches bust measure. As on figure the 44-inch bust size requires with coat in 52-inch length 4⅞ yards of 50-inch cloth, with ½ yard of 54-inch fur cloth.   PRICE, **15** CENTS.

8520—LADIES' BLOUSE. 9 sizes, 32 to 48 inches bust. **8526**—LADIES' FOUR-PIECE PLAITED SKIRT. Lower edge with plaits drawn out about 3¾ yards. 9 sizes, 22 to 38 inches waist to 36 to 54 inches hip. As illustrated on figure the 44-inch bust and 34-inch waist size will require 7¼ yards of 36-inch faille, with 1⅛ yards of 36-inch satin, ⅞ yard of 18-inch lace. **15 CTS EACH.**

8255—LADIES' COAT: 24-Inch Length at the Back; Straight or Cutaway Outline; Notched or Shawl Collar; Long or Short Two-Seam Sleeves. 9 sizes, 32 to 48 inches bust measure. As illustrated on figure the 44-inch bust size will require 2½ yards of 50-inch gabardine, with ⅝ yard of 27-inch velvet for collar and cuffs.   PRICE, **15** CENTS.

8515—LADIES' BLOUSE: Closed to Neck or Rolled Open; Long or Short One-Seam Sleeves. (May be Attached to a Skirt or Worn Separately.) The pattern is cut in 9 sizes from 32 to 48 inches bust measure. As illustrated on figure the 44-inch bust size will require 2⅝ yards of 36-inch taffeta. China silk, pongee and satin may also be used for this blouse.   PRICE, **15** CENTS.

8535—LADIES' BLOUSE: Closed to the Neck or Rolled Open; Long or Short One-Seam Sleeves. (May be Attached to a Skirt or Worn Separately.) The pattern is cut in 8 sizes from 32 to 46 inches bust measure. As illustrated on figure the 44-inch bust size will require 2⅝ yards of 40-inch crêpe de Chine for blouse and ruffles. Tucks form the chief attraction of this blouse.   **15** CENTS.

8438—8536   8523   8520—26

8255   8515   8535

8537

8558

8434

8553

8513

8366

NEW UNDERWEAR AND HOUSE GARMENTS

8537—LADIES' DRESSING-SACK: in Two Lengths; High or Open Neck; Long or Short One-Seam Sleeves. The pattern is cut in 7 sizes, from 32 to 44 inches bust measure. As illustrated on figure, the medium size will require 3½ yards of 27-inch cotton crêpe, with ⅝ yard of 36-inch lawn for collar and frills, and 2½ yards of ribbon. **15 CENTS.**

8558—LADIES' BRASSIERE OR COR-SET COVER: Round Neck or Straight Outline Across the Top; Peplum which may be Omitted. For the embroidery design illustrated use Standard transfer pattern 10010. 9 sizes, 32 to 48 inches bust measure. As illustrated on figure, the medium size will require ⅞ yard of 36-inch long-cloth, with 3⅛ yards of ribbon to trim. **PRICE, 15 CENTS.**

8434—LADIES' DRESSING-SACK: Closed to the Neck or Rolled Open; Long Two-Seam Sleeves or One-Seam Flowing Sleeves. The pattern is cut in 9 sizes from 32 to 48 inches bust measure. As illustrated on figure, the medium size will require 3¾ yards of 27-inch eiderdown, with 5½ yards of ribbon for pipings and 4 ornaments. A practical and comfortable garment. **PRICE, 15 CTS.**

8553 — LADIES' COMBINATION: Slightly High Waistline; One-Piece Corset Cover and Envelope Drawers; Two Outlines at the lower edge. For embroidery design use Standard transfer No. 10198. 9 sizes, 32 to 48 inches bust measure. As illustrated on figure, the medium size will require 2⅛ yards of 36-inch nainsook. **PRICE, 15 CENTS.**

8513—LADIES' DRESS: Long Dart-Fitted or Short Sleeves; Two or Three Piece Skirt. Lower edge about 2½ yards. 9 sizes, 32 to 48 inches bust. As on figure, the medium size requires with three-piece skirt, 5½ yards of 32-inch percale, with ½ yard of 36-inch lawn for collar and cuffs, and ⅛ yard of 36-inch dark lawn for belt. Percale, galatea, gingham are suitable materials. **15 CTS.**

8366—LADIES' EMPIRE NEG-LIGEE: High or Open Neck; Long Sleeves in Two Styles at the Lower Edge, or Short Sleeves; Clearing or Shorter Length. Lower edge about 2¾ yards. The pattern is cut in 9 sizes from 32 to 48 inches bust measure. As illustrated on figure, the medium size will require 6¼ yards of 36-inch cashmere, with ⅞ yard of 22-inch silk for collar and cuffs. **15 CENTS.**

8537

8558

8434

8553   8513   8366

EVENING GOWNS AND A WRAP

Fitted bodices, plain or draped, with full skirts draped at the hips or knees or simply hanging free — here they are again, the styles of yesterday for the women of to-day!

8555 — LADIES' FITTED BODICE OR OVERBLOUSE. 7 sizes, 32 to 44 inches bust. **8556**— LADIES' TWO-PIECE SKIRT. Lower edge about 2 yards. 6 sizes, 22 to 32 inches waist measure, to 36 to 47 inches hip measure. As illustrated on figure, the medium size will require 3⅜ yards of 36-inch satin for bodice and skirt gores, with 3¾ yards of 42-inch chiffon for overskirt and frills and 10¾ yards of velvet ribbon. This style is being worn a great deal.
PRICE, **15** CENTS EACH.

Bodice—**8555**   Skirt—**8556**

8087

8543

Basque—**7935**   Skirt—**8117**

8285

| 8555–56 | 8087 | 8543 | 7935–8117 | 8285 |

8087—LADIES' DRESS. Lower edge about 4¾ yards. 7 sizes, 32 to 44 inches bust measure. As illustrated on figure, the 36-inch size will require 5⅜ yards of 36-inch taffeta, with 1 yard of 40-inch chiffon for bertha, short sleeves and frills and ¾ yard of 1-inch velvet ribbon will be needed for trimming. PRICE, **15** CENTS.

8543—LADIES' COAT: 50 or 45 Inch Length at the Back; High or Open Neck; One-Seam Sleeves in Two Styles at the Wrist and with Slight Fulness at the Top which may be Shrunken Out. The pattern is cut in 7 sizes from 32 to 44 inches bust measure. As illustrated on figure, the 36-inch size will require 6 yards of 36-inch velveteen for coat in 50-inch length. Plush, velvet or broadcloth will make a charming evening wrap. PRICE, **15** CENTS.

7935—LADIES' DRAPED BASQUE. 6 sizes, 32 to 42 inches bust measure. **8117**—LADIES' SKIRT. Lower edge about 2½ yards. 7 sizes, 22 to 34 inches waist measure, to 36 to 49½ inches hip. As on figure the medium size requires 4⅝ yards of 40-inch satin, with ¾ yard of 36-inch chiffon for sleeves, 5¾ yards of fur banding and 1⅛ yards of 36-inch material will be needed for foundation gores. PRICE, **15** CENTS EACH.

8285—LADIES' EMPIRE DRESS. Lower edge of foundation about 2 yards; of gathered skirt about 2½ yards. 6 sizes, 32 to 42 inches bust measure. As illustrated on figure, the 36-inch size will require 7¼ yards of 36-inch faille, with ⅛ yard of 3-inch lace edging for front yoke, 2⅜ yards of 36-inch material for foundation gores and ⅞ yard of 36-inch material for lining. In satin and the soft silks this design will be very pretty. PRICE, **15** CENTS.

THE NEW FASHIONS FOR WINTER

The use of satin and serge in combination is one of the new notes in fashions this season. Plaids and checks are also largely used.

7850—LADIES' BASQUE: Full-Length Dart-Fitted or Shorter Raglan Sleeves. 7 sizes, 32 to 44 inches bust. **7834—LADIES' SKIRT:** Two-Piece Tunic; Two-Piece Skirt with Straight Gathered Ruffles. Lower edge of gores about 1⅝ yards. 8 sizes, 22 to 36 inches waist, to 36 to 52 inches hip. As illustrated on figure the medium size will require 5¼ yards of 42-inch wool faille, with 3¼ yards of fur banding, ¼ yard of 36-inch batiste to face collar and 2⅝ yards of 36-inch material for foundation gores. PRICE, **15** CENTS EACH.

8382

8382—LADIES' DRESS: Chemisette; Blouse Front in One with Front Gore of a Six-Gored Gathered Skirt; **Long** Dart-Fitted or Short Sleeves. Lower edge about 2⅝ yards. 7 sizes, 32 to 44 inches bust measure. The 36-inch bust size will require as illustrated on figure 5⅝ yards of 36-inch plaid cashmere, with ¾ yard of 18-inch satin for chemisette and collar and ¼ yard of 36-inch contrasting satin for belt. PRICE, **15** CENTS.

8089

8089—LADIES' MOYEN AGE DRESS: High or Open Neck; Long or Short Sleeves; Applied Straps which may be Omitted; Three-Piece Circular Skirt; Clearing or Shorter Length. Lower edge about 3 yards. 6 sizes, 32 to **42** inches bust measure. The 36-inch bust size will require as illustrated on figure 5¼ yards of 40-inch prunella cloth, with ½ yard of 36-inch organdy for frilling. A smart **dress** with good lines. PRICE, **15** CENTS.

8159—LADIES' DRESS: Closed at the Back; High Neck with Two Styles of Collar or Open Neck. Lower edge about 3 yards. 7 sizes, 32 to 44 inches bust measure. The **36-inch** bust size will require as illustrated on figure, 1¾ yards of 44-inch serge for bolero and yoke and panel front, with 5½ yards of 27-inch satin for lower part of skirt and **sleeves,** and 1¾ yards of 36-inch organdy will be needed **for blouse.** PRICE, **15** CENTS.

8159

8524—LADIES' OVERBLOUSE. 8 sizes, 32 to 46 **inches** bust. **7924—LADIES' GUIMPE OR BLOUSE** 8 sizes, 32 to 46 inches bust. **8311—LADIES' SEVEN-GORED SKIRT.** Lower edge with plaits drawn out about 2¾ yards. 9 sizes, 22 to 38 waist, to 36 to 54 hip. As on figure the medium size needs 2¾ yards of 44-inch **plaid,** with 3 yards of 44-inch serge and 1⅝ yards of 36-inch **satin.** PRICE, **15** CENTS EACH.

Guimpe **7924**
Over-Blouse **8524**
Skirt **8311**

Basque **7850**
Skirt **7834**

8382   8089   8159   7924—8311   7850—7834

8534

8554

8546

8051

8237

8522

8546

8546—MISSES' AND SMALL WOMEN'S DRESS. Lower edge about 2½ yards. 4 sizes, 14 to 20 years. As on figure the 16-year size requires 3⅝ yards of 50-inch material, with ⅝ yard of 36-inch contrasting material for collar, ½ yard of 20 or more inch satin for pocket and 4 yards of 1-inch ribbon. A charming dance frock for a young girl. PRICE, **15 CENTS.**

8534—MISSES' AND SMALL WOMEN'S SIX-GORED PRINCESS DRESS: Closed at the Front. Lower edge about 2½ yards. 4 sizes, 14 to 20 years. As illustrated on figure, the 16-year size will require 4⅞ yards of 36-inch serge, with 1½ yards of 36-inch satin for bolero and ⅜ yards of 18-inch material will be needed for collar. PRICE, **15 CENTS.**

8546—MISSES' AND SMALL WOMEN'S DRESS: High Neck with Puritan Collar or One-Piece Tucker or Open Neck; Long or Short One-Seam Sleeves; One-Piece Straight Gathered Skirt. Lower edge about 2½ yards. 4 sizes, 14 to 20 years. As illustrated on figure, the 16-year size will require 4¾ yards of 32-inch material, with 10 yards of ribbon. **15** CENTS.

8554—MISSES' AND SMALL WOMEN'S DRESS. Lower edge of skirt about 2½ yards. 4 sizes, 14 to 20 years. As illustrated on figure, the 16-year size will require 3⅞ yards of 36-inch taffeta for blouse and tunic, 2 yards of 72-inch lining net for lower part and yoke, 6¼ yards of 11-inch edging for ruffles and 2½ yards of fur binding. PRICE, **15 CENTS.**

8051—MISSES' AND SMALL WOMEN'S DRESS. Lower edge of lowest ruffle about 2¼ yards. 4 sizes, 14 to 20 years. As on figure, the 16-year size requires 1 yard of 50-inch chiffon for upper part of body front, back and sleeves, 1¾ yards of 9½-inch flouncing for lower part of body, 6⅞ yards of 16-inch for ruffles. **15** CTS.

8237—MISSES' AND SMALL WOMEN'S DRESS. Lower edge of gathered skirt about 2⅝ yards. 4 sizes, 14 to 20 years. As on figure the 16-year size requires 5 yards of 36-inch material, with ⅝ yard of 40-inch lace all-over for sleeves and to face and 2½ yards of 36-inch material for foundation. PRICE, **15 CENTS.**

8522—MISSES' AND SMALL WOMEN'S DRESS: Two-Piece Straight Gathered Skirt. Lower edge about 2½ yards. 4 sizes, 14 to 20 years. As illustrated on figure the 16-year size will require 4⅜ yards of 36-inch material, with 1⅞ yards of 36-inch satin for blouse and 2⅝ yards of fur banding. PRICE, **15 CENTS.**

7670 8527 8532

8561 8551 8557

7670—GIRLS' DRESS: Blouse in One with Tunic; One-Piece Straight Gathered Skirt. 11 sizes, 6 to 16 years. As illustrated on figure, the 8-year size will require 2¾ yards of 36-inch serge, with ½ yard of 24-inch satin for collar and band on sleeves, ⅝ yard of 36-inch linen for shield and 3 yards of braid to trim. PRICE, **15** CENTS.

8527—BOYS' SUIT: Diagonal or Straight Closing; Trousers. The pattern is cut in 6 sizes from 3 to 8 years. As illustrated on figure, the 4-year size will require 1⅞ yards of 40-inch serge, with ½ yard of 44-inch contrasting serge for collar, cuffs and belt. The diagonal closing in this suit is a feature which will commend it. PRICE, **15** CENTS.

8532—LITTLE GIRLS' ONE-PIECE DRESS: Bolero Fronts which may be Omitted. 9 sizes, 4 to 12 years. As illustrated on figure, the 5-year size will require 2 yards of 40-inch novelty mixture, with 7¼ yards of braid, 1 yard of 6-inch ribbon for girdle, ½ yard of 36-inch lawn for collar, ⅞ yard of insertion and 1¼ yards of edging. PRICE, **15** CENTS.

8538 — GIRLS' AND JUNIORS' DRESS: to be Slipped Over the Head; Shield; Two-Piece Skirt Attached Under a Tuck Edge; Inverted Plait at Each Side. 9 sizes, 8 to 16 years. As illustrated on figure, the 10-year size will require 2 yards of 32-inch satin for blouse, with 1½ yards of 42-inch serge for skirt, ½ yard of 36-inch organdy. **15** CTS.

8342 — LITTLE GIRLS' EMPIRE DRESS: Separate Bolero; Straight Gathered Skirt. 9 sizes, 2 to 10 years. As illustrated on figure, the 9-year size will require ½ yard of 36-inch taffeta for bolero, 1⅜ yards of 36-inch striped material for skirt, ⅞ yard of 36-inch lawn for underblouse, 1¾ yards of insertion, and 2⅛ yards of edging. **15** CENTS.

8561—GIRLS' AND JUNIORS' DRESS: Separate Blouse; Two-Piece Jumper Skirt. 9 sizes, 8 to 16 years. As illustrated on figure, the 10-year size will require 2 yards of 32-inch novelty check, with ⅜ yard of 27-inch material for piping, 1½ yards of 36-inch dotted swiss for blouse, and 1 yard of 6-inch ribbon for girdle. PRICE, **15** CENTS.

8548—GIRLS' AND JUNIORS' SMOCKED OR GATHERED DRESS. 9 sizes, 8 to 16 years. As illustrated on figure, the 11-year size will require 2⅝ yards of 40-inch linen, with ⅝ yard of 27-inch contrasting linen for collar and cuffs, and ⅞ yard of 5-inch ribbon for girdle. PRICE, **15** CENTS.

8551—GIRLS' AND JUNIORS' COAT, in Two Lengths; Three-Piece Skirt. 5 sizes from 8 to 16 years. As illustrated on figure, the 10-year size will require 3½ yards of 36-inch velveteen, with ¼ yard of 54-inch fur cloth for collar and cuffs. A dressy coat for best wear. PRICE, **15** CENTS.

8557—GIRLS' AND JUNIORS' DRESS: High or Open Back; Long or Short Sleeves; Five-Gored Skirt. 9 sizes, 8 to 16 years. As on figure, the 12-year size requires 2⅝ yards of 40-inch material, with ⅜ yard of 40-inch satin for turnover collar, belt and cuffs. PRICE, **15** CENTS.

7670 8527 8532 8548 8538 8342 8561 8551 8557

8509

Bodice—8426
Skirt—8211

8542

8424   8542

8509—LADIES' DRESS: High or Open Neck; Long Sleeves in Two Styles at the Wrist or Short Puff Sleeves; One-Piece Straight Skirt Gathered or Gauged at the Waistline; Clearing or Shorter Length. Lower edge about 3½ yard. The pattern is cut in 5 sizes from 32 to 40 inches bust measure. As illustrated on figure the 36-inch size will require 5⅝ yards of 36-inch taffeta, with ⅜ yard of 44-inch tulle for sleeves, 7 yards of jet banding to trim.   PRICE, 15 CENTS.

8426—LADIES' BODICE. 7 sizes, 32 to 44 inches bust measure. **8211**—LADIES' ONE-PIECE STRAIGHT GATHERED TUCKED SKIRT. Lower edge about 2½ yards. 5 sizes, 22 to 30 inches waist, to 36 to 44½ inches hip. As illustrated on figure, the medium size will require 4¼ yards of 44-inch charmeuse, with ¾ yard of 13½-inch lace flouncing for blouse, ⅞ yard of 36-inch lining material and 2½ yards of ribbon for trimming.   PRICE, 15 CENTS EACH.

8424—LADIES' DRESS: Separate Guimpe; High or Open Neck; Long or Short One-Seam Sleeves; Smocked or Gathered Blouse with Long Shoulders; Three-Piece Gathered Skirt; Clearing or Shorter Length. Lower edge about 3¼ yards. The pattern is cut in 4 sizes from 32 to 38 inches bust measure. As illustrated on figure, the 36-inch bust size will require 5 yards of 40-inch crêpe de Chine. A simple and attractive dress with the very popular smocking.   PRCIE, 15 CENTS.

8542—LADIES' DRESS: Low Necked French Lining; Separate Guimpe; One-Piece Straight Gathered Tunic in Three Styles; Three-Piece Foundation Skirt. Lower edge measures about 2⅜ yards, 6 sizes, 32 to 42 inches bust. As illustrated above on figure, the 36-inch size will require 3⅛ yards of 40-inch satin for girdle and foundation, 3⅝ yards of 43-inch flouncing, 1 yard of 40-inch all-over lace for blouse, and ⅝ yard of trimming for straps.   PRICE, 15 CENTS.

8542

8509   8426—8211

One of the most striking innovations the winter brings us is the exaggerated hip line effected by means of draperies, or by wiring, which at once recalls the days of hoops and crinolines. Certainly, they are most bewitching, these draped or wired skirts topped by the draped bodices which in the evening gowns carry the dainty little puffed sleeves and the 1830 shoulder outline. The effect is truly picturesque in the soft silks and pliable fabrics.

8542—LADIES' DRESS: Low Necked French Lining; One-Piece Straight Gathered Tunic in Three Styles; Three-Piece Foundation Skirt; Clearing or Shorter Length; Train in 90 or 72 Inch Length may be Omitted. Lower edge about 2⅜ yards. The pattern is cut in 6 sizes from 32 to 42 inches bust measure. As illustrated on figure, the 36-inch size will require 4½ yards of 44-inch figured taffeta, with 1⅛ yards of 36-inch tulle for blouse, 3½ yards of fur banding and 5⅞ yards of 36-inch plain taffeta for foundation and to trim.   PRICE, 15 CENTS.

8424   8542

FASHION'S FAVORED STYLES

Blouse—**8440**
Skirt—**8441**

Coat—**8185**
Dress—**8409**

Blouse—**8075**   Skirt—**8076**

Blouse—**8602**
Skirt—**8603**

Blouse—**8583**
Skirt—**8584**

| 8440 | 8185 | 8075 | 8602 | 8583 |
| 8441 | 8409 | 8076 | 8603 | 8584 |

8440—LADIES' BLOUSE: Closed to the Neck or Rolled Open; Long or Short One-Seam Sleeves. (May be Attached to a Skirt or Worn Separately.) 9 sizes, 32 to 48 inches bust measure. **8441**—LADIES' SEVEN-GORED PLAITED SKIRT: Slightly High Waistline; Clearing or Shorter Length. Lower edge with plaits drawn out about 3⅝ yards. The pattern is cut in 9 sizes from 22 to 38 inches waist measure, corresponding to 36 to 54 inches hip measure. If combined as illustrated on figure the medium size will require 6¾ yards of 36-inch gabardine, with 1 yard of 36-inch crêpe, 6 yards of braid, and ⅞ yard of 6-inch ribbon for a girdle. There is unusually good style in this dress. The outline of the blouse, and the cluster-plaited skirt are very attractive features.   **15** CENTS EACH.

8185—LADIES' COAT: 26-Inch Length at the Back; Closed to the Neck or Rolled Open; Belt at Regulation Waistline or Gathered at Empire Waistline; Two-Seam Sleeves. For the braiding design illustrated use Standard transfer pattern 10086. 7 sizes, 32 to 44 inches bust measure. **8409**—LADIES' DRESS: Double or Single Cape Collar; Long Dart-Fitted or Short Sleeves; Three or Four Piece Skirt; Single or Double Three or Four Piece Circular Ruffles which may be Omitted. Lower edge of skirt about 2½ yards. 7 sizes, 32 to 44 inches bust measure. If combined as illustrated on figure the medium size will require 2⅞ yards of 36-inch velveteen for coat, with 6⅛ yards of 36-inch cloth for dress with double ruffle.   PRICE, **15** CENTS EACH.

8075—LADIES' BLOUSE: Closed to the Neck or Rolled. Open. 7 sizes, 32 to 44 inches bust measure. **8076**—LADIES' CORSAGE SKIRT: One-Piece Straight Lower Part Gathered All Around or Box-Plaited at Center Back. Lower edge about 3 yards. 6 sizes, 22 to 32 inches waist measure, corresponding to 36 to 47 inches hip measure. As on figure the medium size will require 4½ yards of 44-inch serge, with 1⅞ yards of 36-inch velvet, and 3⅝ yards of fur banding.   **15** CENTS EACH.

8602—LADIES' BLOUSE. For the embroidered design illustrated, use Standard transfer pattern 10176. 7 sizes, 32 to 44 inches bust measure. **8603**—LADIES' SKIRT: Lower edge with plaits drawn out about 2⅜ yards. 9 sizes, 22 to 38 inches waist measure, corresponding to 36 to 54 inches hip measure. If combined as illustrated on figure the medium size will require 3¼ yards of 50-inch broadcloth, with 6¼ yards of braid, and 1½ yards of 40-inch all-over lace.   **15** CENTS EACH.

8583—LADIES' BLOUSE. 7 sizes, 32 to 44 inches bust measure. **8584**—LADIES' FIVE-GORED SKIRT. Lower edge with plaits drawn out about 2¾ yards. 9 sizes, 22 to 38 inches waist measure, corresponding to 36 to 54 inches hip measure. If combined as illustrated on figure the medium size will require 6¾ yards of 40-inch satin for dress, with ⅞ yard of 50-inch chiffon cloth for sleeves, collar and to face lining, and ⅞ yard of 36-inch material for lining. PRICE, **15** CTS EACH.

THE NEW MODES FOR WINTER

Blouse—8608
Skirt—8609   8392   8577

8595   Blouse—8578
                                  Skirt—8579

8608—09   8392   8595   8578—79   8577

8608—LADIES' BLOUSE. 9 sizes, 32 to 48 inches bust measure. **8609**—LADIES' FOUR OR FIVE PIECE SKIRT: Front in One with Front of Two or Three Piece Flounce. Lower edge about 2¾ yards. 9 sizes, 22 to 38 inches waist measure, corresponding to 36 to 54 inches hip measure. Combined as on figure the medium size needs with five-piece skirt and three-piece flounce 4 yards of 44-inch serge, with ⅜ yard of 24-inch satin for collar and cuffs.   PRICE, **15** CENTS EACH.

8392—LADIES' SIX OR SEVEN GORED PRINCESS DRESS: Chemisette; Long Dart-Fitted or Short Sleeves or Long Gathered Sleeves; Clearing or Shorter Length. Lower edge about 2⅝ yards. The pattern is cut in 9 sizes from 32 to 48 inches bust measure. The 36-inch bust size will require as illustrated on figure 4¾ yards of 44-inch fine cloth, with 3¾ yards of fur banding, and 2¾ yards of cord trimming. Broadcloth, serge or wool poplin will develop smartly. PRICE, **15** CENTS.

8595—LADIES' DRESS: Separate Overblouse with Attached Three-Piece Tunic; Two-Piece Skirt. Lower edge about 2 yards. The 36-inch bust size will require as illustrated on figure 2½ yards of 44-inch fine gabardine for overblouse and tunic, with 4 yards of 40-inch satin for blouse and skirt, ⅝ yard of 18-inch net for collar and to face blouse, 4½ yards of wide braid, and 4¾ yards of narrow braid will be needed for one row.   PRICE, **15** CENTS.

8578—LADIES' BLOUSE: Long Dart-Fitted or Short Sleeves; Separate Overblouse. (Desirable for Flouncings, Bordered Materials or Other Fabrics.) 9 sizes, 32 to 48 inches bust measure. **8579**—LADIES' TWO OR THREE PIECE SKIRT: Slightly High Waistline or Gathered at Regulation Waistline; One-Piece Bias Trimming-Bands which may be Omitted. Lower edge about 2 yards. 9 sizes, 22 to 38 inches waist measure, corresponding to 36 to 54 inches hip measure. If combined as illustrated on figure the medium size will require 3½ yards of 40-inch satin for two-piece skirt and overblouse, with 1⅛ yards of 36-inch velvet for bands on skirt, pipings and girdle, 2⅛ yards of 40-inch lace for underblouse, and 1 yard of edging will be needed to trim.   PRICE, **15** CENTS EACH.

8577—LADIES' DRESS: High or Open Neck; Long Dart-Fitted or Short Sleeves; Panel Front and Back in One with the Front and Back of a Six-Gored Skirt; Clearing or Shorter Length. For the braiding design illustrated on the figure, use Standard transfer pattern No. 10301. Lower edge about 2¼ yards. The pattern is cut in 7 sizes from 32 to 44 inches bust measure. The 36-inch bust size will require as illustrated on figure 3⅝ yards of 50-inch broadcloth, with ¾ yard of 24-inch silk for a girdle. Dresses which feature the long unbroken lines obtained by the use of panels are very popular this season. The dress shown here is constructed on very simple lines, and yet possesses a great deal of style and distinction. It is trimmed with a braided motif.   PRICE, **15** CENTS.

LATEST LINGERIE AND DESIGNS FOR THE HOUSE

8618 8612 8586

8577

Corset Cover—8323
Petticoat—8604

8323—LADIES' UNDERBLOUSE OR CORSET COVER: For the scallop design illustrated on the figure use Standard transfer pattern 10064. 7 sizes, 32 to 44 inches bust measure.
8604—LADIES' FIVE-GORED PETTICOAT: Dart-Fitted or Drawn Up on a Casing, or with One-Piece Yoke. Lower edge of petticoat about 1⅞ yards; of circular flounce about 2⅝ yards; of gathered flounce about 2¼ yards. 9 sizes, 22 to 38 inches bust measure, corresponding to 36 to 54 inches hip measure. If combined as illustrated on figure, the medium size will require 1¾ yards of 36-inch nainsook, with ⅞ yards of beading, 2⅞ yards of ribbon for corset cover and 3⅜ yards of 36-inch taffeta for petticoat. PRICE, **15** CENTS EACH.

8323—8604 8577 8618 8612 8586

8577—LADIES' DRESS: High or Open Neck; Long Dart-Fitted or Short Sleeves; Panel Front and Back in One with the Front and Back of a Six-Gored Skirt; Clearing or Shorter Length. Lower edge about 2¼ yards. The pattern is cut in 7 sizes from 32 to 44 inches bust measure. The 36-inch bust size will require as illustrated on figure, 3½ yards of 44-inch linen, with ¾ yard of 36-inch contrasting linen for collar and cuffs. PRICE, **15** CENTS.

8618—LADIES' APRON: in Two Lengths; to be Slipped over the Head. Drawn up on an Elastic or Held in by a Belt; Sleeves which may be Omitted. The pattern is cut in 9 sizes from 32 to 48 inches bust measure. The 36-inch bust size will require as illustrated on figure, 4⅞ yards of 32-inch percale for apron, with ⅜ yards of 32-inch contrasting material for belt and trimming sleeves. PRICE, **15** CENTS.

8612—LADIES' PRINCESS COMBINATION UNDERGARMENT. Chemise and Envelope Drawers; Round or Pointed Neck. The pattern is cut in 9 sizes from 32 to 48 inches bust measure. The 36-inch bust size will require as illustrated on figure, 2¼ yards of 40-inch crêpe de Chine, with 2½ yards of ribbon, 2¾ yards of insertion, 3½ yards of wide edging, 2½ yards of narrow edging and 2 yards of beading. PRICE, **15** CENTS.

8586—LADIES' NIGHTGOWN: to be Slipped Over the Head. The pattern is cut in 9 sizes from 32 to 48 inches bust measure. The 36-inch bust size will require as illustrated on figure, 3¾ yards of 36-inch longcloth, with 1⅛ yards of beading, 1 yard of lace insertion, 2⅝ yards of edging, 2⅜ yards of wide ribbon and 1¾ yards of narrow ribbon. Long-cloth, cambric, nainsook or crêpe de Chine may be used. PRICE, **15** CENTS.

8353

8000

8274

Blouse—8411
Skirt—8412

8413

8353   8000   8274   8413   8411–12

8353—LADIES' DRESS: Collar Rolled in Two Styles; Long Dart - Fitted or Short Sleeves; Slightly High Waistline; Four-Piece Skirt; Yoke Facings which may be Omitted; Clearing or Shorter Length. Lower edge about 2⅝ yards. 9 sizes, 32 to 48 inches bust measure. The 36-inch bust size will require as illustrated on figure 4⅜ yards of 44-inch serge, with 1 yard of 36-inch satin. This is an admirable design for serge, broadcloth, wool poplin, gabardine or whipcord. A band of satin on the skirt and a touch of it on the collar and sleeves illustrates a simple form of trimming which gives tone to the dress. The large pockets are coriously shaped and are also piped with satin.   PRICE, **15** CENTS.

8000—LADIES' DRESS: Closed to the Neck or Rolled Open; Long Dart-Fitted or Short Raglan Sleeves; Three-Piece Tunic in Two Outlines which may be Omitted; Three-Piece Skirt; Clearing or Shorter Length. Lower edge about 1¾ yards. 9 sizes, 32 to 48 inches bust measure. The 36-inch bust size will require as illustrated on figure 3⅞ yards of 44-inch linen, with 18¾ yards of braid to trim.   PRICE, **15** CENTS.

8274—LADIES' DRESS: Long Dart-Fitted or Short Sleeves; Three or Four Piece Skirt; Three-Piece Yoke which may be Omitted. Lower edge about 2⅜ yards. 9 sizes, 32 to 48 inches bust measure. The 36-inch bust size will require as illustrated on figure with four-piece skirt 4 yards of 44-inch cloth, with ⅞ yard of 27-inch plain silk for vest and ¼ yard of 24-inch striped silk. The vest of silk enlivens this smart dress.   PRICE, **15** CENTS.

8413—LADIES' DRESS: Closed to the Neck or Rolled Open or Slightly Open Neck; Long Dart-Fitted or Short Sleeves; Five-Piece Skirt; Inverted Plait or Gathers at the Back; Clearing or Shorter Length. Lower edge about 2⅞ yards. 9 sizes, 32 to 48 inches bust measure. The 36-inch bust size will require as illustrated on figure 6¼ yards of 32-inch percale, with ⅝ yard of 36-inch lawn for collar and belt.   PRICE, **15** CENTS.

8411 — LADIES' SMOCKED OR GATHERED BLOUSE. 9 sizes, 32 to 48 inches bust measure. **8412** —LADIES' THREE-PIECE SKIRT. Lower edge with plaits drawn out about 3⅛ yards. 9 sizes, 22 to 38 inches waist measure, corresponding to 36 to 54 inches hip measure. If combined as illustrated on figure the medium size will require 1⅞ yards of 40-inch crêpe de Chine, and 2⅞ yards of 54-inch cloth.   **15** CENTS EACH.

STREET FROCKS OF DISTINCTION

Blouse—8615
Skirt—8616

Blouse—8373
Skirt—8374

8409

8224

8625

8615—LADIES' BLOUSE. 7 sizes, 32 to 44 inches bust measure. **8616**—LADIES' SIX-GORED JUMPER SKIRT. Lower edge about 2⅝ yards. 9 sizes, 22 to 38 inches waist measure, corresponding to 36 to 54 inches hip measure. If combined as illustrated on figure the medium size will require 2¼ yards of 40-inch crêpe de Chine, with 1 yard of 27-inch satin for collar and pipings and 3⅜ yds. of 50-in. cloth for skirt. **15 CTS. EACH.**

8373—LADIES' BLOUSE. 7 sizes, 32 to 44 inches bust. **8374**—LADIES' TWO-PIECE SKIRT. Lower edge about 3⅜ yards. 7 sizes, 22 to 34 inches waist, to 36 to 49½ inches hip. If combined as illustrated on figure the medium size will require 4¾ yards of 44-inch serge, with 1⅞ yards of 36-inch silk for backs, side body and sleeves, and ⅝ yard of 32-inch crêpe for collar and vest.   PRICE, **15** CENTS EACH.

8409—LADIES' DRESS: Double or Single Cape Collar; Three or Four Piece Skirt; Single or Double Three or Four Piece Circular Ruffles which may be Omitted. Lower edge of skirt about 2½ yards. 7 sizes, 32 to 44 inches bust measure. The 36-inch bust size will require 5⅜ yards of 40-inch plaid serge, with 1⅜ yards of 36-inch crêpe for collar and cuffs. Plaid serge is popular this season.   PRICE, **15** CENTS.

8224—LADIES' DRESS: High or Open Neck; Long Dart-Fitted or Short Sleeves; Two-Piece Skirt with Soft Plaits at the Top; Trimming Pieces which may be Omitted; Clearing or Shorter Length. Lower edge about 2¼ yards. 9 sizes, 32 to 48 inches bust measure. The 36-inch bust size will require as illustrated on figure 3⅛ yards of 50-inch cloth, with 2 yards of 5-inch ribbon for girdle.   PRICE, **15** CENTS.

8615—16   8373—74

Dressing Your Doll Baby

If you want to know the very latest styles for your dolly, send a two-cent stamp and your name and address to the Standard Fashion Company, 12-16 Vandam Street, New York City—and we will send you "Dresses for Dolls," a lovely picture sheet of dolls' patterns.

8625—LADIES' DRESS: High or Open Neck; Long Dart-Fitted Sleeves in Two Styles or Short Sleeves; Revers which may be Omitted; Six-Piece Skirt Gathered at the Sides; Clearing or Shorter Length. Lower edge about 2¾ yards. The pattern is cut in 7 sizes from 32 to 44 inches bust measure. The 36-inch bust size will require as illustrated on figure 5 yards of 36-inch velveteen, with 1¾ yards of 24-inch satin for vest, revers and sleeve frills and 1¼ yards of 36-inch striped satin. The long unbroken lines of the revers and the combination of materials used in developing this dress give a novel and pleasing touch.   PRICE, **15** CENTS.

8625   8409   8224

DRAPERIES OF EVERY DESCRIPTION

8619

Bodice—8587
Skirt—8588

Blouse—8622
Skirt—8623

8611

Bodice—8592
Skirt—8593

8619—LADIES' DRESS: Dart-Fitted Lining in High or Open Neck and with Long Dart-Fitted Sleeves or Long or Three-Quarter Length Tucked Sleeves; Overblouse Front in One with Front of Three-Piece Tunic; Two-Piece Skirt Attached to the Lining; Clearing or Shorter Length. Lower edge about 2 yards. 6 sizes, 32 to 42 inches bust measure. The 36-inch bust size will require as illustrated on figure 6⅞ yards of 44-inch serge, with ⅞ yard of 27-inch fancy silk. PRICE, **15** CENTS.

8587—LADIES' DRAPED BODICE. 8 sizes, 32 to 46 inches bust measure. **8588**—LADIES' TWO-PIECE SKIRT. Lower edge about 2¼ yards. 6 sizes, 22 to 32 inches waist measure, corresponding to 36 to 47 inches hip measure. If combined as illustrated on figure, the medium size will require 5 yards of 36-inch taffeta, with 4 yards of 36 to 50-inch chiffon cloth, 1½ yards of 18-inch all-over lace, 3 yards of ribbon for one row and ⅞ yard of 36-inch lining. **15** CENTS EACH.

8622—LADIES' BLOUSE. 7 sizes, 32 to 44 inches bust measure. **8623**—LADIES' SKIRT. Lower edge of gathered skirt about 3¾ yards. 5 sizes, 22 to 30 inches waist measure, corresponding to 36 to 44½ inches hip measure. If combined as illustrated on figure the medium size will require 7 yards of 36-inch satin for gathered skirt, front, backs and puff, with 2⅝ yards of 44-inch serge for sleeves, bib and facing, and ⅝ yard of 27-inch crêpe for collar and chemisette. **15** CENTS EACH.

8611—LADIES' DRESS with Polonaise: Body Fronts in One with Fronts of Five-Piece Tunic in Two Outlines at the Back; High or Open Neck; Long or Short Dart-Fitted Sleeves; Separate Two-Piece Skirt; Clearing or Shorter Length. Lower edge about 1¾ yards. 6 sizes, 32 to 42 inches bust measure. The 36-inch bust size will require as illustrated on figure with long back 3 yards of 54-inch cloth, with 3⅜ yards of 33-inch satin. This is a striking new model. PRICE, **15** CENTS.

8592—LADIES' DRAPED BODICE: Long or Three-Quarter-Length Dart-Fitted Sleeves with or without the Gauntlet Cuffs; Dart-Fitted Lining. 7 sizes, 32 to 44 inches bust measure. **8593**—LADIES' ONE-PIECE STRAIGHT GATHERED SKIRT: One-Piece Straight Gathered Tunic Draped or Falling Free. Lower edge about 2¼ yards. 7 sizes, 22 to 34 inches waist measure, corresponding to 36 to 49½ inches hip measure. If combined as illustrated on figure the medium size will require 6¼ yards of 27-inch plaid silk, with 3 yards of wide banding, 1¾ yards of narrow banding and 4⅞ yards of 40-inch charmeuse for tunic, cuffs and bodice. PRICE, **15** CENTS EACH.

8619   8587–8588   8622–8623   8611   8592–8593

GRACE MANY A GOWN THIS SEASON

Bodice—8597
Skirt—8598

8605

Bodice—8597
Skirt—8598

Bodice—8426
Skirt—8427

Blouse—8622
Skirt—8623

8597—98   8605   8597—98   8426—27   8622—23

8605—LADIES' DRESS: High, V, or Open Neck; Long One-Seam Sleeves in Two Styles at the Wrist or Short Sleeves; Separate Tie - On Over-blouse; Two-Piece Tunic; Two-Piece Skirt; Straight Gathered Ruffles which may be Omitted; Clearing or Shorter Length. Lower edge of skirt about 2¼ yards. The pattern is cut in 7 sizes from 32 to 44 inches bust measure. The 36-inch bust size will require as illustrated on figure 10 yards of 36-inch satin, with 1¼ yards of 36-inch all-over lace and 4 yards of picot edging.   **15 CENTS.**

8426—LADIES' BODICE. 7 sizes, 32 to 44 inches bust measure. **8427—LADIES' ONE-PIECE STRAIGHT SKIRT:** Plaited or Gathered at Slightly High Waistline or Gathered at Regulation Waistline. Lower edge about 3 yards. 6 sizes, 22 to 32 inches waist measure, corresponding to 36 to 47 inches hip measure. If combined as illustrated on figure, the medium size will require 4⅛ yards of 40-inch chiffon for skirt, with 2⅝ yards of 40-inch satin for bodice and bands on skirt, ¾ yard of 13½-inch lace flouncing and 1 yard of 9-inch flouncing for sleeves.   **PRICE, 15 CENTS EACH.**

8622—LADIES' BLOUSE. 7 sizes, 32 to 44 inches bust measure. **8623—LADIES' SKIRT.** Lower edge of foundation skirt about 2⅛ yards; of gathered skirt about 3¾ yards. 5 sizes, 22 to 30 inches waist measure, corresponding to 36 to 44½ inches hip measure. If combined as illustrated on figure the medium size will require 6⅞ yards of 45-inch taffeta for tunic, front and back bibs and facing gores, with 5½ yards of fur banding, ⅞ yard of ribbon for girdle, ½ yard of 36-inch lace for puffs, 1⅛ yards of edging and 2½ yards of 32 or more inch material for gores.   **PRICE, 15 CENTS EACH.**

8597—LADIES' BODICE: French Lining with Long Dart-Fitted Sleeves or Short Sleeves; Draped Tie-On Overblouse with Two Styles of Open Neck. 6 sizes, 32 to 42 inches bust. **8598—LADIES' SKIRT:** Slightly High Waistline with or without the One-Piece Draped Tunic with Straight Lower Edge or Regulation Waistline; Three-Piece Yoke; Lower edge about 2⅜ yards. 5 sizes, 22 to 30 inches waist, corresponding to 36 to 44½ inches hip. If combined as illustrated in front view on figure the medium size will require 4½ yards of 36-inch taffeta for skirt, yoke and bodice, with 3¾ yards of 40-inch flowered chiffon and 1 yard of 32-inch material for lining; or as in back view on figure 7¼ yards of 40-inch crêpe, with 2¾ yards of lace edging for sleeve ruffles and 1⅛ yards of rose trimming around neck.   **15 CENTS EACH.**

MISSES' STYLES FOR AFTERNOON AND EVENING WEAR

8576   8599

8203

8415

8237

8585

8450

8576—MISSES' AND SMALL WOMEN'S DRESS: Draped Bodice; Long or Short Dart-Fitted Sleeves; Dart-Fitted Lining. Lower edge about 2 yards. 4 sizes, 14 to 20 years. The 16-year size will require as illustrated on figure 7¼ yards of 36-inch satin, with ¾ yard of 18-inch all-over lace, and 3 yards of banding.   PRICE, **15** CENTS.

8599—MISSES' AND SMALL WOMEN'S DRESS. Lower edge about 2½ yards. 4 sizes, 14 to 20 years. The 16-year size will require as illustrated on figure 2¾ yards of 50-inch gabardine, with ¾ yard of 36-inch satin for sleeves, ⅝ yard of 18-inch crêpe, and ⅞ yard of 36-inch material for guimpe.   PRICE, **15** CENTS.

8415—MISSES' AND SMALL WOMEN'S DRESS: Separate Guimpe. Lower edge of skirt about 2⅜ yards. 4 sizes, 14 to 20 years. The 16-year size will require as illustrated on figure 4¾ yards of 40-inch charmeuse, with ¾ yard of 40-inch net, 2 yards of rose trimming, and 2⅛ yards of 36-inch material for gores.   PRICE, **15** CENTS.

8203—MISSES' AND SMALL WOMEN'S DRESS: High or Open Neck; Long or Short One-Seam Sleeves. Lower edge about 2⅝ yards. 4 sizes, 14 to 20 years. The 16-year size will require as illustrated, 5¾ yards of 36-inch taffeta, with 1¼ yards of 40-inch chiffon and 1½ yards of ribbon.   PRICE, **15** CENTS.

8237—MISSES' AND SMALL WOMEN'S DRESS: Two-Piece Foundation. Lower edge of gathered skirt about 2⅝ yards. 4 sizes, 14 to 20 years. The 16-year size will require as illustrated on figure 4½ yards of 40-inch net for dress, with 2¼ yards of 40-inch net for ruching, ½ yard of 18-inch all-over lace.   **15** CENTS.

8450—MISSES' AND SMALL WOMEN'S DRESS: Long One-Seam Sleeves in Two Styles at the Wrist or Three-Quarter-Length Sleeves. Lower edge about 2½ yards. 4 sizes, 14 to 20 years. The 16-year size will require as illustrated on figure 4¼ yards of 40-inch crêpe, with 1⅜ yards of 40-inch chiffon for sleeves and blouse front and back, 2½ yards of ribbon for one row, and 2½ yards of 6-inch ribbon for a girdle and ends.   PRICE, **15** CENTS.

8585—MISSES' AND SMALL WOMEN'S DRESS: Separate Blouse; Draped Bodice with Dart-Fitted Lining; One-Piece Straight Gathered Tunic, Draped in Bustle Style or Falling Free; Two-Piece Skirt. Lower edge about 2⅛ yards. 4 sizes, 14 to 20 years. The 16-year size will require as illustrated on figure 6⅝ yards of 36-inch taffeta for dress, with ⅝ yard of 40-inch all-over lace, and ¼ yard of 40-inch satin for bands.   PRICE, **15** CENTS.

8077 8582

8102 8286 8289 8617

8607 8582

8614

8102—LITTLE GIRLS' DRESS: High or Open Neck; Long or Short Sleeves or Frill Sleeves; Straight Lower Edge. Embroidery design is an adaptation of Standard transfer pattern 10038. 6 sizes, ½ to 5 years. As illustrated on figure the 3-year size will require 1¾ yards of 36-inch batiste. Make this dress of lawn, batiste, nainsook or handkerchief linen. The embroidered design will add to the value of the dress. PRICE, **15** CENTS.

8286—GIRLS' AND JUNIORS' COAT SUIT: Straight or Diagonal Closing; Closed to the Neck or Rolled Open; Two-Seam Sleeves with Slight Fulness at the Top which may be Shrunken Out; Two-Piece Skirt with Suspenders. 9 sizes, 8 to 16 years. As illustrated on figure the 12-year size will require 4⅜ yards of 40-inch cloth, with ⅜ yard of 24-inch velvet for collar and cuffs. A simple coat suit which is very desirable for juniors and younger girls is shown here. PRICE, **15** CENTS.

8077—LITTLE GIRLS' DRESS: Closed to the Neck or Rolled Open; Long or Short Raglan Sleeves; Bloomers. 9 sizes, 2 to 10 years. As illustrated on figure the 6-year size will require 2⅛ yards of 36-inch linen. For play or school this design is equally good. It has bloomers which may be made of the same material as the dress. Gingham, chambray, and poplin are serviceable wash materials, and if a woolen dress is desired, serge and gabardine are recommended. **15** CENTS.

8607—GIRLS' AND JUNIORS' PRINCESS DRESS: High or Open Neck; Long or Short Sleeves. The pattern is cut in 9 sizes from 8 to 16 years. As illustrated on figure the 14-year size will require 3⅛ yards of 44-inch plaid serge, with ¾ yard of 27-inch plain serge for collar, cuffs and belt. Plaid or plain serge makes a practical school frock in this simple design. The one-piece style is very desirable and the novel outline of the pockets is interesting. PRICE, **15** CENTS.

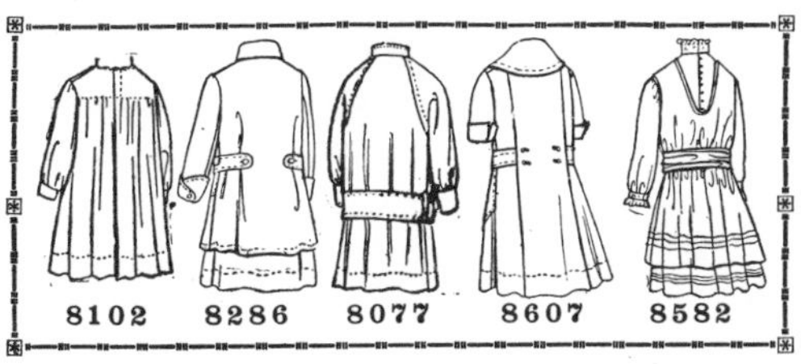

8102 8286 8077 8607 8582

8617—LITTLE GIRLS' DRESS: High or Open Neck; Long or Short Sleeves. The pattern is cut in 9 sizes from 2 to 10 years. As illustrated on figure the 4-year size will require 1¾ yards of 36-inch lawn, with 1½ yards of insertion, 2½ yards of edging, and 2⅝ yards of 5-inch ribbon for a girdle. PRICE, **15** CENTS.

8582—GIRLS' AND JUNIORS' DRESS: Long or Short Sleeves; One-Piece Straight Gathered Skirt Sewed or Buttoned to the Blouse; Separate Over-blouse in One with Tunic; Straight or Pointed Outline at the Lower Edge. 9 sizes, 8 to 16 years. As illustrated on upper figure the 9-year size will require 1⅜ yards of 36-inch crêpe, with 4⅜ yards of 36-inch lawn, 2¼ yards of insertion, and 1 yard of ribbon for a girdle. As illustrated on lower figure the 13-year size will require 2¼ yards of 36-inch taffeta, with 2¾ yards of 23-inch flouncing for skirt, 1 yard of 11½-inch flouncing for sleeves, and ⅞ yard of 40-inch lace for blouse. **15** CENTS.

8289—LITTLE GIRLS' DRESS: High or Open Neck; Long or Short Sleeves. 9 sizes, 2 to 10 years. As illustrated on figure the 5-year size will require 2⅝ yards of 32-inch galatea, with ⅜ yard of 27-inch linen for piping. With the belt arranged at Empire waistline, this dress is very pretty for little girls. It makes a good school frock. PRICE, **15** CENTS.

8614—GIRLS' AND JUNIORS' DRESS: Blouse to be Slipped Over the Head. 9 sizes, 8 to 16 years. As illustrated on figure the 15-year size will require 4¼ yards of 42-inch novelty cloth, with ½ yard of 36-inch silk for collar and belt, ⅝ yard of 27-inch linen for shield and collar, and ¾ yard of 36-inch material will be needed for underbody. PRICE, **15** CENTS.

8289 8617 8614 8582

OVERCOATS AND SUITS FOR YOUR BOYS

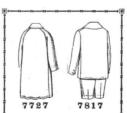

8241   **7990**   **8090**   **7817**

8613

7727

8241—LITTLE BOYS' SUIT: Removable Shield in High or Open Neck; Long or Short Sleeves; Belt and Applied Yokes which may be Omitted; Plain Trousers. 7 sizes, 2 to 8 years. As illustrated on figure the 5-year size will require 1⅛ yards of 36-inch flannel for blouse, with 1⅛ yards of 36-inch serge for collar, band on sleeves and for trousers, ½ yard of 36-inch linen for shield, and 1⅜ yards of white braid for trimming.   PRICE, **15** CENTS.

7990—BOYS' MACKINAW COAT: Applied Yoke and Straps which may be Omitted. The pattern is cut in 7 sizes from 6 to 12 years. As illustrated on figure the 10-year size will require 2⅜ yards of 54-inch novelty plaid. Boys are very fond of the mackinaw coat for outing wear and there are many fancy plaid materials which are used to develop these coats. Every boy would like to have one for winter sports and they are very comfortable too.   PRICE, **15** CENTS.

8613—BOYS' DOUBLE-BREASTED SUIT: Knickerbockers or Plain Trousers. The pattern is cut in 5 sizes from 8 to 14 years. As illustrated on figure the 11-year size will require 3 yards of 44-inch English mixture. This is a very smart suit for boys, with good lines, and above all, it is a model that can be made without any trouble. The pointed pockets and double-breasted style are desirable features. Both knickerbockers and plain trousers are included in the design.   PRICE, **15** CENTS.

8090 — LITTLE BOYS' DOUBLE - BREASTED OVERCOAT: Notched or Shawl Collar; Yoke which may be Omitted. The pattern is cut in 9 sizes from 2 to 10 years. As illustrated on figure the 4-year size will require 1⅞ yards of 50-inch cheviot. This double-breasted overcoat will keep the little boy warm and snug in winter. It is a popular model and especially suited to young boys. Serge, cheviot, mixtures and coatings may be used, and it can be made with notched collar.   PRICE, **15** CENTS.

7817—BOYS' "LITTLE ADMIRAL" SUIT: Coat in Either of Two Outlines; Vest-which may be Omitted; Plain Trousers. The pattern is cut in 5 sizes from 4 to 8 years. As illustrated on figure the 6-year size will require 1¾ yards of 36-inch blue rep, with ¼ yard of 27-inch white rep for collar and vest. Besides being used for general wear, the "Little Admiral" suit for boys is very charming for dressy wear when made up in satin, velvet, corduroy or velveteen. A black velvet suit with white satin vest and collar gives a rich effect.   PRICE, **15** CENTS.

7727—BOYS' RAGLAN OVERCOAT: Closed to the Neck or Rolled Open; Cuffs and Belt which may be Omitted; Two Styles of Pockets. The pattern is cut in 5 sizes from 8 to 16 years. As illustrated on figure the 12-year size will require 2¼ yards of 54-inch novelty cloth. For good, hard service which a boy expects to get from the overcoat he wears for general, daily use, it would be hard to find a better model than this raglan overcoat. It can be made of tweeds, worsteds, cheviot, heavy serge, mixtures, diagonals and coatings. The large pocket will be found a comfort to the boy.   **15** CENTS.

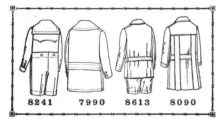

8241   **7990**   **8613**   **8090**

7727   **7817**

SMART WINTER COATS AND SUITS

8590   8581

8575

Coat—8280
Skirt—8258

Coat—8600
Skirt—8085

8590   8581   8575   8280—8258   8600—8085

8590—LADIES' COAT: 50 or 45 Inch Length at the Back; Body and Sleeves in One. The pattern is cut in 7 sizes from 32 to 44 inches bust measure. As illustrated on figure the medium size will require 3⅝ yards of 54-inch novelty cloth. This design will make a serviceable coat in worsteds, mixtures, cheviots and tweeds. It is also suitable for zibeline, army cloth, plush or velvet.   PRICE, **15** CENTS.

8581—LADIES' COAT: 56-Inch Length at the Back; Closed to the Neck or Rolled Open. The pattern is cut in 9 sizes from 32 to 48 inches bust measure. As illustrated on figure the medium size will require 4½ yards of 40-inch serge, with ⅝ yard of 24-inch velvet for collar and cuffs.   PRICE, **15** CENTS.

8575—LADIES' COAT: 50 or 45 Inch Length at the Back. The pattern is cut in 7 sizes from 32 to 44 inches bust measure. As illustrated on figure the medium size will require 3¼ yards of 54-inch plush, with 1 yard of 50-inch Krimmer fur, or 3 yards of fur banding will be needed.   PRICE, **15** CENTS.

8280—LADIES' COAT. 8 sizes, 32 to 46 inches bust measure. **8258**—LADIES' FIVE-GORED SKIRT. Lower edge with plaits drawn out about 2⅝ yards. 9 sizes, 22 to 38 inches waist measure, corresponding to 36 to 54 inches hip measure. As on figure the medium size requires 5¼ yards of 44-inch novelty check. **15** CTS. EACH.

8600—LADIES' COAT. 8 sizes, 32 to 46 inches bust measure. **8085**—LADIES' TWO-PIECE SKIRT. Lower edge about 2½ yards. 7 sizes, 22 to 34 inches waist, 36 to 49½ inches hip. As on figure the medium size requires 4½ yards of 50-inch broadcloth, with 1 piece of fur 18 by 22 for collar, 5¼ yards of fur banding. **15** CTS. EACH.

Coat—8694 Skirt—8732

8728

8728

Coat—8685 Skirt—8623 Blouse—8696 Skirt—8697

8694—8732 8728 8685—8623 8696—97 8685—8726

8694—LADIES' COAT: 20 Inch Length at the Back; Straight or Cutaway Closing; Three-Quarter Length One-Seam Flowing Sleeves or Long Two-Seam Sleeves with Slight Fulness at the Top which may be Shrunken Out. 5 sizes, 32 to 40 inches bust. **8732**—LADIES' TWO OR THREE PIECE SKIRT: Lower edge with plaits drawn out about 3 yards. 8 sizes, 22 to 36 inches waist, corresponding to 36 to 52 inches hip. Combined as on figure, the medium size needs 4½ yards of 50-inch gabardine with 6¼ yards of braid for one row. PRICE, **15** CENTS EACH.

8728—LADIES' DRESS: Chemisette; Three Styles of Collar; Long Dart-Fitted or Short Sleeves; One-Piece Gathered Tunic in Cascade Effect at the Back; Three-Piece Skirt. Lower edge about 2½ yards. 6 sizes, 32 to 42 inches bust measure. The 36-inch bust size will require as illustrated in front view on figure, 9¼ yards of 36-inch striped taffeta, with ½ yard of 24 inch plain taffeta for collar and belt and 2 yards of ribbon. As illustrated in back view on figure, 6 yards of 54-inch cloth, with 10 yards of 2-inch braid to trim. PRICE, **15** CENTS.

8685—LADIES' FITTED COAT: 26 or 20 or 15 Inch Length at the Back; Flare Collar which may be Omitted; Two Styles of Two-Seam Sleeves. 7 sizes, 32 to 44 inches bust. **8623**—LADIES' SKIRT: Slightly High or Regulation Waistline. Lower edge of gathered skirt about 3¾ yards. 5 sizes, 22 to 30 inches waist measure, corresponding to 36 to 44½ inches hip measure. If combined as illustrated on figure, the medium size will require with coat in 20-inch length 3¼ yards of 50-inch plain cloth for coat and skirt facing, with 5⅜ yards of 44-inch plaid cloth for skirt, cuffs and collar. PRICE, **15** CENTS EACH.

8696—LADIES' BLOUSE: Chemisette; Back Extending Over the Shoulders to Form a Yoke. 9 sizes, 32 to 48 inches bust. **8697**—LADIES' SKIRT. Lower edge with plaits drawn out about 2¾ yards. The pattern is cut in 9 sizes from 22 to 38 inches waist measure, corresponding to 36 to 54 inches hip measure. If combined as illustrated on figure, the medium size will require 1¾ yards of 36-inch silk for blouse, with ⅝ yard of 27-inch silk for vest and cuffs, ⅝ yard of 18-inch all-over lace for collar and to face chemisette, 1 yard of 27-inch material for chemisette and 2½ yards of 54-inch cheviot for skirt. **15** CENTS EACH.

Description of figure on cover

8685—LADIES' FITTED COAT: 26 or 20 or 15 Inch Length at the Back; Flare Collar which may be Omitted; Two Styles of Two-Seam Sleeves. 7 sizes, 32 to 44 inches bust. **8726**—LADIES' ONE-PIECE GATHERED SKIRT: Slightly High Waistline; Draped with Pockets or Falling Free. Lower edge about 3 yards. 5 sizes, 22 to 30 inches waist to 36 to 44½ inches hip measure. As illustrated on the cover the medium size will require 2½ yards of 40-inch satin for coat in 26-inch length, with 2½ yards of 54-inch broadcloth for skirt. PRICE, **15** CENTS EACH.

THE VERY NEWEST NOTES
IN SUITS AND DRESSES

*B*LEAK and dreary though the February days be, our thoughts begin to turn towards our Spring clothes, and it is not really premature to give them some attention for many of us at present are planning trips to warmer climes. Suit coats are generally hip length or shorter, invariably flaring at the edges. The fitted coats with short circular peplums and in direct contrast, the loose box-coats with rippling edges, as well as the semi-fitted belted models, are among the most popular styles. The materials most favored are broadcloths, serges and gabardines, with satins, taffetas and silk poplins for dressy afternoon suits. Just at present wool jersey cloths are immensely popular for outing and skating and are to be had in all the most attractive colorings. Silk jersey cloths are also very smart.

In afternoon dresses there are charming soft styles which are lovely in taffetas, silk poplins, satins and crêpe de Chines. The skirt and overblouse or bolero, which is a feature of many dresses, are generally of the same material, with the underblouse or sleeves of lace, silk voile, Georgette crêpe or other sheer material.

Apron tunics and side tunics are used freely to increase the pretty, full effect of skirts. The attractive princess dresses are often fashioned of two materials. A deep facing almost reaching the hips forms the lower part of the dress when this style is worked out.

Coat—8722
Skirt—8653

8722—LADIES' COAT: 26 or 20 Inch Length at the Back. 7 sizes, 32 to 44 inches bust measure. **8653**—LADIES' TWO-PIECE SKIRT. Lower edge about 2½ yards. 6 sizes, 22 to 32 inches waist measure, corresponding to 36 to 47 inches hip measure. Combined as on figure, the medium size will require 4¼ yards of 50-inch cloth, with ⅛ yard of 20-inch velvet for collar. **15** CENTS EACH.

8708—LADIES' BLOUSE. 8 sizes, 32 to 46 inches bust measure. **8709**—LADIES' TWO-PIECE SKIRT. Lower edge about 2½ yards. 6 sizes, 22 to 32 inches waist measure, corresponding to 36 to 47 inches hip measure. Combined as illustrated on figure, the medium size will require 5¼ yards of 40-inch satin, with 2 yards of 40-inch all-over lace. PRICE, **15** CENTS EACH.

8578—LADIES' BLOUSE. 9 sizes, 32 to 48 inches bust. **8579**—LADIES' TWO OR THREE PIECE SKIRT. Lower edge about 2 yards. 9 sizes, 22 to 38 inches waist,

Transfer 10255
Blouse—8708
Skirt—8709

Blouse—8578
Skirt—8579

8717

Transfer 10290
Blouse—8511
Skirt—8526

corresponding to 36 to 54 inches hip. Combined as on figure, the medium size requires 3¾ yards of 44-inch cloth, with 2¼ yards of 36-inch silk for blouse, and ¾ yard of 27-inch silk for girdle. **15** CENTS EACH.

8511—LADIES' BLOUSE. 7 sizes, 32 to 44 inches bust. **8526**—LADIES' FOUR-PIECE SKIRT. Lower edge with plaits drawn out about 3¼ yards. 9 sizes, 22 to 38 inches waist, corresponding to 36 to 54 inches hip. Combined as on figure, the medium size requires 2⅝ yards of 36-inch crêpe for blouse, with 1 yard of 27-inch net and 5⅛ yards of 44-inch serge for skirt. **15** CENTS EACH.

8717—LADIES' PRINCESS DRESS; Separate Guimpe. Lower edge about 2¾ yards. The pattern is cut in 6 sizes from 32 to 42 inches bust. The 36-inch bust size will require as illustrated on figure, 3⅜ yards of 36-inch satin, with 3½ yards of 27-inch velvet for facing, and 1¾ yards of 36-inch striped voile for guimpe. PRICE, **15** CENTS.

8722—8653   8708—8709

8578—79   8717   8511—26

FROCKS FOR THE SUNNY SOUTH

Are you preparing for a trip to the South? Then you will need light lingerie dresses of sheer texture, and pretty suggestions for making them will be found in the dainty models illustrated on this page.

Blouse—8145   Skirt—8072

8145—LADIES' BLOUSE. For the embroidery design use Standard transfer 10114. 8 sizes, 32 to 46 inches bust measure. **8072—LADIES' SKIRT.** Lower edge about 2⅝ yards. 7 sizes, 22 to 34 inches waist, corresponding to 36 to 49½ inches hip measure. Combined as on figure, the medium size requires 5 yards of 40-inch cotton voile, with 5 yards of insertion, ⅝ yard of 18-inch net for collar and to face chemisette, and 1 yard of 27-inch silk for girdle. **15 CENTS EACH.**

8701—LADIES' BLOUSE. 6 sizes, 32 to 42 inches bust measure. **8702—LADIES' SKIRT.** Lower edge about 2⅞ yards. 5 sizes, 22 to 30 inches waist measure, corresponding to 36 to 44½ inches hip measure. Combined as illustrated on figure, the medium size will require 6¼ yards of 36-inch net for dress, with 3¾ yards of lace insertion, ⅞ yards of wide ribbon for girdle, 1¼ yards of narrow ribbon and 6 yards of net footing for ruffles on skirt. **PRICE, 15 CENTS EACH.**

Blouse—8701   Skirt—8702

8327—LADIES' BLOUSE. 6 sizes, 32 to 42 inches bust. **8593—LADIES' ONE - PIECE STRAIGHT GATHERED SKIRT.** Lower edge about 2¼ yards. 7 sizes, 22 to 34 inches waist, corresponding to 36 to 49½ inches hip. Combined as on figure, the medium size requires 4⅝ yards of 40-inch figured cotton crêpe, with 1¾ yards of 36-inch plain crêpe for underblouse, 3⅞ yards of 40-inch dark crêpe for underskirt, and ⅜ yard of 18-inch all-over lace for yoke. **PRICE, 15 CENTS EACH.**

Blouse—8327   Skirt—8593

Blouse—8737
Skirt—8738

8737—LADIES' BLOUSE. 5 sizes, 32 to 40 inches bust measure. **8738—LADIES' SKIRT.** Lower edge about 2½ yards. 5 sizes, 22 to 30 inches waist measure, corresponding to 36 to 44½ inches hip measure. Combined as illustrated on figure the medium size will require 4¼ yards of 36-inch embroidered cotton, with 1¾ yards of 36-inch plain material for blouse, ⅞ yard of 27-inch silk for girdle and 2⅛ yards of lace edging to trim. **PRICE, 15 CENTS EACH.**

8544—LADIES' BLOUSE. 7 sizes, 32 to 44 inches bust. **8556—LADIES' TWO-PIECE SKIRT.** Lower edge about 2 yards. 6 sizes, 22 to 32 inches waist, corresponding to 36 to 47 inches hip. Combined as on figure, the medium size requires 3⅝ yards of 39-inch flouncing for tunic, with 1⅝ yards of 9-inch flouncing for lower part of blouse, 4 yards of 36-inch lawn and ⅞ yard of 27-inch silk for girdle. **PRICE, 15 CENTS EACH.**

Blouse—8544   Skirt—8556

8145
8072

8737—38

8327
8593

8701—02

8544—56

SOME OF THE LATE DESIGNS

Apron tunics and graceful draperies continue to be very popular features of skirts, while many of the blouses are characterized by wide bretelles and overblouses in a number of styles.

Blouse—8719 Skirt—8720

8717

8711

Bodice—8714
Skirt—8715

Blouse—8708 Skirt—8709

8719—20
8717
8711
8714—15
8708—09

8719—LADIES' LOW-NECKED BLOUSE. 6 sizes, 32 to 42 inches bust. **8720**—LADIES' TWO-PIECE SKIRT. Lower edge of skirt about 2½ yards. 5 sizes, 22 to 30 inches waist, corresponding to 36 to 44½ inches hip. If combined as on figure, the medium size needs 6⅞ yards of 36-inch light taffeta, with ⅝ yard of 36-inch all-over lace, 1¾ yards of 36-inch dark taffeta, and ⅞ yard of 36-inch material for guimpe. **15** CTS. EACH.

8717—LADIES' PRINCESS DRESS: Closed on the Shoulders; Separate Guimpe with Long Dart-Fitted or Short Sleeves; Two-Piece Skirt Facing which may be Omitted. Lower edge about 2¾ yards. 6 sizes, 32 to 42 inches bust measure. The 36-inch bust size will require as illustrated on figure 3⅜ yards of 40-inch serge, with 1¾ yards of 36-inch taffeta for guimpe, 4¾ yards of braid trimming and 1¾ yards of ribbon. **15** CENTS.

8711—LADIES' PRINCESS DRESS, in Jumper Style: Closed at the Left Side; Jumper Front and Back in One with Four-Piece Skirt. Lower edge about 3¼ yards. The pattern is cut in 5 sizes from 32 to 40 inches bust measure. The 36-inch bust size will require as illustrated on figure 6⅛ yards of 36-inch taffeta, with 1¼ yards of 36-inch crêpe for sleeves, chemisette, collar and frill, ¾ yard of 24-inch satin for girdle and pipings and ⅞ yard of 36-inch material for front and back of guimpe. **15** CTS.

8708—LADIES' BLOUSE: High or Open Neck; Overblouse. 8 sizes, 32 to 46 inches bust measure. **8709**—LADIES' TWO-PIECE SKIRT: Two-Piece Tunic with Straight Lower Edge which may be Omitted. Lower edge about 2½ yards. 6 sizes, 22 to 32 inches waist measure, corresponding to 36 to 47 inches hip measure. If combined as illustrated on figure, the medium size will require 3⅛ yards of 50-inch broadcloth, with 1⅝ yards of 40-inch satin for front, back, cuffs and collar and 17½ yards of braid to trim. PRICE, **15** CENTS EACH.

8714—LADIES' DRAPED BODICE. 7 sizes, 32 to 44 ins. bust measure. **8715**—LADIES' TWO-PIECE SKIRT. Lower edge about 2½ yards. 5 sizes, 22 to 30 inches waist measure, corresponding to 36 to 44½ inches hip measure. If combined as illustrated on figure the medium size will require 3⅜ yards of 36-inch satin for sleeves and underskirt, with ½ yard of 32-inch crêpe for collar and yoke, 4⅜ yards of 40-inch figured crêpe for bodice and apron tunic and ⅞ yard of 36-inch material for lining. PRICE, **15** CENTS EACH.

NEW LINGERIE AND NEGLIGEES

8703

8703—LADIES' NEGLIGEE: High or Open Neck; Long or Short One-Seam Sleeves; Round or Square Corners; Clearing or Shorter Length. Lower edge about 2¼ yards. The pattern is cut in 8 sizes from 32 to 46 inches bust measure. The 36-inch bust size will require as illustrated on figure 4½ yards of 36-inch cotton crêpe, with ½ yard of 36-inch silk for collar and bands on sleeves and 2⅜ yards of 6-inch ribbon for a girdle. Such a simple negligee as this model is sure to be a favorite. It will make up attractively in cotton crêpe, lawn, batiste, silk mull or crêpe de Chine. Lace edging may be used to finish the neck and sleeves, or contrasting material as shown on the figure. The outline of the yoke is quite attractive and graceful.
PRICE, **15** CENTS.

Brassiere—**8558**
Petticoat—**8723**

Brassiere—**7193**   Corset Cover—**8101**
Petticoat—**8723**   Drawers—**8686**

8558—LADIES' BRASSIERE OR CORSET COVER. **9** sizes, 32 to 48 inches bust. **8723**—LADIES' COMBINATION ENVELOPE DRAWERS AND LONG OR SHORT GATHERED PETTICOAT. Lower edge of petticoat about 2 yards. 8 sizes, 22 to 36 inches waist, corresponding to 36 to 52 inches hip. As illustrated on figure, the medium size will require ⅞ yard of 36 inch cambric, with 3 yards of edging, 1⅜ yards of insertion, 1¼ yards of beading and 3½ yards of 36-inch lawn for petticoat, with 2⅝ yards of edging.   PRICE, **15** CENTS EACH.

7193—LADIES' ONE-PIECE BRASSIERE: Straight Upper Edge. 8 sizes, 32 to 46 inches bust measure. **8723**—LADIES' COMBINATION ENVELOPE DRAWERS AND LONG OR SHORT GATHERED PETTICOAT. 8 sizes, 22 to 36 inches waist measure, corresponding to 36 to 52 inches hip measure. As illustrated on figure, the medium size will require 1¼ yards of 10½-inch flouncing for brassiere, with 1¾ yards of ribbon; 2⅜ yards of 17-inch flouncing for petticoat and 1½ yards of 36-inch material for drawers. PRICE, **15** CENTS EACH.

8703   8558-8723   7193-8723   8101-8686   8735-8540

8101 — LADIES' BRASSIERE OR CORSET COVER. 9 sizes, 32 to 48 bust. **8686** — CIRCULAR OPEN DRAWERS. For the embroidery illustrated use Standard transfer pattern 10198. Lower edge of each leg about 1½ yards. 9 sizes, 22 to 38 inches waist, to 36 to 54 inches hip. As on figure, the medium size will require ⅞ yard of 36-inch nainsook, with 3⅛ yards of lace edging for corset cover; 1⅞ yards of 36-inch nainsook, with 3⅞ yards of edging for drawers.   **15** CTS. EACH.

8735 — LADIES' ONE-PIECE DRESSING-SACK. 9 sizes, 32 to 48 inches bust. **8540**—LADIES' THREE OR FOUR PIECE SKIRT. Lower edge about 2¾ yards. 9 sizes, 22 to 38 inches waist, corresponding to 36 to 54 inches hip. As illustrated on figure, the medium size will require 2⅝ yards of 32-inch challis, with 3¾ yards of ribbon for frills, 2⅛ yards of 3-inch ribbon for girdle and 2 yards of 54-inch cloth is needed for two-piece skirt.
PRICE, **15** CENTS EACH.

Dressing-Sack—**8735**
Skirt—**8540**

SIMPLE BLOUSES AND SKIRTS

8731—LADIES' MIDDY BLOUSE: to be Slipped Over the Head. 6 sizes, 32 to 42 inches bust measure. **8732**—LADIES' TWO OR THREE-PIECE SKIRT. Lower edge with plaits drawn out about 3 yards. 8 sizes, 22 to 36 inches waist measure, corresponding to 36 to 52 inches hip measure. If combined as illustrated on figure, the medium size will require 4⅛ yards of 44-inch French serge, with ⅜ yard of 36-inch contrasting serge. **15** CENTS EACH.

8515—LADIES' BLOUSE. 9 sizes, 32 to 48 inches bust. **8412**—LADIES' THREE-PIECE SKIRT. Lower edge with habit back about 2⅞ yards; with plaits drawn out about 3⅛ yards. 9 sizes, 22 to 38 inches waist, corresponding to 36 to 54 inches hip. For the embroidery design use Standard transfer pattern 10122. If combined as on figure, the medium size requires 2 yards of 36-inch cotton voile, with 3¾ yards of 44-inch cloth for skirt. **15** CENTS EACH.

8491—LADIES' BLOUSE: Back Extending Over the Shoulders to Form a Yoke. 8 sizes, 32 to 46 inches bust. **8492**—LADIES' SKIRT: Three-Piece Yoke Having the Right Front in One with Panel Front of Three-Piece Lower Part. Lower edge about 2½ yards. 8 sizes, 22 to 36 inches waist, corresponding to 36 to 52 inches hip. If combined as illustrated on figure, the medium size needs 3¾ yards of 50-inch broadcloth. **15** CENTS EACH.

8687—LADIES' BLOUSE. For the embroidery design use Standard Transfer pattern 10225. 7 sizes, 32 to 44 inches bust. **8688**—LADIES' SEVEN-GORED SKIRT. Lower edge with plaits drawn out about 2½ yards; with habit back about 2¼ yards. 9 sizes, 22 to 38 inches waist, corresponding to 36 to 54 inches hip. If combined as on figure, the medium size will require 1⅞ yards of 40-inch crêpe for blouse, with 3 yards of 44-inch cheviot. **15** CENTS EACH.

Blouse—8731
Skirt—8732

8691—LADIES' BLOUSE. 8 sizes, 32 to 46 inches bust. **8692**—LADIES' FOUR-PIECE SKIRT. Lower edge with plaits drawn out about 2⅝ yards. 9 sizes, 22 to 38 inches waist, corresponding to 35 to 54 inches hip. Combined as on figure, the medium size requires 1⅞ yards of 44-inch crêpe de Chine, with ¾ yard of 18-inch net, 2⅝ yards of 44-inch Shepherds' check and ¾ yard of 36-inch satin. PRICE, **15** CENTS EACH.

Blouse—8491
Skirt—8492

Blouse—8691
Skirt—8692

Blouse—8515
Skirt—8412

Blouse—8687
Skirt—8688

8515-8412   8731-32   8691-92   8491-92   8687-88

PUFFED, RUFFLED AND DRAPED ARE THE NEW EVENING GOWNS

Blouse—8461   Skirt—8556

Bodice—8714   Skirt—8715

Blouse—8737   Skirt—8738

Blouse—8719   Skirt—8720

Bodice—8426   Skirt—8211

8461—LADIES' EVENING BLOUSE. 9 sizes, 32 to 48 inches bust measure. **8556**—LADIES' TWO-PIECE SKIRT: One-Piece Straight Gathered Tunic Hanging Free at Slightly High Waistline or Draped at Regulation Waistline. Lower edge about 2 yards. 6 sizes, 22 to 32 inches waist measure, corresponding to 36 to 47 inches hip measure. If combined as on figure, the medium size will require 3⅝ yards of 38-inch flouncing for tunic, with 1 yard of 40-inch lace for overblouse, 1¾ yards of 40-inch tulle for sleeves and blouse, 3 yards of 36-inch faille taffeta for skirt and girdle. This gown is extremely dainty.
PRICE, **15** CENTS EACH.

8714—LADIES' DRAPED BODICE: Low-Necked French Lining. 7 sizes, 32 to 44 inches bust measure. **8715**—LADIES' TWO-PIECE SKIRT: Gathers at the Back; Lower edge about 2½ yards. 5 sizes, 22 to 30 inches waist, to 36 to 44½ inches hip. If combined as on figure, the medium size will require 4⅝ yards of 36-inch embroidered taffeta for outside front, back and tunic, with 2½ yards of 36-inch plain taffeta for foundation, ⅝ yard of 36-inch lace for sleeves, and ⅞ yard of 36-inch material for lining. **15** CENTS EACH.

8737—LADIES' BLOUSE. 5 sizes, 32 to 40 inches bust measure. **8738**—LADIES' SKIRT: Two-Piece Yoke Lengthened by a Straight Gathered Lower Part; Lower edge about 2½ yards. 5 sizes, 22 to 30 inches waist, to 36 to 44½ inches hip. If combined as illustrated on figure the medium size will require 4⅛ yards of 40-inch Georgette crêpe for bolero and tunic, with 1¾ yards of 36-inch lace for blouse, 6⅛ yards of 40-inch charmeuse for girdle, lower part and yokes and bands on tunic, and 2¼ yards of velvet ribbon.
15 CENTS EACH.

8719—LADIES' LOW-NECKED BLOUSE: For embroidery on bretelles and tunic use transfer No. 10255. 6 sizes, 32 to 42 inches bust. **8720**—LADIES' TWO-PIECE SKIRT: Lower edge of skirt about 2½ yards. 5 sizes, 22 to 30 inches waist measure, to 36 to 44½ inches hip. If combined as illustrated on figure, the medium size will require 6½ yards of 36-inch taffeta for skirt, tunic and bretelles, with 9 yards of 8-inch edging for ruffles, 1⅜ yards of 12-inch edging for blouse, and ⅞ yard 36 for lining guimpe.
15 CENTS EACH.

8426—LADIES' BODICE: High, Round or Low Neck; Long One-Seam Sleeves in Two Styles at the Wrist or Short Sleeves; Low-Necked French Lining. 7 sizes from 32 to 44 inches bust measure. **8211**—LADIES' ONE-PIECE STRAIGHT GATHERED TUCKED SKIRT. Lower edge about 2½ yards. 5 sizes from 22 to 30 inches waist measure, corresponding to 36 to 44½ inches hip measure. If combined as illustrated on figure the medium size will require 4¼ yards of 44-inch crêpe de Chine, with ¾ yard of 40-inch tulle for upper portion of bodice, and 1¾ yards of pearl trimming will be needed.
PRICE, **15** CENTS EACH.

8461
8556

8714
8715

8737
8738

8719—8720

8426—8211

BOLEROS SHARE HONOR WITH OVERBLOUSES IN THE NEW MODELS

Blouse—8602 Skirt—8311

8602—LADIES' BLOUSE: Body in One with Long or Short Sleeves. 7 sizes from 32 to 44 inches bust measure. **8311—LADIES' SEVEN - GORED SKIRT.** Lower edge with habit back about 2½ yards. Lower edge with plaits drawn out about 2¾ yards. The pattern is cut in 9 sizes from 22 to 38 inches waist measure, corresponding to 36 to 54 inches hip measure. If combined as illustrated on figure, the medium size will require 1⅞ yards of 40-inch Georgette crêpe for blouse, with ¼ yard of 24-inch satin for collar, 4½ yards of 50-inch gabardine for skirt, overblouse and cuffs and 2⅛ yards of 36-inch taffeta for bands. **15 CENTS EACH.**

**Blouse—8583
Skirt—8441**

8583 — LADIES' BLOUSE. 7 sizes, 32 to 44 inches bust measure. **8441—LADIES' SEVEN-GORED PLAITED SKIRT.** Lower edge with plaits drawn out about 3⅝ yards. 9 sizes, 22 to 38 inches waist measure, corresponding to 36 to 54 inches hip measure. If combined as illustrated on figure the medium size will require 2 yards of 36-inch taffeta for blouse, with ⅞ yard of 40-inch net for underblouse, ⅞ yard of 36-inch material for lining, and 4½ yards of 50-inch broadcloth for skirt. **PRICE, 15 CENTS EACH.**

Dress—8711

8711—LADIES' PRINCESS DRESS IN JUMPER STYLE: Closed at the Left Side. For the braiding design use Standard transfer pattern No. 10086. Lower edge about 3¼ yards. The pattern is cut in 5 sizes from 32 to 40 inches bust measure. The 36-inch bust size will require as illustrated on figure, 6¼ yards of 36-inch velveteen, with 1¼ yards of 36-inch all over lace for collar, sleeves and chemisette, ¾ yard of 24-inch satin for a girdle, and ⅞ yard of 36-inch material will be needed for guimpe fronts and back. **PRICE, 15 CENTS.**

Dress—8734

8734—LADIES' DRESS: High or Open Neck; Bolero with or without the Panel Back. (Desirable for Flouncings, Bordered Materials or Other Fabrics). Lower edge about 3 yards. The pattern is cut in 5 sizes from 32 to 40 inches bust measure. The 36-inch bust size will require, as illustrated on figure, 2⅜ yards of 36-inch serge for bolero and sleeves, with 3⅞ yards of 40-inch plaid serge for skirt, 1⅛ yards of 40-inch net for front, collar, and back of blouse, ¾ yard of 27-inch velvet will be needed for girdle. **PRICE, 15 CENTS.**

Bodice—8592 Skirt—8436

8592—LADIES' DRAPED BODICE: High or Open Neck; Long or Three-Quarter-Length Dart-Fitted Sleeves with or without the Gauntlet Cuffs. 7 sizes, 32 to 44 inches bust measure. **8436 — LADIES' SHIRRED OR GATHERED THREE-PIECE SKIRT.** Lower edge about 3¼ yards. The pattern is cut in 7 sizes from 22 to 34 inches waist measure, corresponding to 36 to 49½ inches hip measure. If combined as illustrated on figure, the medium size will require 8⅝ yards of 36-inch velveteen for blouse and skirt, with ¾ yard of 40-inch chiffon for vest and collar, and 1⅛ yards lining for body and stay. **15 CENTS EACH.**

8602—8311   8583—8441

8711   8734   8592—8436

8695 8729

8445 8736 8712

8718

8695—LITTLE GIRLS' DRESS: Separate Blouse; Back Extending Over the Shoulders to Form a Yoke; Long or Short Sleeves; Straight Gathered Skirt Attached to an Underbody. 9 sizes, 4 to 12 years. The 5-year size will require as illustrated on figure 2⅛ yards of 13-inch flouncing, with 1¼ yards of 42-inch batiste, ⅜ yard of 18-inch all-over embroidery to face underbody, ½ yard of 36-inch material for underbody, 1 yard of insertion, and 1⅛ yards of edging. PRICE, **15** CENTS.

8729—LITTLE BOYS' SUIT: Blouse to be Slipped Over the Head; Removable Shield; Long or Short Sleeves; Straight Trousers. 5 sizes, 2 to 6 years The 5-year size will require as illustrated on figure 2⅞ yards of 27-inch striped galatea, with 1 yard of 27-inch dark galatea for collar and belt, ⅝ yard of 27-inch light galatea for shield and 3 yards of braid will be needed for three rows on collar. PRICE, **15** CENTS.

8718—GIRLS' AND JUNIORS' COAT in Two Lengths: Closed to the Neck or Rolled Open; One-Seam Sleeves with Slight Fulness at the Top which may be Shrunken Out. The pattern is cut in 5 sizes from 8 to 16 years. The 12-year size will require as illustrated on figure 2½ yards of 54-inch serge for coat, with ½ yard of 24-inch velvet for collar and cuffs. Broadcloth and gabardine are also suitable. PRICE, **15** CENTS.

8445—LITTLE GIRLS' SMOCKED OR GATHERED DRESS: High or Open Neck; Long or Short Sleeves; Bloomers. The pattern is cut in 9 sizes from 2 to 10 years. The 4-year size will require as illustrated on figure 1⅞ yards of 36-inch crêpe, with ⅜ yard of 36-inch figured crêpe for collar, cuffs and pockets, and 1 yard of 36-inch material for bloomers. Linen, poplin or chambray may be used. PRICE, **15** CENTS.

8736—GIRLS' AND JUNIORS THREE-PIECE SUIT: Coat Closed to the Neck or Rolled Open; Two-Seam Sleeves with Slight Fulness at the Top which may be Shrunken Out; Three Piece Jumper Skirt. 9 sizes, 8 to 16 years. The 11-year size will require as illustrated on figure 3¼ yards of 44-inch serge for suit, with ¼ yard of 36-inch contrasting serge for collar and 3¼ yards of braid. PRICE, **15** CENTS.

8712—LITTLE GIRLS' COAT: Two Seam Sleeves with Slight Fulness at the Top which may be Shrunken Out. The pattern is cut in 5 sizes from 2 to 10 years. The 6-year size will require as illustrated on figure 2⅛ yards of 44-inch shepherd's check for coat. PRICE, **15** CENTS.

8713—GIRLS' AND JUNIORS' REDINGOTE: Closed on the Left Shoulder; Separate Guimpe; Two Styles of Collar. For the braiding design illustrated use Standard transfer pattern 10176. 9 sizes, 8 to 16 years. The 13-year size requires as on figure 2¾ yards of 40-inch cloth for dress, with 1⅞ yards of 36-inch silk for guimpe. **15** CTS.

8693—GIRLS' AND JUNIORS' ETON SUIT: Separate Bolero; Long Sleeves in Two Styles at the Wrist or Short Sleeves; Straight Plaited Skirt Attached to an Underbody. 9 sizes, 8 to 16 years. The 14-year size will require as on figure 4 yards of 36-inch serge, with 1¼ yards of 36-inch contrasting serge. PRICE, **15** CENTS.

8706—GIRLS' AND JUNIORS' DRESS: Jacket Fronts which may be Omitted; Six-Piece Skirt. 9 sizes, 8 to 16 years The 13-year size will require as illustrated on figure 3 yards of 42-inch cloth, with ¾ yard of 36-inch silk for front of blouse and ⅜ yard of 27-inch satin will be needed for collar. PRICE, **15** CENTS.

8713 8706 8693

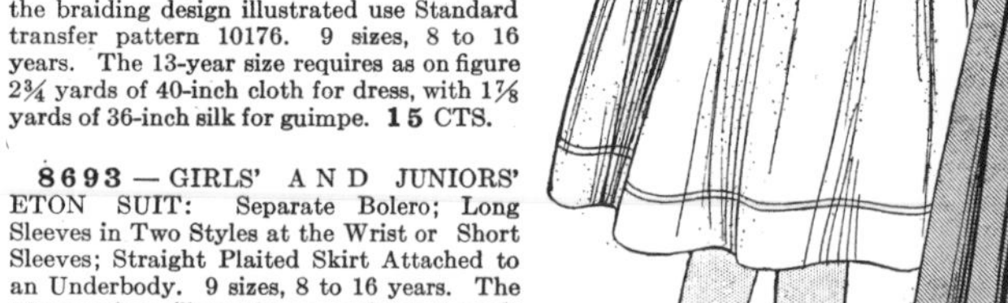

8695 8729 8718 8445 8736 8712

8713 8693 8706

8739

8699

8690

Blouse—8701   Skirt—8702

8701—LADIES' BLOUSE: High or Open Neck; Long or Short One-Seam Sleeves. 6 sizes, 32 to 42 inches bust measure. **8702**—LADIES' SKIRT: Three-Piece Yoke; Panel Back in One-Piece Lower Part Draped or Falling Free. Lower edge about 2⅝ yards. 5 sizes, 22 to 30 inches waist measure, corresponding to 36 to 44½ inches hip measure. If combined as illustrated on figure the medium size will require 6¼ yards of 36-inch taffeta, and ½ yard of 40-inch chiffon will be needed for collar.   PRICE, **15** CENTS EACH.

8739—LADIES' DRESS: Closed to the Neck or Rolled Open; Long Dart-Fitted or Short Sleeves; Slightly High Waistline; Two-Piece Shirred Tunic and Trimming-Band which may be Omitted; Two-Piece Skirt. For the embroidery design use Standard transfer pattern 10122. Lower edge about 2½ yards. 6 sizes, 32 to 42 inches bust measure. The 36-inch bust size will require as illustrated on figure 6⅛ yards of 36-inch taffeta, with 1 yard of 36-inch contrasting taffeta for band and 2¼ yards of 36-inch material for gores.   PRICE, **15** CENTS.

8690—LADIES' COAT: 50 or 45 Inch Length at the Back; Body and Sleeves in One; Closed to the Neck or Rolled Open; Pockets in One with Sides of Four-Piece Belt or Regulation Belt. The pattern is cut in 6 sizes from 32 to 42 inches bust measure. The 36-inch bust size will require as illustrated on figure for coat in 50-inch length 4¼ yards of 54-inch novelty check, with ¾ yard of 24-inch velvet for collar, belt and straps. An up-to-date coat developed in the popular checked coating as illustrated here will be found useful for many occasions. The large pockets and belt are noteworthy.   PRICE, **15** CENTS.

Blouse—8725   Skirt—8726

8699—LADIES' PRINCESS DRESS: Closed on the Left Side; High or Open Neck; Long Dart-Fitted or Short Sleeves; Four-Piece Skirt Attached Under a Tuck Edge; Clearing or Shorter Length. For the embroidery design illustrated on the figure use Standard transfer pattern 10176. Lower edge with plaits drawn out about 2⅞ yards. The pattern is cut in 6 sizes from 32 to 42 inches bust measure. The 36-inch bust size will require as illustrated on figure 4½ yards of 50-inch gabardine, with braid trimming.   PRICE, **15** CENTS.

8725—LADIES' BLOUSE: High or Open Neck. 9 sizes, 32 to 48 inches bust measure. **8726**—LADIES' ONE-PIECE GATHERED SKIRT: Draped with Pockets or Falling Free. Lower edge about 3 yards. 5 sizes, 22 to 30 inches waist measure, corresponding to 36 to 44½ inches hip measure. If combined as illustrated on figure the medium size requires 6¼ yards of 36-inch polka-dot taffeta, with 1¾ yards of 24-inch satin for revers, cuffs, pocket-drops and a girdle and ⅝ yards of 40-inch chiffon for vest and collar.   PRICE, **15** CENTS EACH.

8701—02   8739   8690   8699   8725—26

9150—LADIES' BLOUSE. 7 sizes, 32 to 44 inches bust measure. **9151**—LADIES' THREE-PIECE SKIRT. Lower edge about 1⅝ yards. The pattern is cut in 5 sizes from 22 to 30 inches waist measure, corresponding to 36 to 44½ inches hip measure. If combined as illustrated on figure, the medium size will require 6¼ yards of 40-inch satin for blouse and tunic and to face skirt, with 1 yard of 27-inch crêpe for collar and frills, and 2⅝ yards of 32 or 36 inch material for foundation skirt.   Price, 20 cents each.

9159—LADIES' COAT: 50 or 42 Inch Length at the Back; Two-Seam Sleeves with Slight Fulness at the Top which may be Shrunken Out. 7 sizes, 32 to 44 inches bust measure. **8683**—LADIES' THREE OR FOUR PIECE SKIRT. Lower edge about 2½ yards. 9 sizes, 22 to 38 inches waist measure, corresponding to 36 to 54 inches hip measure. If combined as illustrated on figure, the medium size will require 3¾ yards of 50-inch material for coat, with 3 yards 36 for collar and skirt. 20 cts. for coat and 15 cts. for skirt.

Coat—**9072** Skirt—**9032**

Coat—**9137**
Skirt—**9003**

9072—LADIES' COAT. 7 sizes, 32 to 44 inches bust measure. **9032**—LADIES' TWO-PIECE SKIRT, Lower edge of gores about 1¾ yards. 7 sizes, 22 to 34 inches waist measure, to 36 to 49½ inches hip measure. If combined as illustrated on figure, the medium size will require 3⅝ yards of 54-inch cheviot for coat and skirt, with ½ yard of 24-inch velvet for collar and cuffs.
Price, 20 cents for coat and 15 cents for skirt.

9137—LADIES' COAT: 50 or 36 Inch Length at the Back. The pattern is cut in 9 sizes from 32 to 48 inches bust measure. **9003**—LADIES' SIX-GORED SKIRT. Lower edge with plaits drawn out about 3⅜ yards. 9 sizes, 22 to 38 inches waist measure, corresponding to 36 to 54 inches hip measure. If combined as illustrated on figure, the medium size will require 5½ yards of 54-inch novelty cloth for coat and skirt. 20 cents for coat and 15 cents for skirt.

Blouse—**9150** Skirt—**9151**   9150—9151   9072—9032   9137—9003 9159—8683   Coat—**9159** Skirt—**8683**

8994—LADIES' TWO-PIECE PRINCESS SLIP: to be Slipped Over the Head; Round Neck or Straight Outline Across the Top. Lower edge of flounce about 2⅞ yards. 7 sizes, 32 to 44 inches bust measure. The 36-inch bust size will require as illustrated on figure, 3⅜ yards of 36 or 45 inch nainsook for slip with gores cut away, with 7¾ yards of edging, 3½ yards of beading, 9 yards of ribbon and 5¾ yards of insertion. Price, 15 cents.

9164—LADIES' CORSET COVER. Use transfer No. 10297 and 10155 for the embroidery designs. 9 sizes, 32 to 48 bust. **9176**—LADIES' CIRCULAR OPEN DRAWERS. Lower edge of each leg about 1½ yards. 9 sizes, 22 to 38 waist; 36 to 54 hip. If combined as on figure, the medium size will require 1 yard of 36-inch nainsook for corset cover, with 2 yards of ribbon; 1⅝ yards of 36-inch nainsook for drawers, with 3 yards of insertion, 3⅝ yds. of 4-in. edging. 20 cts. each.

8994

9164—9176

8994

9182—9183   9175   9155 9156

Corset-Cover—**9164**
Drawers—**9176**

Shirt—**9155**
Skirt—**9156**

9175   Blouse—**9182** Skirt **9183**

Now is the Time When Our Thoughts

9182—LADIES' BLOUSE: High or Open Neck; Collar and Tie in One; Yoke in One with Long or Short Sleeves. (May be Attached to a Skirt or Worn Separately.) 6 sizes, 32 to 42 inches bust measure. **9183**—LADIES' TWO-PIECE SKIRT: High Waistline; One-Piece Belt which may be Omitted; Clearing or Shorter Length. Lower edge about 2 yards. 7 sizes, 22 to 34 inches waist measure, corresponding to 36 to 49½ inches hip measure. If combined as illustrated on figure, the medium size will require 2⅜ yards of 40-inch voile for blouse, with ⅝ yards of 36-inch contrasting voile for bias bands and 2⅞ yards of 50-inch cheviot for skirt. Price, 20 cents each.

9175—LADIES' BATHROBE OR KIMONO: Body in One with Long or Short Sleeves; High or Open Neck. The pattern is cut in 7 sizes from 32 to 44 inches bust measure. The 36-inch bust size will require as illustrated on figure, 3⅜ yards of 64-inch blanket cloth. This garment is a comfortable and simple model which may be worn as a bathrobe or as a kimono. As a bathrobe, it might be made of flanelet, Turkish toweling or eider-down, with the large collar that buttons up close to the neck. As a kimono, this large collar might be omitted, and the garment made of albatross or cotton crêpe. Large patch pockets on the gown are a great convenience. Price, 20 cents.

9155—LADIES' SHIRT: Neckband with Separate Turnover Collar or Open Neck with Large Collar; Back Yoke Facing which may be Omitted; Two Styles of Long One-Seam Sleeves. 9 sizes, 32 to 48 inches bust measure. **9156**—LADIES' TWO-PIECE SKIRT: High Waistline or Gathered at Regulation Waistline; One-Piece Box-Plaited Sections. Lower edge with plaits drawn out about 2⅞ yards. 6 sizes, 22 to 32 inches waist measure, corresponding to 36 to 47 inches hip measure. If combined as illustrated on figure, the medium size will require 2½ yards of 36-inch linen for shirt, with 2½ yards of 54-inch serge for skirt. Price, 20 cents each.

For All Hours of the Day and for All Manner

9150—Ladies' Blouse. 7 sizes, 32 to 44 bust. **9151**—Ladies' Three-Piece Skirt. Lower edge about 1⅝ yards. 5 sizes, 22 to 30 waist, 36 to 44½ hip. Combined as on figure, the medium size requires 6¼ yards of 40-inch poplin for blouse, tunic and to face skirt, with 15½ yards of ribbon for girdle with bow and ends and to trim, ¾ yard of 18-inch all-over lace for vest and standing collar, and 2⅝ yards of 32 or 36-inch material will be needed for foundation gores.   Price, 20 cents each.

9184—Ladies' Dress: High or Open Neck; Long Dart-Fitted or Short Sleeves; Slightly High Waistline; Four-Piece Tunic; Two-Piece Skirt; Clearing or Shorter Length. Lower edge about 1¾ yards. 8 sizes, 32 to 46 inches bust measure. The 36-inch bust size will require as illustrated on figure, 5 yards of 36-inch satin for blouse and tunic, with 1¾ yards of 36-inch contrasting satin for large collar and to face skirt, and 2⅝ yards of 32-inch material will be needed for foundation skirt.   Price, 20 cents.

Blouse—8997
Skirt—9077

Blouse—9144
Skirt—9145

8997—Ladies' Blouse. 6 sizes, 32 to 42 bust. **9077**—Ladies' Two-Piece Skirt. Lower edge about 2 yards. 7 sizes, 22 to 34 waist, 36 to 49½ hip. Combined as on figure, the medium size requires 2⅝ yards of 36-inch silk, with 2½ yards of braid, and 2⅜ yards of 44-inch cloth. 15 cents for blouse; 20 cents for skirt.

9144—Ladies' Blouse. 8 sizes, 32 to 46 bust. **9145**—Ladies' Two-Piece Skirt. Lower edge about 2¼ yards. 5 sizes, 22 to 30 waist, 36 to 44½ hip. Combined as on figure, the medium size requires 3 yards of 36-inch silk, with 3½ yards of 50-inch striped cloth.   Price, 20 cents each.

8997–9077   9144–45   9192   9184   9150–51

Blouse—9150
Skirt—9151

9192

9184

9192—Ladies' Evening Dress: Closed at the Front; Fichu or Short Sleeves. Lower edge about 1¾ yards. 6 sizes from 32 to 42 inches bust measure. The 36-inch bust size will require as illustrated on figure, 5¾ yards of 36-inch taffeta for overblouse and tunic, with 2⅝ yards of 36-inch contrasting taffeta for skirt, ½ yard of 18-inch net for tucker, 1 yard of 18 or more inch net for draped fichu and ½ yard of 36-inch material for underblouse. This charming dress has the new Empire waistline. Price, 20 cents.

# of Occasions—Here Are Your New Fall Clothes

9166—LADIES' BLOUSE: Back Extending Over the Shoulders to Form a Yoke. 8 sizes, 32 to 46 inches bust. **9167**—LADIES' THREE-PIECE SKIRT: Three-Piece Belt which may be Omitted. Lower edge about 2¼ yards. 7 sizes, 22 to 34 inches waist, corresponding to 36'to 49½ inches hip. If combined as on figure, the medium size will require 2⅝ yards of 32-inch washable satin for blouse, with ½ yard of 32-inch contrasting satin for collar and revers, and 2⅝ yards of 44-inch cloth for skirt.   Price, 20 cents each.

9172—LADIES' BLOUSE. 8 sizes, 32 to 46 inches bust measure. **9173**—LADIES' SIX-PIECE TUCK-SEAMED SKIRT: High Waistline. Lower edge about 2⅛ yards. 9 sizes, 22 to 38 inches waist measure, corresponding to 36 to 54 inches hip measure. If combined as illustrated on the figure, the medium size will require 2⅜ yards of 36-inch linen for blouse, with ½ yard of 27-inch contrasting linen for piping on collar, cuffs and pocket, and 2¾ yards of 44-inch serge for skirt.   Price, 20 cents each.

9142—LADIES' COAT: 50 or 45 Inch Length at the Back; Closed to the Neck or Rolled Open; Large Collar with Stand away Effect at the Back; Two-Seam Sleeves with Slight Fulness at the Top which may be Shrunken Out. The pattern is cut in 7 sizes from 32 to 44 inches bust measure. The 36-inch bust size will require as illustrated on figure, for coat in 45-inch length, 5 yards of 50-inch tweed. A smart coat of this type might be developed in tweeds, coatings, mixtures, broadcloth or serge. Price, 20 cents.

Blouse—9166   Skirt—9167

Blouse—9172
Skirt—9173

8879   9159

9159—LADIES' COAT: 50 or 42 Inch Length at the Back; Two-Seam Sleeves with Slight Fulness at the Top which may be Shrunken Out; Sash or Belt. 7 sizes, 32 to 44 inches bust measure. The 36-inch bust size will require as illustrated on figure 4¼ yards of 50 or 54 inch double-faced cloth.   Price, 20 cents.

8879—LADIES' COAT: 50 or 36 Inch Length at the Back; Circular Capes which may be Omitted. 7 sizes, 32 to 44 inches bust measure. The 36-inch bust size will require as illustrated on figure 5¾ yards of 44-inch cloth for coat, with ½ yard of 24-inch velvet for collar and bands.   Price, 15 cents.

9172–73   9166–67   9142   8879   9159

9177—LADIES' SHIRT: Convertible Collar. 8 sizes, 32 to 46 inches bust measure. **9178**—LADIES' THREE-PIECE SKIRT: High Waistline; Inverted Plait or Gathers at the Back. Lower edge about 2⅜ yards. 7 sizes, 22 to 34 waist measure, corresponding to 36 to 49½ inches hip measure. If combined as on figure the medium size will require 2½ yards of 40-inch linen for blouse, with 3⅛ yards of 44-inch cheviot.   Price, 20 cents each.

9076—LADIES' BLOUSE. For embroidery design use Standard transfer pattern 10361. 6 sizes, 32 to 42 bust. **8979**—LADIES' ONE-PIECE STRAIGHT GATHERED SKIRT. Lower edge about 3½ yards. 5 sizes, 22 to 30 waist, corresponding to 36 to 44½ hip. If combined as illustrated on figure the medium size will require 3¾ yards of 36-inch taffeta for blouse, with 3⅞ yards of 44-inch cloth for skirt.
20 cents for blouse; 15 cents for skirt.

October Brings New Draped Skirts, Also New Long Tunics Over Narrow

Blouse—9177   Skirt—9178

Blouse—9138   Skirt—9139

9185—LADIES' DRESS: High Neck or Open Neck, with Large Collar in Standaway Effect at the Back. Lower edge about 1¾ yards. 6 sizes, 32 to 42 inches bust measure. The 36-inch bust size will require, as illustrated on figure, 4⅝ yards of 45-inch taffeta, with 2 yards of 45-inch contrasting taffeta for cape collar and cuffs, and facing skirt, and 2½ yards of 32-inch material will be needed for foundation gores.   Price, 20 cents.

9141—LADIES' DRESS: Dart-Fitted Lining; High or Open Neck; Long Dart-Fitted or Short Sleeves; Separate Draped Overbodice; Two-Piece Draped Skirt Attached to the Lining. Lower edge about 2½ yards. 7 sizes, 32 to 44 inches bust measure. The 36-inch bust size will require, as illustrated on figure, 5⅞ yards of 36-inch satin for dress, with ⅜ yard of 27-inch contrasting satin for collar.   Price, 20 cents.

9138—LADIES' BLOUSE. 5 sizes, 32 to 40 inches bust. **9139**—LADIES' STRAIGHT SKIRT. Lower edge about 2½ yards. 7 sizes, 22 to 34 inches waist, corresponding to 36 to 49½ inches hip. If combined as illustrated on figure the medium size requires 6⅜ yards of 36-inch silk poplin, with ½ yard of 18-inch all-over lace for collar, 18¼ yards of narrow ribbon to trim and ⅞ yard of 5-inch ribbon will be needed for girdle. Price, 20 cents each.

Blouse—9076   Skirt—8979

9185

9141

9141

9076—8979   9177—78   9138—39   9185

Draped on Two Sides or Just One, Foundation Skirts, and New Coats

9046—Ladies' Waist. 7 sizes, 32 to 44 bust. **9047**—Ladies' Two-Piece Straight Gathered Skirt. Lower edge of foundation skirt about 1¾ yards. **5** sizes, 22 to 30 waist, 36 to 44½ hip. Combined as on figure, the medium size needs 6¾ yards of 40-inch crêpe for overbodice, sleeves and gathered skirt, with 1⅜ yards of 36-inch silk for collar, cuffs and to face skirt, and 3 yards of 36-inch material for gores and lining.   Price, 20 cents each.

9165—Ladies' Dress: Back Extending Over the Shoulders to Form a Yoke. Lower edge about 1¾ yards. The pattern is cut in 7 sizes from 32 to 44 inches bust measure. The 36-inch bust size will require as illustrated on figure 6⅜ yards of 44-inch prunella cloth for dress, with ⅞ yard of 24-inch satin for overblouse and cuffs, ⅝ yard of 27-inch crêpe for collar and vestee, and 2½ yards of 32-inch material for foundation skirt.   Price, 20 cents.

9153—Ladies' Empire Coat: 50-Inch Length at the Back; One or Two Seam Sleeves; Three-Piece Gathered Skirt. The pattern is cut in 7 sizes from 32 to 44 inches bust measure. The 36-inch bust size will require as illustrated on figure 4½ yards of 54-inch duvetyn for coat, with ¾ yard of 36-inch silk for collar and cuffs. Other suitable materials are velveteens and coatings. Price, 20 cents.

9148—Ladies' Coat Dress: Crushed Collar in Standaway Effect at the Back; Long Dart-Fitted or Short Sleeves. Lower edge about 1¾ yards. The pattern is cut in 6 sizes from 32 to 42 inches bust measure. The 36-inch bust size will require as illustrated on figure 3⅝ yards of 44-inch cloth for blouse and tunic, with 1⅞ yards of 44-inch striped cloth for skirt and ½ yard of 36-inch satin for collar and cuffs.   Price, 20 cents.

9169—Ladies' Dress: Long Dart-Fitted of Short Sleeves; Three-Piece Belt which may be Omitted; Two-Piece Straight Gathered Skirt. Lower edge about 2 yards. The pattern is cut in 7 sizes from 32 to 44 inches bust measure. The 36-inch bust size will require as illustrated on figure, 3¾ yards of 50-inch serge for dress, with ½ yard of 50-inch contrasting serge for collar and cuffs, and 6½ yards of braid.   Price, 20 cents.

9153

Blouse—9046
Skirt—9047

9169

9148

9153   9169   9165   9148

9046—9047

9165

8991—MISSES' AND SMALL WOMEN'S DRESS: Long or Short One-Seam Sleeves. Lower edge about 3 yards. 4 sizes, 14 to 20 years. The 16-year size will require as illustrated on figure 5⅝ yards of 40-inch crêpe de Chine, with 1¾ yards of 36-inch silk for trimming-bands and cuffs. 15 cents.

9158—MISSES' AND SMALL WOMEN'S DRESS. Lower edge about 2 yards. 4 sizes, 14 to 20 years. The 16-year size will require as illustrated on figure 2½ yards of 44-inch serge, with 2¾ yards of 36-inch checked silk for underblouse and to face skirt, and 2¼ yards 32 for skirt. Price 15 cents.

9163—MISSES' AND SMALL WOMEN'S DRESS. For the embroidery design illustrated, use Standard transfer pattern 10036. Lower edge about 2¼ yards. 4 sizes, 14 to 20 years. The 16-year size needs as illustrated on figure 4 yards of 54-inch gabardine, with ½ yard 24 for collar. 15 cents.

9035—MISSES' AND SMALL WOMEN'S BLOUSE. 4 sizes, 14 to 20 years. **9036**—MISSES' AND SMALL WOMEN'S SKIRT. Lower edge about 2¾ yards. 4 sizes, 14 to 20 years. As on figure, the 16-year size needs 6½ yards of 36-inch flowered silk, with ¼ yard of 36-inch plain silk. 15 cents each.

8991

Blouse 9035 Skirt 9036

9163

9143

9158

9158

9035—9036

9163

9143   9147   9152

9152   Emblem—No. 10015

9147

9143—MISSES' AND SMALL WOMEN'S DRESS. Long Dart-Fitted or Short Sleeves. Lower edge about 2¼ yards. 4 sizes, 14 to 20 years. The 16-year size will require as illustrated on figure 2⅞ yards of 36-inch silk for blouse and facing on skirt, with 2⅝ yards of 36-inch cashmere for skirt, revers, collar, and straps. The use of contrasting materials is effective. 15 cents.

9152—MISSES' AND SMALL WOMEN'S DRESS. Lower edge with plaits drawn out about 2½ yards. 4 sizes, 14 to 20 years. The 16-year size will need as illustrated on figure 4½ yards of 44-inch serge for dress, with 1¼ yards of 27-inch white flannel for collars and chemisette and 4 yards of braid will be needed for two rows on collar and cuffs. Price, 15 cents.

9147—MISSES' AND SMALL WOMEN'S COAT: in Two Lengths; Large Collar with Standaway Effect; Two-Seam Sleeves with Slight Fulness at the Top which may be Shrunken Out; Two Styles of Belt. The pattern is cut in 4 sizes, from 14 to 20 years. The 16-year size will require as illustrated on figure 4¼ yards of 54-inch wool cloth for coat. Price, 15 cents.

9146

9170

9180

9157
8286

Guimpe—**9157**
Skirt of Suit—**8286**

9189

9154

9186

9186

9180

9179

9170   9154   9146   9189   9189   8286   8286

9157—Girls' and Juniors' Blouse or Guimpe. 8 sizes, 2 to 16 years. **8286** —Juniors' and Girls' Skirt of Suit: 9 sizes, 8 to 16 years. The 10-year size requires as on figure, 1½ yards of 36-inch lawn for guimpe, with 2 yards of 27-inch gingham for skirt and suspenders. Guimpes are very practical.   Price, 15 cents each.

9170—Little Girls' Rompers: Long or Short Sleeves; Bloomers Sewed or Buttoned to the Blouse. The pattern is cut in 5 sizes from 2 to 6 years. The 3-year size will require as illustrated on figure, 2⅜ yards of 27-inch chambray for rompers, with ¼ yard of 36-inch linen for collar. A very comfortable garment.   Price, 15 cents.

9189—Child's Apron or Dress: Bloomers. 9 sizes, 2 to 10 years. The 6-year size will require, as illustrated on figure, 2½ yards of 32-inch percale for apron, with ½ yard of 36-inch linen for collar, cuffs and belt and 1¼ yards of 32 or more inch percale will be needed for bloomers.   Price, 15 cents.

9186—Girls' and Juniors' Dress: Long or Short Sleeves; Separate Overblouse; Straight Gathered Skirt. The pattern is cut in 9 size from 8 to 16 years The 15-year size will require as illustrated on figure, 4¼ yards of 44-inch serge for dress, and 7 yards of ribbon will be needed for one row.   Price, 15 cents.

9154—Girls' and Juniors' Dress: High or Open Neck; Long or Short Sleeves; Five-Piece Skirt. The pattern is cut in 11 sizes from 6 to 16 years. The 12-year size requires as on figure, 4 yards of 32-inch rep for dress, with ⅜ yard of 27-inch voile for collar. The front closing is novel and smart.   Price, 15 cents.

9179 — Little Girls' Dress: Separate Jacket; Straight Gathered Skirt. The pattern is cut in 9 sizes from 4 to 12 years. The 8-year size will require as shown on figure, 2⅞ yards of 32-inch galatea for dress, with 1 yard of 32-inch contrasting galatea for overblouse and collar. Materials in combination are very smart. Price, 15 cents.

9180—Little Girls' Dress: Two-Piece Skirt Sewed or Buttoned to the Blouse. The pattern is cut in 9 sizes from 4 to 12 years. The 6-year size requires as on figure, 2⅛ yards of 44-inch cashmere for dress, with ⅝ yard of 36-inch voile for collar and cuffs. This cunning little dress will be found unusually smart.   Price, 15 cents.

9146—Girls' and Juniors' Dress. For the embroidery design on figure use Standard transfer 10167. The pattern is cut in 9 sizes from 8 to 16 years. The 11-year size will require as shown on figure, 1⅞ yards of 44-inch linen for dress, with 1⅝ yards of 36-inch batiste for blouse. Belt of linen or leather.   Price, 15 cents.

8286—Girls' Coat Suit: Straight or Diagonal Closing; Closed to Neck or Rolled Open; Two-Seam Sleeves with Slight Fulness at the Top which may be Shrunken Out. 9 sizes, 8 to 16 years. The 13-year size will require as shown on figure, 4⅝ yards of 40-inch serge for suit, with 1¼ yards of 24-inch silk for collar, belt and cuffs. Price, 15 cents.

9153— LADIES' EMPIRE COAT: 50-Inch Length at the back; One or Two-Seam Sleeves with Slight Fulness at the Top which may be Shrunken Out; Three-Piece Gathered Skirt. 7 sizes, 32 to 44 inches bust measure. The 36-inch size requires as an figure, 4 yards of 54-inch checked velours, with ¾ yard of 36-inch velvet for collar and revers. The double belt is very smart.   Price, 20 cents.

9148—LADIES' COAT DRESS. Lower edge about 1¾ yards. 6 sizes, 32 to 42 inches bust measure. The 36-inch size will require as illustrated on figure, 4⅜ yards of 36-inch taffeta for blouse and tunic, with 3¼ yards of 36-inch striped taffeta for skirt and belt, ⅝ yard of 18-inch lace for collar and facing chemisette, and ⅝ yard of 27-inch material for chemisette.
Price, 20 cents.

9193—LADIES' BLOUSE. 7 sizes, 32 to 44 bust. **9194**—LADIES' SKIRT. Lower edge about 2⅝ yards. 6 sizes, 22 to 32 waist, or 36 to 47 hip. Combined as on figure the medium size requires 2⅛ yards of 36-inch satin, with 4⅝ yards of 44-inch striped serge, 1¼ yards of 6-inch lace edging and 2⅜ yards of 32-inch material for foundation.   20 cents each.

9141—LADIES' DRESS. Lower edge about 2½ yards. 7 sizes, 32 to 44 bust. The 36-inch size requires as on figure, 5¼ yards of 32-inch foulard for overbodice and skirt, with 1¼ yards of 36-inch satin for large collar, turnover collar and sleeves, ½ yard of 18-inch net for yoke and to face lining, and ⅞ yard of 36-inch material for lining.   Price, 20 cents.

9153   9185   Blouse—9193
Skirt—9194

Variety is One Great Charm of the New Fashions for Fall

9185—LADIES' DRESS: High Neck or Open Neck with Large Collar in Standaway Effect at the Back; Long Dart-Fitted or Short Sleeves; Slightly High Waistline; Two-Piece Straight Gathered Skirt. Lower edge about 2½ yards. The pattern is cut in 6 sizes from 32 to 42 inches bust measure. The 36-inch size will require as illustrated on figure, 5¼ yards of 54-inch gabardine, with ½ yard of 24-inch satin for small collar and pockets.   Price, 20 cents.

9148   9153   9185   9193—9194   9141

9148   9141

A Plaited Russian Blouse—A New Coat

9197—Ladies' Tucked or Gathered Blouse: Closed to the Neck or Rolled Open, or Open Neck; Long Dart-Fitted or Short Sleeves. 5 sizes, 32 to 40 inches bust measure. **9198**—Ladies' Three-Piece Skirt: Slightly High Waistline, with Three-Piece Belt, or Regulation Waistline; Clearing or Shorter Length. (May be Attached to a Blouse or Worn Separately.) Lower edge about 2 yards. 9 sizes, 22 to 38 inches waist, or 36 to 54 inches hip measure. If combined as illustrated on figure, the medium size will require 2⅝ yards of 36-inch satin for blouse, with 2½ yards of 50-inch suiting for skirt.
Price, 20 cents each.

Blouse—9239   Skirt—9240

9239—Ladies' Plaited Russian Blouse: In Two Lengths; Convertible Collar; Long or Short One-Seam Sleeves. The pattern is cut in 6 sizes from 32 to 42 inches bust measure. **9240**—Ladies' Three-Piece Skirt: Slightly High Waistline; Clearing or Shorter Length. (May be Attached to a Blouse or Worn Separately.) Lower edge about 2⅛ yards. The pattern is cut in 6 sizes from 22 to 32 inches waist measure, corresponding to 36 to 47 inches hip measure. If combined as illustrated on figure, the medium size will require 4½ yards of 36-inch black satin for blouse, with ⅜ yard yard of 24-inch white satin for collar and cuffs, and 3¾ yards of 36-inch striped serge for skirt. A smart Russian blouse worn with a tailored skirt makes an attractive street costume.
Price, 20 cents each.

9195

9195—Ladies' Coat: 50 or 45 Inch Length at the Back; Lapped Seams at the Front; Convertible Collar; Two-Seam Sleeves with Slight Fulness at the Top which may be Shrunken Out. The pattern is cut in 8 sizes from 32 to 46 inches bust measure. As illustrated on figure, the 36-inch bust size will require 3⅝ yards of 54-inch diagonal for coat, with ⅜ yard of 50-inch fur cloth for collar and cuffs. The keen and bracing winter air has enticed this young lady out for an early morning walk. She has not neglected to dress warmly in a smart coat of diagonal material, with fur cuffs and a fur collar, which may be buttoned up close to the neck. The pockets which form a continuous line with the front seams are large and warm enough to protect her fingers from the biting frost. The coat may be made of tweeds, cheviots, coatings and broadcloth.   Price, 20 cents.

Blouse—9197
Skirt—9198

9214

9227 — Ladies' Blouse: Closed to the Neck or Rolled Open, or Open Neck; Long Dart-Fitted or Short Sleeves. (May be Attached to a Skirt or Worn Separately.) 9 sizes, 32 to 48 inches bust measure. **9228**—Ladies' Seven-Gored Skirt: High Waistline; Clearing or Shorter Length. Lower edge with plaits drawn out about 3¾ yards. 8 sizes, 22 to 36 inches waist, or 36 to 52 inches hip. If combined as illustrated on figure, the medium size will require 2¾ yards of 32-inch striped satin for blouse, with ⅞ yard of 36-inch chiffon for collar and sleeve frills, and 4½ yards of 50-inch broadcloth for skirt. Price, 20 cents each.

Blouse—9227
Skirt—9228

9214—Ladies' Dress: Separate Guimpe; High or Open Neck; Blouse Front in One with Front of Three-Piece Yoke; Standaway Collar; Long Dart-Fitted or Short Sleeves Sewed in the Blouse or Guimpe; Four-Piece Gathered Tunic; Two-Piece Gathered Skirt; Clearing or Shorter Length. Lower edge about 2⅛ yards. The pattern is cut in 7 sizes from 32 to 44 inches bust measure. As illustrated on figure, the 36-inch bust size will require 3⅛ yards of 42-inch serge for dress, with 2¼ yards of 40-inch white satin for sleeves, pipings, cuffs, facing guimpe, and three bands on skirt, and 1 yard of 27-inch material for guimpe fronts and back.   Price, 20 cents.

9195   9239—40   9197—98   9227—28   9214

Winter Blouses and Skirts—A One-Piece Frock

9216—Ladies' Blouse: Long or Short One-Seam Sleeves. 7 sizes, 32 to 44 inches bust measure. 9217—Ladies' Three-Piece Skirt. Lower edge with plaits drawn out about 3⅜ yards. 9 sizes, 22 to 38 inches waist measure, corresponding to 36 to 54 inches hip measure. If combined as illustrated on figure, the medium size will require 2 yards of 40-inch Georgetta crêpe for blouse, with 3⅞ yards of 36-inch velveteen for suspenders and skirt.   Price, 20 cents each.

9245—Ladies' Blouse. 6 sizes, 32 to 42 inches bust measure. 9246—Ladies' Fourteen - Gored Box - Plaited Skirt. Lower edge with plaits drawn out about 3⅜ yards. 8 sizes, 22 to 36 inches waist measure, corresponding to 36 to 52 inches hip measure. If combined as illustrated on figure, the medium size will require 2⅜ yards of 36-inch silk for blouse, with ⅜ yard of 36-inch contrasting silk for collar and cuffs, and 3 yards of 54-inch serge for skirt.   20 cents each.

9233—Ladies' Blouse. 6 sizes, 32 to 42 inches bust measure. 9217—Ladies' Three-Piece Skirt. Lower edge with plaits drawn out about 3⅜ yards. 9 sizes, 22 to 38 inches waist measure, or 36 to 54 inches hip measure. If combined as illustrated on figure, the medium size will require 2 yards of 36-inch silk for blouse, with ⅜ yard 27 or more inch crêpe for collar, and 3⅞ yards of 36-inch corduroy for skirt.   Price, 20 cents each.

8995—Ladies' Dress: High or Open Neck; Long One-Seam Sleeves in Two Styles or Short Sleeves, Four or Five Piece Skirt; Clearing or Shorter Length. Lower edge about 2¾ yards. 7 sizes, 32 to 44 inches bust measure. The 36-inch size will require, as illustrated on figure, 3½ yards of 50-inch cheviot for dress, with ½ yard of 36-inch silk for collar and front of belt. A very smart model is this, which might be developed in serge or gabardine. Price, 15 cents.

Blouse—9216   Shirt—9201   Blouse—9233
Skirt—9217   Skirt—9202   Skirt—9217

9201—Ladies' Shirt. 9 sizes, 32 to 48 bust. 9202—Ladies' Skirt. Lower edge with plaits drawn out about 2⅝ yards. 9 sizes, 22 to 38 waist, corresponding to 36 to 54 hip. If combined as illustrated on figure, the medium size will require 2½ yards of 40-inch linen for blouse, with 2⅝ yards of 50-inch gabardine for skirt, and 10 yards of braid.   Price, 20 cents each.

Blouse—9245   Skirt—9246

9245—9246   9201—9202   9216—9217   9233—9217   8995

8995

Modes Which Make Us All Thankful

9205—Ladies' Blouse: Convertible Collar or Open Neck with Standaway Collar. 7 sizes, 32 to 44 inches bust. **9206**—Ladies' Skirt. Lower edge with plaits drawn out about 3 yards. 8 sizes, 22 to 36 inches' waist, or 36 to 52 inches hip. If combined as illustrated on figure, the medium size will require 1⅞ yards of 40 or 44 inch linen for blouse, with ½ yard of 36-inch contrasting linen and 3⅝ yards of 44-inch serge for skirt.   Price, 20 cents each.

9220—Ladies' Coat: 50 or 36 Inch Length at the Back; Standaway Collar Closed to the Neck or Rolled Open; One or Two-Seam Sleeves with Slight Fulness at the Top which may be Shrunken Out. 7 sizes from 32 to 44 inches bust. As illustrated on figure, the 36-inch size will require for coat in 50-inch length, 5¼ yards of 50-inch Chinchilla cloth, with 2½ yards of narrow fur banding for collar and sleeves and 3½ yards of wide fur banding on edge of coat.   Price, 20 cents.

Blouse—9205
Skirt—9206

[9205—9206]

9220

9209—9210

9232

9220

9222—9223

Blouse—9222
Skirt—9223
Scarf—9215

Blouse—9209
Skirt—9210

9209—Ladies' Blouse. 7 sizes, 32 to 44 inches bust measure. **9210**—Ladies' Skirt: Two-Piece Yoke; Three-Piece Lower Part; Inverted Plaits at Sides and Back. Lower edge with plaits drawn out about 2½ yards. 6 sizes, 22 to 32 inches waist, or 36 to 47 inches hip. If combined as illustrated on figure, the medium size will require 2 yards of 40-inch checked chiffon for blouse, with 2⅞ yards of ribbon to trim and 2⅜ yards of 50-inch gabardine for skirt.
Price, 20 cents each.

9232—Ladies' Coat: 45 or 34 Inch Length at the Back; Convertible Collar; Two-Seam Sleeves with Slight Fulness at the Top which may be Shrunken Out. The pattern is cut in 7 sizes from 32 to 44 inches bust measure. As illustrated on figure, the 36-inch size will require 3¾ yards of 50-inch diagonal cloth, with ⅝ yard of 24-inch velvet for collar and cuffs. The side closing and fitted waist give this coat attractive lines.   Price, 20 cents.

9222—Ladies' Blouse. 7 sizes. 32 to 44 inches bust. **9223**—Ladies, Three-Piece Skirt. Lower edge about 1⅞ yards. 7 sizes, 22 to 34 inches waist, to 36 to 49½ inches hip. **9215**—Ladies' Scarf: in Two Lengths. One size, ladies. If combined as on figure, the medium size requires 5½ yards of 40-inch chiffon for blouse, tunic and collar, with 3¾ yards of 36-inch satin for overblouse, underskirt, cuffs and to trim and 2⅝ yards of 20 or more inch material for scarf.   Price, 20 cents each.

A Negligée, Apron and a Gymnasium Suit

9218-A

9218-B

9225

9230

9257

9256

9218 — LADIES' NEGLIGÉE. Drawn Up on an Elastic; High or Open Neck; Long, Three-Quarter Length or Short One-Seam Sleeves; Separate Bolero; Clearing or Shorter Length. The pattern is cut in 8 sizes from 32 to 46 inches bust measure. As shown on figure A, the 36-inch size will require 6⅜ yards of 27-inch chambray for negligee, with ¼ yard of 36-inch linen for collar. As illustrated on figure B, 5½ yards of 32-inch cotton crêpe for negligee, with 1½ yards of 27-inch sheer crêpe for overblouse and collar, 4¾ yards of lace edging, 3¾ yards of insertion, and 2½ yards of ribbon for girdle with ends. Negligées were designed with a view to comfort, and surely no more comfortable and attractive garment than this one could be found anywhere. The A view suggests a warm house dress for winter, while the B view shows a dressy garment with separate bolero.   Price, 20 cents.

9225 — LADIES' GYMNASIUM SUIT: Blouse to be Worn Inside or Outside the Plaited Bloomers; Closed to the Neck or Rolled Open; Long or Short One-Seam Sleeves. The pattern is cut in 5 sizes from 32 to 40 inches bust measure. As illustrated on figure, the 36-inch size will require 7⅜ yards of 36-inch serge for gymnasium suit, with ¼ yard of 27-inch linen for collar. Don't you envy this young lady her slim and athletic figure? If you do, you should attend a gymnasium class the way she does, and in order to be considered among those best prepared, you must have a smart suit like hers. The plaited bloomers will permit great freedom of movement, and the simple blouse will also be found very comfortable. The blouse may be worn outside the bloomers, and held at the waistline by a novelty belt. A sailor collar of contrasting material may be used instead of the small collar with the high neck.   Price, 20 cents.

9257 — LADIES' DRESS: Back Extending Over the Shoulders to Form a Yoke; Closed to the Neck or Rolled Open or Open Neck; Long Dart-Fitted or Short Sleeves. (Suitable for Invalid or Maternity Wear.) Lower edge about 2½ yards. 8 sizes, 32 to 46 inches bust measure. As on figure, the 36-inch size will require 4⅝ yards of 50-inch gabardine for dress, ⅝ yard of 36-inch silk for vestee and collar and ¾ yard of 27-inch striped silk for girdle.   Price, 20 cents.

9256 — LADIES' APRON: In Two Lengths; High or Open Neck; Long or Short Raglan Sleeves; Cap. The pattern is cut in 9 sizes from 32 to 48 inches bust measure. As illustrated on figure, the 36-inch size will require 6¼ yards of 27-inch gingham for apron, with ⅝ yard of 27-inch chambray for collar and belt. You will find an apron of this kind with long sleeves and high neck a good protection for a fancy dress. It might be made of gingham, percale, or chambray.   Price, 20 cents.

9230 — LADIES' NIGHTGOWN: High or Open Neck; Long Gathered Sleeves or Short Sleeves. The pattern is cut in 9 sizes from 32 to 48 inches bust measure. As illustrated on figure the 36-inch size will require 4 yards of 36-inch flannelette for nightgown. This nightgown is a desirable garment for winter wear. The round yoke with gathered lower section will be found very comfortable. It might be made of flannelette, nainsook or lawn.   Price, 20 cents.

9218   **9218**   **9225**   **9230**   **9257**   **9256**

Winter Accessories—Skating Sets, Fur Sets, Fichus

9229—LADIES' SET: Cap with Two Styles of Crown, Scarf, Bags. One size, and requires as illustrated on figure A 1⅛ yards of 27 or more inch velvet for two-piece crown of cap and to line scarf, with 1⅛ yards of 20-inch striped silk for band of cap and for scarf; as on figure B 1⅛ yards of 40 or more inch broadcloth for scarf and one-piece crown of cap, with 1⅛ yards of 20-inch contrasting broadcloth for band of cap and to line scarf; ¼ yard 27 to line cap.   20 cents.

9215—LADIES' SET: Scarf in Two Lengths; Cape; Hat; Muff. 1 size, and requires as on figure A 3 yards of 40-inch velvet for cape and muff, with ⅞ yard of 20-inch lining for muff; as on figure B 2⅝ yards of 20 to 40 inch satin for scarf; as on figure C 1⅛ yards of 42 or 54 inch fur cloth for scarf and muff, with 1 yard of ribbon for tie; as on view D 2⅝ yards of 50-inch broadcloth for scarf and hat, with 6 yards of fur banding to trim.   Price, 20 cents.

9242—LADIES' FICHUS, in Various Styles. For the embroidery design on figure B use Standard transfer No. 10290. The pattern is cut in 1 size. and requires as illustrated on figure A 1¾ yards of 40-inch Georgette crêpe for fichu and ruffles. The edges of ruffles are picot; as in figure B ⅝ yard of 36 or more inch voile; as in figure C ⅞ yard of 40-inch chiffon for fichu, with 2⅛ yards of insertion and 2¾ yards of edging. Fichus of Georgette crepe are very fashionable.   Price, 20 cents.

9251—CAP, SCARF AND MUFF. 2 sizes, misses and children. The children's size will require as on figure A 1 yard of 27 or more inch chinchilla for cap and scarf; as on figure C 1 yard of 6-inch Angora banding for scarf and band of cap, with ⅝ yard of 4-inch contrasting Angora banding for crown of cap. The misses' size requires as on figure B 1¼ yards of 30 or more inch velvet for cap, scarf and muff, with 3¾ yards of banding, and 1¼ yards 32 for lining scarf, muff and cap.   15 cents.

8787—CHILD'S CAP. For the emblem illustrated use Standard transfer pattern 10015. 4 sizes, 2 to 8 years. The 4-year size requires ⅝ yard of 24 or more inch material, with ¾ yard of 2-inch ribbon to trim, and ⅜ yard of 27-inch material for lining. The cap shown above is very popular both for little girls and boys. It can be made of the same material as the suit or dress with which it is intended to be worn. Wash materials may be used.   Price, 10 cents.

8419—HAT in Various Styles. 4 sizes, ladies, misses, girls and little girls. The ladies' and misses' size requires as in view A ⅜ yard 36 or more inches wide, with ¾ yard of 18-inch contrasting material for band and to trim; as in view B2 ½ yard of 27-inch material for crown, with ¾ yard of 18-inch contrasting material for band; as in view B3, ¾ yard 27 or more, with ¾ yard of 24-inch material for interlining and ¾ yard of 27 inch material for lining.   Price, 10 cents.

Graceful Suggestions for Afternoon Frocks, Evening Gowns and Wraps

9226—LADIES' EMPIRE DRESS: Low Neck; Short One-Seam Puff Sleeves; One-Piece Straight Gathered Skirt Draped or Falling Free. Fichu, Straight Bands and Three-Piece Foundation Skirt may be Omitted. Lower edge of gathered skirt about 3½ yards. 5 sizes, 32 to 40 inches bust measure. As on figure, the 36-inch size requires 6⅛ yards of 40-inch Georgette crêpe for dress, with 2⅞ yards of 36-inch satin for straight bands, girdle and band on sleeves. Price, 20 cents.

9253—LADIES' BLOUSE. 8 sizes, 32 to 46 bust. **9254**—LADIES' TWO-PIECE SKIRT. For the embroidery design use Standard transfer 10361. Lower edge about 1¾ yards. 8 sizes, 22 to 36 inches waist, or 36 to 52 hip. If combined as illustrated on figure, the medium size will require 4 yards of 50-inch broadcloth, 1⅝ yards of 36-inch satin for lining, and sleeves, 2⅞ yards of wool fringe and 2½ yards of 32-inch material for foundation gores. Price, 20 cents each.

9247—LADIES' EMPIRE EVENING DRESS: One-Piece Gathered Tunic; Three-Piece Skirt; Overblouse, Sleeves, Train in 72-Inch Length. Lower edge about 1¾ yards. 5 sizes, 32 to 40 inches bust measure. As illustrated on figure, the 36-inch size will require 4¼ yards of 40-inch satin for skirt and train, with 4¾ yards of 40-inch chiffon for shoulder straps and tunic, 1⅜ yards of sequin banding and ¾ yard of 27-inch material for lining. Price, 20 cents.

9214—LADIES' DRESS: Separate Guimpe; High or Open Neck; Blouse Front in One with Front of Three-Piece Yoke; Standaway Collar; Long Dart-Fitted or Short Sleeves Sewed in the Blouse or Guimpe; Four-Piece Gathered Tunic; Two-Piece Gathered Skirt. Lower edge about 2⅛ yards. 7 sizes, 32 to 44 inches bust measure. As illustrated on figure, the 36-inch size will require 6¾ yards of 36-inch Mohair for dress, with ¾ yards of 36-inch satin for collar, cuffs and belt. Price, 20 cents.

9213—LADIES' CAPE: 50 Inch Length at the Back; Cutaway or Straight Outline; High Neck with Hood or Open Neck with Standaway Collar. The pattern is cut in 4 sizes from 32 to 44 years. As illustrated on figure, the 36-inch size will require 5 yards of 50-inch broadcloth for cape, with 7⅛ yards of 36-inch silk for lining hood and cape and 1¼ yards of ribbon. Women will welcome the return to fashion of these simple graceful and becoming evening capes. Price, 20 cents.

9214

9213

9226

9253—9254

9247

9214   9213   9226   9253—9254   9247   Blouse **9253**—Skirt **9254**

Graceful Empire Evening Gowns and An Evening Cape in Burnoose Style

9238—LADIES' DRESS: High Neck with Flare Collar or Open Neck with Overblouse and Standaway Collar; Long Dart-Fitted or Short Sleeves; Four-Piece Skirt; Clearing or Shorter Length. Lower edge about 3¼ yards. 7 sizes from 32 to 44 inches bust measure. The embroidery design is an adaptation of Standard transfer 10057. As illustrated on figure, the 36-inch size will require 5⅜ yards of 44-inch cloth for dress, with ¾ yard of 27-inch silk for girdle. 20 cents.

9253—LADIES' BLOUSE: French Lining; Overblouse. 8 sizes, 32 to 46 bust. **9254**—LADIES' TWO-PIECE SKIRT: Two or Four Piece Tunic with or without the Train. Lower edge about 1¾ yards. 8 sizes, 22 to 36 inches waist, or 36 to 52 hip. Combined as on figure, the 36-inch size will require 5 yards of 40-inch satin, with 1¼ yards of 40-inch net for blouse, tucker and sleeves, and 3 yards 36-inch material for foundation gores and lining. Price, 20 cents each.

9226—LADIES' EMPIRE DRESS: Low Neck; One-Piece Straight Gathered Skirt; Three-Piece Foundation Skirt. Lower edge of foundation about 1⅞ yards. Lower edge of gathered skirt about 3½ yards. 5 sizes, 32 to 40 inches bust measure. As illustrated on figure, the 36-inch size will require 9½ yards of 40-inch chiffon for blouse, tunic and ruffles, with 2⅜ yards of 36-inch satin for skirt and 3⅝ yards of 7-inch satin ribbon for fichu and sash. Price, 20 cents.

9238

9213

9247

9253—9254

9226

Blouse 9253—Skirt 9254

9247—LADIES' EMPIRE EVENING DRESS: One-Piece Gathered Tunic; Three-Piece Skirt; Overblouse, Train in 72-Inch Length (not shown) and Straight Gathered Peplum may be Omitted. Lower edge about 1¾ yards. 5 sizes, 32 to 40 inches bust measure. As illustrated on figure, the 36-inch size will require 5¼ yards of 36-inch taffeta for overblouse and tunic, with 2⅜ yards of 36-inch contrasting taffeta for blouse and skirt facing, and 3 yards 36 for foundation gores and lining. Price, 20 cents.

9213—LADIES' CAPE: 50-Inch Length at the Back; Cutaway or Straight Outline; High Neck with Hood or Open Neck with Standaway Collar. The pattern is cut in 4 sizes from 32 to 44 inches bust measure. As illustrated on figure, the 36-inch size will require 7¾ yards of 36-inch satin for cape, with ⅜ yard of 36-inch velvet for collar. Your frock may be frilly and fluffy with puffs and ruffles innumerable, but not a bit will it be crushed if you wear a sleeveless cape like this. Price, 20 cents.

9226   9238   9213   9247

9255

9255

9236-A

9219

9241

9248

9237

9237

9207

9252   9252   9207

9219   9236-B   9236   9236   9241   9248   9207

9255—Girls' and Juniors' Dress. 9 sizes from 8 to 16 years. As illustrated on figure, the 12-year size will require 2½ yards of 40-inch net, with 2½ yards of 36-inch taffeta for underskirt, girdle and straps and 2 yards of rosebud trimming. Georgette crêpe and satin might also be combined.   Price, 15 cents.

9219—Girls' and Juniors' Dress: To be Slipped Over the Head; High or Open Neck; Long or Short Sleeves. 9 sizes, 8 to 16 years. As illustrated on figure, the 14-year size will require 3⅛ yards of 42-inch serge for dress, with ⅜ yards of 27-inch satin for collar and tabs on cuff.   Price, 15 cents.

9241—Girls' and Juniors' Dress: to be Slipped Over the Head; Back Extending Over the Shoulders to Form a Yoke. 11 sizes, 6 to 16 years. As illustrated on figure, the 9-year size will require 3⅜ yards of 27-inch striped gingham, with 1¼ yards of 24-inch silk for collar, cuffs, belt and pockets.   Price, 15 cents.

9248—Girls' Coat: Convertible Collar; One-Seam Sleeves with Slight Fulness at the Top which may be Shrunken Out. 5 sizes, 6 to 14 years. As illustrated on figure, the 10-year size will require 2½ yards of 54-inch velours, with ⅞ yards of 36-inch velvet. Suitable materials are broadcloth, velvet, zibeline and duvetyn   15 cents.

9236—Girls' Coat. 5 sizes, 4 to 12 years. As illustrated on figure A, the 10-year size will require 2¼ yards of 50-inch broadcloth, with ⅜ yard of 54-inch fur cloth. As on figure B, the 12-year size needs 2¾ yards of 54-inch diagonal, with ⅛ yard of 36-inch velveteen for scarf collar and cuffs.   Price, 15 cents.

9237—Boys' Overcoat: Closed to the Neck or Rolled Open; Two-Seam Sleeves. 5 sizes, 2 to 10 years. As illustrated on figure, the 8-year size will require 2¼ yards of 50 or 54 inch chinchilla. A serviceable coat for the boy made up in cheviot, melton or serge, just the thing for winter.   Price, 15 cents.

9207—Girls' and Juniors' Dress: High or Open Neck; Long Shoulders. 11 sizes, 6 to 16 years. As illustrated on figure, the 9-year size will require 1⅞ yards of 42-inch plain serge, with ½ yard of 44-inch plain serge for front and back sections, collar and cuffs and 2½ yards of braid.   Price, 15 cents.

9252—Little Girls' Dress: High or Open Neck; Long or Short Sleeves. The pattern is cut in 9 sizes from 4 to 12 years. As illustrated on figure, the 6-year size will require 2½ yards of 36-inch poplin, with 1 yard of 24-inch silk for collar and belt. The yoke and panel in one produces smart lines.   Price, 15 cents.

9239—Ladies' Plaited Russian Blouse: In Two Lengths; Convertible Collar; Long or Short One-Seam Sleeves. 6 sizes, 32 to 42 inches bust measure. **8993**—Ladies' Two or Three Piece Skirt. Lower edge about 2¼ yards. 8 sizes, 22 to 36 inches waist measure, corresponding to 36 to 52 inches hip measure. If combined as illustrated on figure, the medium size will require 5 yards of 50-inch serge, with 1 yard of 36-inch satin, and 2 yards of 9-inch ribbon for sash.
20 cents for blouse; 15 cents for skirt.

9220—Ladies' Coat: 50 or 36 Inch Length at the Back. 7 sizes from 32 to 44 inches bust measure. **9246**—Ladies' Fourteen-Gored Box Plaited Skirt. Lower edge with plaits drawn out about 3⅜ yards. 8 sizes from 22 to 36 inches waist measure, or to 36 to 52 inches hip measure. As illustrated on figure, the medium size will require 3⅜ yards of 54-inch cheviot for coat, with ⅜ yards of 54-inch fur cloth for collar and cuffs, 2½ yards of 36-inch satin for gores, and 2½ yards of 44-inch serge. Price, 20 cents each.

9243—Ladies' Coat: 50 or 34 Inch Length at the Back; Waistline Gathered to a Stay or Held in by a Belt; Convertible Collar or Closed to the Neck in Russian Style with Chin Collar. 7 sizes, 32 to 44 inches bust measure. As illustrated on figure, the 36-inch size will require 4½ yards of 54-inch checked velours, with ⅜ yard of 54-inch fur cloth. This coat in Russian style is very warm and comfortable. Price, 20 cents.

9232—Ladies' Coat: 45 or 34 Inch Length at the Back. 7 sizes, 32 to 44 bust. **9198**—Ladies' Three-Piece Skirt. Lower edge about 2 yards. 9 sizes, 22 to 38 inches waist, or 36 to 54 hip. As on figure, the medium size will require 2⅞ yards of 50-inch serge for coat, with ½ yard of 50-inch white broadcloth, and 1¼ yards of fur banding, 1⅞ yards of 54-inch plaid serge for skirt. 20 cents each.

Blouse—**9239**
Skirt—**8993**

9238

9243

Dresses and Coats for the Winter

9238—Ladies' Dress: High Neck with Flare Collar or Open Neck, with Overblouse and Standaway Collar; Long Dart-Fitted or Short Sleeves; Four-Piece Skirt; Clearing or Shorter Length. Lower edge with plaits drawn out about 3¼ yards. The pattern is cut in 7 sizes from 32 to 44 inches bust measure. As illustrated on figure the 36-inch size will require 5⅜ yards of 50-inch broadcloth for dress, with ⅝ yard of 36-inch satin for collar, cuffs, and trimming on belt, and 4⅞ yards of braid. The design of this dress is an unusually attractive one. Price, 20 cents.

9220—9246   9239—8993   9238   9243   9232—9198

Coat—**9220**   Skirt—**9246**

Coat—**9232**
Skirt—**9198**

Straight from Shoulder to Hem the Lines of Our New Frocks Mean to go

8559—LADIES' DRESS: Blouse in One with Skirt or Tunic; Back Extending Over the Shoulders to Form a Yoke; Closed to the Neck or Rolled Open; Long or Three-Quarter Length Dart-Fitted Sleeves. Lower edge of skirt about 2⅝ yards. The pattern is cut in 6 sizes, from 32 to 42 inches bust measure. The 36-inch size will require as illustrated on figure, 3⅝ yards of 54-inch checked gabardine, with ⅜ yard of 27 or more inch broadcloth to face collar and 9¼ yards of braid to trim.   Price, 15 cents.

9295—LADIES' REDINGOTE COAT: 48 or 42 Inch Length at the Back; Convertible Collar; Two-Seam Sleeves with Slight Fulness at the Top which may be Shrunken Out; Three-Piece Gathered Skirt in Two Styles. The pattern is cut in 7 sizes from 32 to 44 inches bust measure. The 36-inch size will require as illustrated on figure, 4¼ yards of 54-inch prunella cloth for coat, with ½ yard of 54-inch fur cloth for collar, cuffs and tabs on pockets. This model is unusually smart.   Price, 20 cents.

9288—LADIES' DRESS: High or Open Neck; Long Dart-Fitted or Short Sleeves; Slightly High Waistline; Loose Front in One with Front of Four-Piece Skirt. Lower edge about 3⅝ yards. The pattern is cut in 5 sizes from 32 to 40 inches bust measure. As illustrated on figure, the 36-inch size will require 5 yards of 50-inch serge for dress, with ⅝ yard of 36-inch organdy for collar and to face fronts, and 1¼ yards of ribbon. The long lines of this dress are interesting and becoming. Price, 20 cents.

Blouse 9263   Skirt—9264

9263—LADIES' BLOUSE: Standaway Collar; Long or Short One-Seam Sleeves. (May be Attached to a Skirt or Worn Separately.) 6 sizes, 32 to 42 inches bust measure.   **9264**—LADIES' FOUR-PIECE SKIRT: Slightly High Waistline with Four-Piece Belt or Regulation Waistline; Clearing or Shorter Length. (May be Attached to a Blouse or Worn Separately.)   Lower edge with plaits drawn out about 2⅝ yards. 8 sizes, 22 to 36 inches waist measure, corresponding to 36 to 52 inches hip measure. If combined as illustrated on figure, the medium size will require 3 yards of 36-inch silk for blouse, with ¾ yard of 24-inch silk for collar, pockets, trimming piece and cuffs, and 2⅞ yards of 50-inch velours for skirt.   Price, 20 cents each.

8559

9263—9264   8559   9295   9288

9295   9288

Blouse—9263 Skirt—9139

9040

9269

Blouse—9297 Skirt—9298

9263—Ladies' Blouse: Overblo se. 6 sizes, 32 to 42 inches bust. **9139**—Ladies' Straight Skirt: Lower edge about 2½ yards. 7 sizes, 22 to 34 inches waist, or 36 to 49½ hip. Combined as on figure, the medium size will require 3¼ yards of 44-inch cloth, with 3¼ yards of 36-inch satin for blouse and lower part of skirt, ⅝ yard of 18 or more inch chiffon for collar and to face chemisette, and 5¼ yards of fur banding.   Price, 20 cents each.

9274—Ladies' Russian Coat: To be Slipped Over the Head; 50 or 42 Inch Length at the Back; Convertible Collar; Two-Seam Sleeves with Slight Fulness at the Top which may be Shrunken Out; Waistline Drawn Up on a Sash or Held in by Belt. 5 sizes, 32 to 40 inches bust measure. As illustrated on figure, the 36-inch size will require 3⅞ yards of 54-inch fancy cloth, with 1¼ yards of 54-inch fur cloth for collar, cuffs, etc.   Price, 20 cents.

9269—Ladies' Russian Dress: To be Slipped Over the Head; Long or Short One-Seam Sleeves; Separate Two-Piece Skirt. Lower edge about 2⅝ yards. 5 sizes, 32 to 40 inches bust measure. The embroidery design illustrated on skirt and belt is an adaptation of Standard transfer 10347. As illustrated on figure, the 36-inch size will require 4⅝ yards of 50-inch French serge, with ¼ yard of 18-inch satin for turnover collar.   Price, 20 cents.

9040—Ladies' Coat: 45 or 36 Inch Length at the Back; Held in by a Belt or Hanging Free; Closed to the Neck or Rolled Open; Deep Armhole; Two-Seam Sleeves. The pattern is cut in 7 sizes from 32 to 44 inches bust measure. As illustrated on figure, the 36-inch size will require 4 yards of 54-inch double-faced coating. This coat might be developed in chinchilla, cheviot, velveteen, prunella or broadcloth and is simple of construction.   Price, 20 cents.

9297—Ladies' Surplice Blouse: Chemisette; Long or Short One-Seam Sleeves. 7 sizes from 32 to 44 inches bust measure. **9298**—Ladies' Skirt: High Waistline or Gathered at Regulation Waistline; Two-Piece Yoke; Eight-Piece Lower Part. Lower edge with plaits drawn out about 4 yards. The pattern is cut in 6 sizes from 22 to 32 inches waist measure, corresponding to 36 to 47 inches hip measure. If combined as illustrated on figure the medium size will require 5¼ yards of 54-inch duvetyn, with ⅞ yard of 24-inch satin for collar and lining frill on sleeves.   Price, 20 cents each.

9040   9263—9139   9274   9269   9297   9297—9298

9285—Ladies' Blouse: Convertible Collar; Long Shoulders; Long Dart-Fitted or Short Sleeves. 6 sizes, 32 to 42 inches bust measure. **9286**—Ladies' Four-Piece Skirt: High Waistline; Jumper which may be Omitted; Clearing or Shorter Length. The embroidery design is an adaptation of Standard transfer 10319. Lower edge with plaits drawn out about 3⅜ yards. 6 sizes, 22 to 32 inches waist, or 36 to 47 inches hip measure. If combined as illustrated on figure, the medium size will require 1⅞ yards of 40-inch voile for blouse, with 4½ yards of 44-inch serge for jumper skirt and 4 yards of ribbon. Price, 20 cents each

9288—Ladies' Dress: High or Open Neck; Long Dart-Fitted or Short Sleeves; Slightly High Waistline; Loose Front in One with Front of Four-Piece Skirt; Clearing or Shorter Length. The embroidery design is an adaptation of Standard transfer 10216. Lower edge about 3⅜ yards. The pattern is cut in 5 sizes from 32 to 40 inches bust measure. As illustrated on figure, the 36-inch size will require 5 yards of 50 or 54 inch duvetyn for dress, with ⅜ yard of 18-inch net for collar. A fine edging may be used to trim collar. Price, 20 cents.

Clothes for Daytime Pleasures

9278—Ladies' Dress: Gathered to a Stay at High Waistline or Held in by a Belt at Regulation Waistline; High Neck or Open Neck with Standaway Collar; Long or Short Dart-Fitted Sleeves. Lower edge of dress about 2½ yards. 6 sizes from 32 to 42 inches bust measure. As illustrated on figure the 36-inch size will require 4¾ yards of 44-inch wool plaid, with 3 yards of fur banding. The straight lines of this dress form a new and fashionable silhouette. Price, 20 cents.

9307—Ladies' Dress: in Moyen Age Style; Long Dart-Fitted or Short Sleeves; One-Piece Straight Gathered Skirt or Tunic; Two-Piece Foundation Skirt. Lower edge about 2¼ yards. 6 sizes, 32 to 42 inches bust. As illustrated on figure, the 36-inch size will require 4⅞ yards of 50-inch broadcloth, with 3⅞ yards of 7-inch fur banding and 2⅝ yards of 36-inch material for skirt. The Moyen Age waistline and gathered tunic make this model very attractive. Price, 20 cents.

9280—Ladies' Tie-On Blouse: One-Piece Gathered Peplum. 6 sizes, 32 to 42 inches bust measure. **9281**—Ladies' Nine-Gored Skirt. Lower edge with plaits drawn out about 3¾ yards. 6 sizes, 22 to 32 inches waist, or 36 to 47 inches hip. If combined as illustrated on figure, the medium size will require 3½ yards of 32-inch brocaded velvet, with ⅜ yard of 24-inch silk and 6¼ yards of 36-inch velveteen. Both blouse and skirt are novel designs. Price, 20 cents each.

Blouse—9285
Skirt—9286

9285-9286   9278

9288   9280-9281   9307

9288   9307

Blouse—9280   Skirt—9281

Hours of Leisure and Night Time

9291—LADIES' BLOUSE: 6 sizes, 32 to 42 inches bust measure. **9292**—LADIES' SKIRT: Lower edge about 2¼ yards. 7 sizes, 22 to 34 inches waist measure, corresponding to 36 to 49½ inches hip measure. If combined as illustrated on figure, the medium size will require 2 yards of 40-inch linen for blouse, with ⅜ yard of 36 or more inch contrasting linen for collar and cuffs, ¼ yard of 24-inch silk to inlay collar and 2⅛ yards of 54-inch novelty cloth for skirt.   Price, 20 cents each.

9289—LADIES' NIGHTGOWN: Drawn Up On a Ribbon in Empire Style or Falling Free. The pattern is cut in 9 sizes from 32 to 48 inches bust measure. The 36-inch size will require as illustrated on figure, 4 yards of 36-inch nainsook for nightgown, with 3¾ yards of insertion and 3¾ yards of ribbon. Suitable materials which you might use in making this pretty and dainty nightgown are nainsook, batiste, wash satin, crêpe de Chine, cotton crêpe, silk mull, long-cloth and cambric.   20 cents.

9287—LADIES' SURPLICE DRESSING-SACK. 8 sizes, 38 to 46 inches bust measure. **9314**—LADIES' THREE-PIECE PETTICOAT: Lower edge of gores about 2⅛ yards; of flounce about 2¾ yards. 9 sizes, 22 to 38 inches waist measure, corresponding to 36 to 54 inches hip measure. If combined as illustrated on figure, the medium size will require 2¾ yards of 40-inch wool crêpe, with 3 yards of pleating, and 6 yards of 36-inch silk for petticoat with gores in full length. Price, 20 cents each.

9293—LADIES' DRESS: Convertible Collar; Long or Short One-Seam Sleeves; Clearing or Shorter Length. Lower edge about 3 yards. The pattern is cut in 7 sizes from 32 to 44 inches bust measure. The 36-inch size will require as illustrated on figure, 8 yards of 27-inch gingham for dress, with 1⅛ yards of 27-inch plain gingham for collar, cuffs and belt. What could be more attractive for a house dress than this simple model? It has very smart lines and very roomy pockets which are a great convenience. Suitable materials for this dress are gingham, chambray, percale, serge, gabardine and duvetyn.   Price, 20 cents.

8183—LADIES' BATHROBE: Long or Short Raglan Sleeves; Clearing or Shorter Length. The pattern is cut in 9 sizes from 32 to 48 inches bust measure. The 36-inch size will require as illustrated on figure, 3 yards of 64-inch blanket cloth for bathrobe, with 1⅝ yards of 27-inch silk for collar, trimming on front, cuffs and pocket edge. Simple to make and very comfortable to wear is this bathrobe of blanket cloth. The raglan sleeves may be either long or short. Suitable materials which might be used for this bathrobe are eider-down, flannelet, Turkish toweling or albatross, with contrasting silk for trimming bands. Price, 15 cents.

Blouse—**9291**
Skirt—**9292**

9293

9289

9291—9292

Scallop Outline **10307**

Dressing-Sack—**9287**   Petticoat—**9314**

9289

9287—9314   **9293**   **8183**

8183

Afternoon Frocks of Simple Charm

9269—LADIES' RUSSIAN DRESS: to be Slipped Over the Head. Lower edge of foundation skirt about 1¾ yards. 5 sizes, 32 to 40 inches bust measure. The 36-inch size will require as illustrated on figure, 3⅝ yards of 40-inch Georgette crêpe for dress, with 2⅜ yards of 36-inch velveteen for cuffs, girdle and band on edge of tunic, and 2½ yards of 36-inch silk for skirt.   Price, 20 cents.

9278—LADIES' DRESS: Gathered to a Stay at High Waistline or Held in by a Belt at Regulation Waistline. Lower edge of foundation skirt about 1¾ yards. 6 sizes, 32 to 42 inches bust measure. The 36-inch bust size will require as shown on figure, 4¾ yards of 54-inch gabardine for dress, with ½ yard of 36-inch organdy for standaway collar and cuffs, ⅞ yard of insertion, and 2½ yards of 32 or more inch material for foundation skirt.   Price, 20 cents.

9301—LADIES' DRESS: High, French or Open Neck; Long, Three-Quarter or Short One-Seam Sleeves; One-Piece Straight Gathered Tunic which may be Omitted; Loose Front and Back Panels; the Back Panel in Train or Shorter Length; One-Piece Straight Gathered Skirt; Clearing or Shorter Length. (Desirable for Flouncings, Bordered Materials or Other Fabrics.) The embroidery design illustrated on the figure is an adaptation of Standard transfer pattern 10271. Lower edge about 3⅜ yards. The pattern is cut in 6 sizes from 32 to 42 inches bust measure. The 36-inch bust size will require as illustrated on figure, 5¾ yards of 36-inch silk for dress, with 2⅛ yards of 50-inch serge for panel and facing the skirt, and ½ yard of 27-inch crêpe will be needed for yoke and collar.
Price, 20 cents.

9269

Blouse—9304   Skirt—9305

9304—LADIES' BLOUSE: Body in One with Long, Three-Quarter Length or Short Sleeves; High Neck or Open Neck with or without Standaway Collar. 7 sizes, 32 to 44 inches bust measure. **9305**—LADIES' THREE-PIECE SKIRT: Slightly High Waistline; Straight Plaited Tunic; Clearing or Shorter Length. Lower edge about 1¾ yards. The pattern is cut in 6 sizes from 22 to 32 inches waist measure, corresponding to 36 to 47 inches hip measure. If combined as on figure, the medium size will require 2 yards of 36-inch taffeta for overblouse, cuffs, collar and facing skirt, with 6⅞ yards of 36-inch figured taffeta for blouse and overskirt, and 2½ yards 32 for foundation skirt.   Price, 20 cents each.

9265

9265—LADIES' DRESS: High Neck or Open Neck with Standaway Collar. The embroidery design is an adaptation of Standard transfer pattern 10207. Lower edge about 2⅛ yards. 7 sizes, 32 to 44 inches bust measure. The 36-inch size will require as on figure, 4⅝ yards of 50-inch broadcloth for dress and facing skirt, with 2⅝ yards of fur banding on edge of tunic, ½ yard of 22-inch filet lace for collar and frill on cuff, and 1⅜ yards of filet lace edging on collar and frill.   Price, 20 cents.

9265   9278   9269   9304—9305   9301   9301

8987—LADIES' DRESS: Lower edge about 2½ yards. 6 sizes, 32 to 42 inches bust measure. The 36-inch bust size requires as on figure, 4¼ yards of 44-inch crêpe for overblouse and tunic, with 1¾ yards of 12-inch lace flouncing for blouse, 3¾ yards of 36-inch messaline for skirt, 20¼ yards of fur banding, ¾ yard of 27-inch silk for a girdle and ¾ yard 36, for guimpe.   15 cents.

9301—LADIES' DRESS. Lower edge about 3⅜ yards. 6 sizes, 32 to 42 bust. The 36-inch size requires as on figure, 1 yard of 36 or 40 inch net for blouse, with 1 yard of 8-inch edging for sleeves, 2¼ yards of 36-inch velveteen, 2⅝ yards of 35-inch lace flouncing for tunic, 2⅝ yards of 44-inch flouncing for skirt and ¾ yard of 4-inch ribbon.   20 cents.

Delectable Gowns for Gay Evenings

9304—LADIES' BLOUSE. 7 sizes, 32 to 44 inches bust measure. **8427**—LADIES' ONE-PIECE STRAIGHT SKIRT. Lower edge about 3 yards. 6 sizes, 22 to 32 inches waist measure, corresponding to 36 to 47 inches hip measure. Combined as on figure, the medium size requires 2 yards of 30-inch lace flouncing for blouse, with 8⅜ yards of 36-inch taffeta for overblouse and skirt.   20 cents for blouse and 15 cents for skirt.

8461—LADIES' EVENING BLOUSE. 9 sizes, 32 to 48 bust. **8738**—LADIES' SKIRT. Lower edge about 2½ yards. 5 sizes, 22 to 30 waist; 36 to 44½ hip. Combined as on figure, the medium size requires 7 yards of 40-inch chiffon for sleeves, overblouse, tunic and train, with 2¾ yards of 36-inch white satin for blouse, 3½ yards of 36-inch dark satin for skirt and girdle and ¾ yard of 40-inch material to line train.
Price, 15 cents each.

Blouse—9304
Skirt 8427

8987

9301

Blouse—8461
Skirt—8738

Bodice—8597
Skirt—8715

9301   8987   9304
8427   8461
8738   8597
8715

8597—LADIES' BODICE. 6 sizes, 32 to 42 inches bust measure. **8715**—LADIES' TWO-PIECE SKIRT. Lower edge of skirt measures about 2½ yards. The pattern is cut in 5 sizes from 22 to 30 inches waist measure, corresponding to 36 to 44½ inches hip measure. If combined as illustrated on figure, the medium size will require 1⅝ yards of 40-inch beaded chiffon for bodice, with ¾ yard of 40-inch net for sleeve ruffles, 1 yard of 32-inch material to line bodice, ¼ yard of 36-inch material for sleeve foundation, 6¼ yards of 36-inch velveteen for skirt and tunic and 1⅜ yards of fur banding.   Price, 15 cents each.

One-Piece Frocks and Some Modish

9266—Misses' and Small Women's Coat. 4 sizes, 14 to 20 years. **8495**—Misses' and Small Women's Three or Four-Piece Skirt. Lower edge about 2⅛ yards. 4 sizes, 14 to 20 years. As on figure, the 16-year size requires 2½ yards of 50-inch broadcloth, with ¼ yard of 24-inch velvet and 2⅛ yards of 44-inch striped suiting for four-piece skirt. Price, 15 cents each.

9270—Misses' and Small Women's Coat. 4 sizes, 14 to 20 years. **8352**—Misses' and Small Women's Five-Gored Skirt. Lower edge with plaits drawn out about 2⅜ yards. 4 sizes, 14 to 20 years. As on figure, the 16-year size requires 2⅞ yards of 54-inch plaid coating, with ½ yard of 27 or more inch fur and 3⅝ yards of 36-inch gabardine for skirt. Price, 15 cents each.

9262—Misses' and Small Women's Dress: Drawn Up on a Ribbon at High Waistline or Held in by a Belt at Regulation Waistline. For the embroidery design use Standard transfer pattern 10319. Lower edge about 2¾ yards. 4 sizes, 14 to 20 years. As on figure, the 16-year size requires 5⅛ yards of 36-inch broadcloth, with ½ yard of 24 or more inch satin for collar and cuffs. Price, 15 cents.

Coat—9266
Skirt—8495

B
9275

A
9275

Coat—9266
Skirt—9132

9270—8352

9275—Misses' and Small Women's Dress. Lower edge of skirt about 2⅝ yards. 4 sizes from 14 to 20 years. As illustrated on figure A, the 16-year size requires 3¾ yards of 36-inch plain serge, with ¾ yard of 36-inch satin for collar, cuffs and tie, 4 yards of braid and 2¾ yards of 42-inch checked serge; as on figure B 4¾ yards of 50-inch serge, with ⅝ yard of 20 or more inch contrasting serge and ¾ yard of 24-inch satin for tie. Price, 15 cents.

9266—Misses' and Small Women's Coat: Convertible Collar; Two-Seam Sleeves. 4 sizes, 14 to 20 years. **9132**—Misses' and Small Women's Two or Four Piece Skirt. Lower edge about 2 yards. 4 sizes, 14 to 20 years. If combined as on figure, the 16-year size will require 2½ yards of 50-inch Angora cloth, with ¼ yard of 24 or more inch fur for collar and 3 yards of 50-inch broadcloth for four-piece skirt. Separate coats in this length will be found very practical for wearing with separate skirts. Price, 15 cents each.

9290—Misses' and Small Women's Empire Dress: Long Dart-Fitted or Short Puff Sleeves; Separate Draped Overblouse which may be Omitted; One-Piece Straight Gathered Skirt. Lower edge about 2½ yards. 4 sizes, 14 to 20 years. As illustrated on figure, the 16-year size will require 4¼ yards of 42-inch satin, with ¾ yard of 32-inch contrasting satin for collar and cuffs, ¾ yard of 18-inch lace for standing collar and to face blouse fronts and back and ⅝ yard 36 for blouse front and back. Price, 15 cents.

9275   9275   9266—9132   9266—8495   9290

9290

Coat—9270   Skirt—8352

9262

9262

9300

9310   9308

9313

9294   9279

9306

9299

9284

9299

9306   9284

Foundation Skirts, and New Coats

9294—GIRLS' AND JUNIORS' EM-
PIRE DRESS. 11 sizes, 6 to 16 years.
The 13-year size requires as on figure,
1 yard of 44-inch serge, with 2¼
yards of 36-inch striped serge, ⅞ yard
of 24-inch satin, and ¾ yard 27 for
underbody.   Price, 15 cents.

9313—LITTLE GIRLS' EMPIRE
DRESS. 9 sizes, 4 to 12 years. The
10-year size requires as on figure, 2⅞
yards of 50-inch broadcloth, with ¾
yard of 27-inch checked satin for
collar, tie and pockets and 3¼ yards
of braid.   Price, 15 cents.

9300—LITTLE GIRLS' COAT. 5
sizes, 4 to 12 years. The 8-year size
requires as on figure, 2 yards of 54-
inch velours, with 1 yard of 18-inch
velvet for facing and cuffs, and ¼
yard of 27 or more inch fur for collar.   Price, 15 cents.

9306—JUNIORS' AND GIRLS'
DRESS. 11 sizes, 6 to 16 years. The
15-year size will require as illustrated
on figure, 4¼ yards of 42-inch
checked serge, with ¾ yard of 36-
inch contrasting serge, and 3 yards
of braid.   Price, 15 cents.

9279—GIRLS' AND JUNIORS'
COAT. The pattern is cut in 6 sizes
from 6 to 16 years. The 12-year size
will require as illustrated on figure,
2½ yards of 54-inch coating, with
⅜ yard of 50-inch broadcloth for collar.   Price, 15 cents.

9308—GIRLS' AND LITTLE
GIRLS' BOX-PLAITED DRESS. 11
sizes, 4 to 14 years. The 8-year size
requires as on figure, 3 yards of 44-
inch serge, with ½ yard of 40-inch
linen, ¾ yard of 24-inch striped satin
for tie.   Price, 15 cents.

9310—LITTLE GIRLS' DRESS. 9
sizes, 4 to 12 years. The 8-year size
will require as illustrated on figure,
3 yards of 36-inch flowered voile for
dress, with 1 yard of 36-inch satin for
collar, sash and bands. This is a
pretty dressy frock. Price, 15 cents.

9284—JUNIORS' AND GIRLS'
DRESS. 11 sizes, 6 to 16 years. The
16-year size will require as illustrated
on figure, 3½ yards of 50-inch broadcloth for dress, with 1 yard of 27-inch
satin for collar, cuffs, pockets and
belt.   Price, 15 cents.

9299—JUNIORS' AND GIRLS'
DRESS: 11 sizes, 6 to 16 years. The
14-year size will require as illustrated
on figure, 3½ yards of 40-inch satin
for dress, with 1⅜ yards of 48-inch
serge for overblouse and band on
skirt.   Price, 15 cents.

9300   9310   9308   9313   9294   9279

One-Piece Dresses—A Redingote Coat—Low Waistlines

This is essentially a season of one-piece dresses and long separate coats, but there are many new and fashionable coat suits and blouses for those women who prefer them. At the present time the smartest of the one-piece dresses are made of serge, combined with satin. Faille, taffeta, Georgette crepe and gabardine are other materials.

Coat—9261
Skirt—9264

9261—LADIES' COAT: 32-Inch Length at the Back; Convertible Collar. 8 sizes, 32 to 46 inches bust measure. 9264—LADIES' FOUR-PIECE SKIRT: Clearing or Shorter Length. Lower edge with plaits drawn out about 2⅝ yards. 8 sizes, 22 to 36 inches waist, or 36 to 52 inches hip. As illustrated on figure, the medium size will require 5¼ yards of 54-inch novelty woolen goods. Price, 20 cents each.

9295

9295—LADIES' REDINGOTE COAT: 48 or 42 Inch Length at the Back; Convertible Collar; Two-Seam Sleeves with Slight Fulness at the Top which may be Shrunken Out; Three-Piece Gathered Skirt in Two Styles. The pattern is cut in 7 sizes from 32 to 44 inches bust measure. As illustrated on figure, the 36-inch bust size will require 3¾ yards of 54-inch duvetyn for coat, with 1¼ yards of 54-inch fur cloth. Price, 20 cents.

9315—LADIES' DRESS in Redingote Style; High Neck or Open Neck with Standaway Collar; Long Dart-Fitted or Shorter Sleeves; High Waistline; Three-Piece Tunic in Two Lengths; Separate Two-Piece Skirt; Clearing or Shorter Length. Lower edge about 1¾ yards. The pattern is cut in 6 sizes from 32 to 42 inches bust measure. As illustrated on figure the, 36-inch bust size will require 3⅜ yards of 50-inch French serge for blouse and tunic, with ¾ yard of 36-inch white satin for collar and cuffs, 2⅞ yards of braid to trim collar and cuffs, and 2½ yards of 36-inch satin for skirt. Price, 20 cents.

9307

9307—LADIES' DRESS: in Moyen Age Style: Chemisette; Collar with or without the Trimming Piece; Long Dart-Fitted or Short Sleeves; One-Piece Straight Gathered Skirt or Tunic; Two-Piece Foundation Skirt. Lower edge about 2¼ yards. The pattern is cut in 6 sizes from 32 to 42 inches bust measure. As illustrated on figure, the 36-inch bust size will require 4⅞ yards of 50-inch broadcloth for dress, with 1¼ yards of 18-inch satin for trimming-band on collar and 2¾ yards of 36-inch material for foundation skirt. A dress which embodies some of the smartest as well as some of the most fashionable features is shown in the above illustration. The long, straight lines of the fitted blouse and gathered tunic are extremely popular. The trimming piece on the collar is very new and unusual. Price, 20 cents.

9307   9261—9264   9315   9315   9295   9283

9283—LADIES' COAT in Moyen-Age Style; 42 or 48 Inch Length at the Back; Convertible Collar; Two-Seam Sleeves with Slight Fulness at the Top which may be Shrunken Out. The pattern is cut in 6 sizes from 32 to 42 inches bust measure. As illustrated on figure, the 36-inch bust size will require 4⅜ yards of 54-inch checked cloth for coat, with ⅝ yard of 50-inch contrasting cloth for collar, cuffs and belts. You surely can't deny that this coat has both style and comfort. Just look at the big collar that may be worn open so that it looks like a cape in the back, or which may be partly buttoned up, or which, best of all, may be buttoned up close around the chin to keep out the bitter cold. The pockets, too, are roomy enough to protect the hands from the frost.   Price, 20 cents.

9253

8461

Blouse—9412
Skirt—8222

9412—Ladies' Blouse. 6 sizes, 32 to 42
bust. **8222**—Ladies' Five-Piece Skirt.
Lower edge about 2½ yards. 7 sizes, 22 to 34
waist, or 36 to 49½ hip.   20 cents each.

8461—Ladies' Evening Blouse. 9
sizes, 32 to 48 bust. As on figure, for 36-inch
size 1¾ yards of 40-inch Georgette, 1⅜ yards
of 13½-inch banding, ¾ yard 24 for girdle, ⅞
yard 32 for lining.   Price, 20 cents.

9253—Ladies' Blouse. 8 sizes, 32 to 46
bust. As on figure, for 36-inch size ⅞ yard of
brocaded silk 36, 1¼ yard of tulle 40, and 1
yard 32 for lining.   Price, 20 cents.

9416—Ladies' Dress: One-Piece Un-
derblouse; Separate Draped Overblouse; One-
Piece Straight Gathered Tunic or Pointed
Tunic with or without the Train; One-Piece
Skirt. Lower edge of skirt about 2 yards. 6
sizes, 32 to 42 inches bust.   25 Cents.

9192—Ladies' Dress. Lower edge
about 1¾ yards. 6 sizes, 32 to 42 bust. As
on figure, the 36-inch size requires 7¼ yards
of 40-inch Georgette crêpe, ½ yard of 36-inch
silk for overblouse and 4 yards of ribbon each
width.   Price, 20 cents.

9416

9412—8222   8461   9192

9192

9416

9416   9253   9416

Coat—9371

Coat—9409 Skirt—9277

9371—Ladies' Coat: 45 or
42 or 36 Inch Length at the Back.
8 sizes, 32 to 46 inches bust measure. As illustrated on figure
the 36-inch size requires 4 yards
of 54-inch novelty cloth coating.   Price, 20 cents.

9409—Ladies' Coat. 7
sizes, 32 to 44 bust. 9277—
Ladies' Skirt. Lower edge
about 2¼ yards. 7 sizes, 22 to
34 waist, or 36 to 49½ hip.
As on figure for medium size 4½
yards 54.   20 cents each.

9423

9420

9420   9371   9409—9277   9423

9420—Ladies' Dress.
The embroidery design is an
adaptation of Standard transfer 10317. Lower edge measures about 2¼ yards. 6 sizes,
32 to 42 bust. As on figure
the 36-inch size requires 5⅝
yards of 54-inch cloth, with 2⅝
yards of 24-inch satin, and 3
yards 36 inches for foundation
skirt.   Price, 25 cents.

9423 — Ladies' Red-
ingote Dress. Lower edge
about 2 yards. The pattern is
cut in 6 sizes from 32 to 42
inches bust measure. As illustrated on figure the 36-inch
size will require 6⅞ yards of
40-inch satin, with ⅝ yard of
27-inch contrasting satin, and
⅞ yard of 32-inch material for
lining.   Price, 25 cents.

9376

Blouse—9285
Skirt—9198

Blouse—
9150
Skirt—
9281

9376

Guimpe—8284 Skirt—9400

8284—9400

9285
9198

9150—9281

9388—9273

9416

Blouse—9388 Skirt—9273

9416

8284—Ladies' Guimpe. 9 sizes, 32 to 48 bust. **9400**—Ladies' Jumper Skirt: Two-Piece Foundation Skirt. Lower edge about 2 yards. 6 sizes, 32 to 42 bust.
Guimpe 15 cents; Skirt 20 cents.

9376—Ladies' Dress. Lower edge of separate skirt about 2⅛ yards. 7 sizes, 32 to 44 bust. As on figure, the 36-inch size requires 3⅝ yards of 50-inch serge, 4⅛ yards of 40-inch satin.   25 cents.

9285—Blouse. 6 sizes, 32 to 42 bust. **9198**—Skirt. Lower edge about 2 yards. 9 sizes, 22 to 38 waist, or 36 to 54 hip. As on figure, the medium size needs 4 yds. of figured silk 36, and 1⅞ yds. 54.   20 cents each.

9150—7 sizes, 32 to 44 bust. **9281**— Lower edge about 3¾ yards. 6 sizes, 22 to 32 waist, or 36 to 47 hip. As on figure, the medium size needs 2½ yards of crêpe 36, 2⅝ yds. of insertion, 3½ yds. of edging, 3¾ yards of serge 54.   20 cents each.

9416—Ladies' Dress: Underblouse; Draped Overblouse; Guimpe; Tunic; One-Piece Skirt. 6 sizes; 32 to 42 bust. Lower edge of skirt about 2 yards.   25 cents.

9388—7 sizes, 32 to 44 bust. **9273**— Lower edge about 2¾ yards. 9 sizes, 22 to 38 waist, or 36 to 54 hip. As on figure, the medium size requires 4½ yds. of striped silk 32 and 4 yds. of plain 36.   20 cts. each.

Blouse—9377
Skirt—9198

Blouse—9276
Skirt—9389

Coat—9371
Skirt—9264

Blouse—9373
Skirt—9374

9276—7 sizes, 32 to 44 bust. **9389**—Lower edge about 2½ yards. 9 sizes, 22 to 38 waist, 36 to 54 hip. As on figure the medium size requires 1¾ yards 42 for blouse, with ⅝ yard 36; for skirt 2¾ yards 44 inches wide. Price, 20 cents each.

9377—7 sizes, 32 to 44 bust. **9198**—Lower edge about 2 yards. 9 sizes, 22 to 38 waist, or 36 to 54 hip. As on figure the medium size needs 4¾ yards 32 of striped, with 2⅝ yards 36 of plain. 20 cents each.

9371—8 sizes, 32 to 46 bust. **9264**—Lower edge about 2⅝ yards. 8 sizes, 22 to 36 waist, or 36 to 52 hip. As on figure the medium size needs 8½ yards 36, with ¾ yard of striped material 36. Price, 20 cents each.

9373—LADIES' BLOUSE. 8 sizes, 32 to 46 bust. **9374**—LADIES' SKIRT. Lower edge about 2¼ yards. 6 sizes, 22 to 32 waist, or 36 to 47 hip. As on figure the medium size needs 3⅞ yards of taffeta 45, 1½ yards of crepe 40. Price, 20 cents.

9130—LADIES' DRESS. Lower edge about 1¾ yards. 6 sizes, 32 to 42 bust. As on figure the 36-inch size requires 6½ yards 36, with ¾ yard 27. Price, 20 cents.

Embroidery design an adaptation of transfer
10112
Blouse—9382
Skirt—9378

9382—LADIES' BLOUSE. 6 sizes, 32 to 42 bust. **9378**—LADIES' SKIRT. Lower edge about 2⅝ yards. 9 sizes, 22 to 38 waist, or 36 to 54 hip. As on figure the medium size requires 2⅞ yards 40 for blouse, and 2⅞ yards 50 inches wide for skirt. 20 cents each.

9130

9377—9198 9371—9264 9373—74

9130   9276—9389 9382—9378

9376

9133

9376   9164—9384   9133

9417   9424   9105

9105

9424

Corset-cover
9164
Drawers 9384
*Embroidery
design an adap-
tation of
Transfer
4414*

9417

9417 — LADIES' APRON AND
CAP. 7 sizes, 32 to 44 bust. The
36-inch size requires as on figure,
6¾ yards 27 for apron, ¾ yard 27
for cap, and ¾ yard of 27-inch striped
gingham.   Price, 15 cents.

9164—LADIES' CORSET COVER.
9 sizes, 32 to 48 bust. **9384**—
LADIES' CLOSED DRAWERS. 5 sizes,
22 to 30 waist. As on figure the medium size requires 1 yard 36 for corset cover, 1½ yards 36 for drawers.
Corset Cover 20 cts., Drawers 15 cts.

9133—LADIES' DRESS. Lower
edge of skirt about 2½ yards. 9
sizes, 32 to 48 bust. The 36-inch
size requires as on figure, 6 yards 32,
with ½ yard of 32-inch striped galatea.   Price, 20 cents.

9376—LADIES' DRESS. Lower
edge about 3⅛ yards. 7 sizes, 32
to 44 bust. The 36-inch size requires as on figure, 6¼ yards of 36-
inch percale, and 1⅛ yards of 36-
inch lawn.   Price, 25 cents.

9424—LADIES' NIGHT-
GOWN. 9 sizes, 32 to 48 bust.
The 36-inch size requires as
on figure, 4¾ yards 36-inch
batiste, with 2¾ yards of
edging. Price, 20 cents.

9105—LADIES' BATHROBE. 9
sizes, 32 to 48 bust. The 36-inch
size requires as on figure, 6½ yards
32, with ½ yard 36 for collar, 1¼
yards of edging, and 1¾ yards of
ribbon.   Price, 20 cents.

A VARIETY OF MODES
⚜ FOR SPRING DAYS ⚜

Blouse—9394
Skirt—9395

Blouse—9405
Skirt—9406

Blouse—9216
Skirt—9383

9380

Coat—9386
Skirt—9198

9394—LADIES' BLOUSE: Back Extending Over the Shoulders to Form a Yoke. **7 sizes, 32 to 44 inches bust measure. 9395**—LADIES' FOUR-PIECE SKIRT. The embroidery design is an adaptation of Standard transfer 10290. Lower edge with plaits drawn out about 2½ yards. 6 sizes, 22 to 32 inches waist, or 36 to 47 inches hip. Combined as illustrated on figure, the medium size will require 2⅞ yards of 40-inch cotton voile, with 2¾ yards of edging and 2⅝ yards of 54-inch cloth for skirt.   Price, 20 cents each.

9405—LADIES' TUCKED BLOUSE. Convertible Collar or Open Neck with Sailor Collar. **5 sizes, 32 to 40 inches bust measure. 9406**—LADIES' SKIRT: One-Piece Shirred or Gathered Upper Part; One-Piece Lower Part. For the embroidery design use Standard transfer 10013. Lower edge about 2¼ yards. 6 sizes, 22 to 32 inches waist, or 36 to 47 inches hip. Combined as illustrated on figure, the medium size will require 6 yards of 40-inch crêpe de Chine, with ½ yard of 36-inch satin for collar.   Price, 20 cents each.

9216—LADIES' BLOUSE. **7 sizes, 32 to 44 inches bust measure. 9383**—LADIES' SIX-PIECE SKIRT: Slightly High Waistline; Front Gore in One with Yoke Front; Clearing or Shorter Length. Lower edge with plaits drawn out 2⅝ yards. 6 sizes, 22 to 32 inches waist measure, or 36 to 47 inches hip measure. Combined as illustrated on figure, the medium size will require 2⅜ yards of 36-inch lawn for blouse, with 3¾ yards of lace banding to trim collar and jabot and 3⅜ yards of 50-inch broadcloth for skirt. 20 cents each.

9380—LADIES' COAT: 50 or 36 Inch Length at the Back; Convertible Collar in Two Outlines at the Back; Deep Armhole; One-Seam Sleeves in Two Styles at the Wrist. The pattern is cut in 8 sizes from 32 to 46 inches bust measure. As illustrated on figure, the 36-inch size will require 4⅜ yards of 54-inch coating, with ⅝ yard of 24 or more inch velvet for collar. Corduroy will be suitable for the coat in shorter length and serge, gabardine, broadcloth and coatings for the full length.   Price, 20 cents.

9386—LADIES' COAT: Tuck Seams; 27-Inch Length at the Back; Convertible Collar; Two-Seam Sleeves with Slight Fulness at the Top which may be Shrunken Out; Three-Piece Peplum which may be Omitted. **7 sizes from 32 to 44 inches bust measure. 9198**—LADIES' THREE-PIECE SKIRT. Lower edge about 2 yards. 9 sizes, 22 to 38 inches waist, or 36 to 54 inches hip. Combined as on figure, the medium size requires 5¼ yards of 50-inch broadcloth, with ½ yard of 50-inch contrasting broadcloth.   Price, 20 cents each.

9394—9395   9405—9406   9216—9383   9380   9386—9198

STYLES WE WILL WEAR
IN THE SPRING

Waist—9399
Skirt—9032

9393

Blouse—9382   Skirt—9167   Coat—9380   Skirt—9281   9398

9399-9032   9393   9382-9167   9380-9281   9398

9398—LADIES' DRESS: High Neck or Open Neck with Standaway Collar; Long Dart-Fitted or Short Sleeves; Two-Piece Gathered Skirt. Lower edge about 2½ yards. 6 sizes, 32 to 42 inches bust measure. As illustrated on figure, the 36-inch size will require 4½ yards of 44-inch French serge, with ½ yard of 27-inch silk to trim collar and top of pockets. The arrangement of the pockets to follow the lines of the gathered skirt gives very smart and attractive lines.   Price, 25 cents.

9380—LADIES' COAT: 50 or 36 Inch Length at the Back; Deep Armhole; One-Seam Sleeves. 8 sizes, 32 to 46 inches bust measure. **9281**—LADIES' NINE-GORED SKIRT. Lower edge with plaits drawn out about 3¾ yards. 6 sizes, 22 to 32 inches waist measure, or 36 to 47 inches hip measure. As on figure, the medium size will require 4¼ yards of 44-inch cloth for coat, with 1½ yards of 44-inch contrasting cloth and 5 yards of 44-inch cloth for skirt.   Price, 20 cents each.

9382—LADIES' BLOUSE: in Russian Style. 6 sizes, 32 to 42 inches bust measure. **9167**—LADIES' THREE-PIECE SKIRT. Lower edge about 2¼ yards. 7 sizes, 22 to 34 inches waist measure, corresponding to 36 to 49½ inches hip measure. As on figure, the medium size requires 3⅜ yards of 36-inch cotton voile for blouse, with ½ yard of 36-inch contrasting voile for collar, 2 yards of lace insertion and 3½ yards of 36-inch striped pongee for skirt.   Price, 20 cents each.

9393—LADIES' DRESS: Box-Plaited Blouse to be Slipped Over the Head; Convertible Collar or Open Neck with Large Collar; Yoke Facing which may be Omitted; Long or Short One-Seam Sleeves; Two-Piece Skirt; Clearing or Shorter Length. Lower edge about 2½ yards. 7 sizes, 32 to 44 inches bust measure. As illustrated on figure, the 36-inch size will require 3¾ yards of 32-inch galatea for blouse and 3 yards of 32-inch contrasting galatea for collar, cuffs and skirt.   Price, 25 cents.

9399—LADIES' WAIST: One-Piece Straight Gathered Tunic in Two Lengths; Long Dart-Fitted or Short Sleeves. 6 sizes, 32 to 42 inches bust measure. **9032**—LADIES' TWO-PIECE SKIRT. Lower edge of gores about 1¾ yards. 7 sizes, 22 to 34 inches waist, or 36 to 49½ inches hip. The embroidery design is an adaptation of standard transfer 10086. Combined as illustrated on figure, the medium size will require 6 yards of 44-inch cloth, with ½ yard of 36-inch silk for collar and 5½ yards of braid.   20 cents each.

ONE SEES EVERYWHERE ⚜

Blouse—9411
Knickerbockers—2742

9375

9401

9404

9396

9410

Coat—9117 Hat—8341

9418   9390

9375—Little Girls' Coat: Three-Piece Skirt. 5 sizes, 4 to 12 years. As on figure, the 10-year size requires 2½ yards of 50-inch broadcloth, with ⅜ yard of 36 or more inch contrasting broadcloth for collar and cuffs.   Price, 15 cents.

9401—Girls' and Juniors' Two-Piece Suit: One-Piece Straight Plaited Skirt. 6 sizes, 6 to 16 years. As on figure, the 14-year size requires 5½ yards of 44-inch linen, with 1⅜ yard of 36-inch contrasting linen.   Price, 20 cents.

9411—Boys' Shirt Blouse. 11 sizes, 4 to 14 years. **2742**—Little Boys' Knickerbockers. 7 sizes, 2 to 8 years. As on figure the 7 year size requires 1¾ yard of linen 40 inches wide, and ¾ yard of cheviot 54 inches wide.   15 cents each.

9396—Little Girls' Dress. Bloomers. 9 sizes, 2 to 10 years. As on figure, the 5-year size requires 2⅜ yards of 32-inch galatea, with ⅝ yard of 36-inch plain galatea for collar, cuffs and belt and 1 yard 32 for bloomers.   Price, 15 cents.

9410—Little Girls' Dress: Straight Gathered Skirt. 7 sizes, 4 to 10 years. As on figure, the 8-year size requires 1 yard of 27-inch checked gingham, 3 yards of 27-inch plain gingham and ¼ yard of 36-inch lawn.   Price, 15 cents.

9390—Girls' and Juniors' Dress: High or Open Neck; Jacket Front with Two Styles of Pockets. 11 sizes, 6 to 16 years. As on figure, the 9-year size requires 2⅛ yards of 48-inch gabardine, and ⅜ yard of 50-inch broadcloth.   15 cents.

9117—Child's Coat: For the embroidery design use Standard transfer 10290. 7 sizes, ½ to 6 years. **8341**—Hat. 2 sizes, girls and little girls. As on figure, the 4-year size needs 2⅝ yards 44 for coat, ⅞ yards 27 for hat, 2 yards of pleating, ⅝ yds. of rose-bud trimming.   15 cts. each.

9404—Girls' and Juniors' Dress: Straight Gathered or Cartridge Plaited Side Tunics in Two Lengths which may be Omitted. 11 sizes from 6 to 16 years. As on figure, the 11-year size needs 4¼ yards of 40-inch serge and ½ yard of 27-inch linen for collar and cuffs.   Price, 15 cents.

9418—Little Girls' Dress: Closed to the Neck with Round Collar or Convertible Collar; Bloomers. 9 sizes, 2 to 10 years. As on figure, the 4-year size needs 2¼ yards of 32-inch chambray, with 1¼ yards of 27-inch plain chambray and 1 yard 32 for bloomers.   Price, 15 cents.

9375   9401   9404   9411   2742   9117   9396   9410   9418   9390

⚜ TO ADD CHARMS TO THE CHARMING ⚜

Coat—9409
Skirt—9087

Blouse—9412   Skirt—9413

9402 B

9412 — LADIES' BLOUSE: Separate Guimpe; Draped Overblouse and Lower Part of Sleeve may be Omitted. 6 sizes, 32 to 42 bust. 9413—LADIES' FOUR-PIECE SKIRT. Lower edge about 2⅔ yards. 7 sizes, 22 to 34 waist, or 36 to 49½ hip. 20 cents each.

9402 A

9402 — LADIES' DRESS: Two-Piece Skirt or Tunic. Lower edge about 2½ yards. 7 sizes, 32 to 44 bust. As on figure A the 36-inch size requires 4 yards of 50-inch velours, with ½ yard of 20 or more inch broadcloth. 25 cents.

9420 — LADIES' DRESS: to be Slipped Over the Head. Lower edge of dress about 3 yards. 6 sizes, 32 to 42 bust. As on figure, the 36-inch size requires 5⅝ yds. of duvetyn 54, ⅞ yard of net 18, ¾ yard of silk 40.
Price, 25 cents.

9409 — LADIES' COAT. 7 sizes, 32 to 44 bust. 9087 — LADIES' SKIRT. Lower edge about 3¾ yards. 9 sizes, 22 to 38 waist, or 36 to 54 hip. As on figure, the medium size needs 5 yards 50, and ⅜ yard 27 for collar. 20 cts. each.

9386—7 sizes, 32 to 44 bust. 9151 —Lower edge about 1⅝ yards. 5 sizes, 22 to 30 waist, or 36 to 44½ hip. As on figure, the medium size needs 3⅞ yds. checked cloth 48, 3 yds. of plain 44, 2⅝ yds. 32 for foundation. 20 cents each.

9402   9402   9412—9413   9409—9087   9386—9151   9420

9420

Coat—9386   Skirt—9151

A New Silhouette Appears—

"*THE MORE THE MERRIER*," *thought the barrel silhouette, as it came rolling back into fashion to rival the straight-lined skirts and dresses and reduce the flaring ones to a state of innocuous desuetude This silhouette is really an old friend of yesteryear, which we knew familiarly as the "peg-top." It has its more formal appellations, too, such as jupe tonneau, Turkish and Hindu. The point of the whole thing is that the barrel silhouette is wide at the hips or just below, and narrow at the lower part. You will notice that shaped bands produce the narrowness in the case of the two examples on this page. Many women will find skirts with straight lines more becoming to their figures, and for them there are extremely smart, new two or three piece models and new draped, gathered and plaited skirts, which hang straight, as the materials of the season are uniformly soft.*

9578   Blouse—9583   Skirt—9584

9566

9578   9583   9566   9558   9555
         9584   9559

Blouse—9558   Skirt—9559   9555

9578—Ladies' One-Piece Dress. Lower edge in regulation style about 2⅝ yards. 6 sizes, 32 to 42 bust. The 36-inch size requires as on figure 4½ yards of 40-inch novelty voile, with ⅝ yard of 40-inch white voile.   Price, 25 cents.

9555—Ladies' Dress. Lower edge about 2¼ yards. 5 sizes, 32 to 40 bust. The 36-inch size requires as on figure, 7¼ yards of Georgette crepe 40, with 1¼ yards of white Georgette 22 and ¾ yard of 32-inch striped silk.   Price, 25 cents.

9566—Ladies' Semi-Fitted Dress. Lower edge about 2 yards. 6 sizes, 32 to 42 bust. The 36-inch size requires as on figure 2¾ yards of 40-inch plain satin, with 3⅞ yards of 36-inch figured satin.   Price, 25 cents.

9558—Ladies' Blouse. 7 sizes, 32 to 44 bust. **9559**—Ladies' Two-Piece Skirt. Lower edge in barrel style about 1½ yards. 7 sizes, 22 to 34 waist; 36 to 49½ hip. For braiding design use transfer 10310. As on figure, the medium size requires 4¾ yards 40 with ¾ yard 18 for collar.   Price, 20 cents each.

9583—Ladies' Blouse. 6 sizes, 32 to 42 bust. **9584**—Ladies' Skirt. Lower edge about 4 yards. 5 sizes, 22 to 30 waist, 36 to 44½ hip. As on figure, the medium size requires 4⅛ 5 inch bordered material, with 2¼ in for overblouse and 1⅞ for blouse. 20 cts. each.

Coat—**9561**   Blouse—**9568**
Skirt—**9554**   Skirt—**9575**
             Transfer—**10372**

9568—LADIES' BLOUSE. 6 sizes, 32 to 42 bust. **9575**—LADIES' SKIRT. Lower edge about 2 yards. 6 sizes, 22 to 32 waist; 36 to 47 hip. As on figure the medium size requires 7⅛ yards of 48-inch linen. 20 cents each.

9561—LADIES' COAT. 6 sizes, 32 to 42 bust. **9554**—LADIES' SKIRT. Lower edge about 2⅛ yards. 9 sizes, 22 to 38 waist, or 36 to 54 hip. As on figure, the medium size requires 4⅝ yds. of serge 48, ⅛ yd. of velvet 36, ⅜ yd. of broadcloth 48.   Price, 20 cents each.

9588—LADIES' BLOUSE. 7 sizes, 32 to 44 bust. **9589**—LADIES' SKIRT. Lower edge about 2 yards. 6 sizes, 22 to 32 waist, 36 to 47 hip. As on figure, the medium size requires 2⅜ yards of flowered chiffon 40, with 4¼ yards of taffeta 36.   Price, 20 cents each.

9563—LADIES' CHEMISE BLOUSE. 6 sizes, 32 to 42 bust. **9564**—LADIES' SKIRT. Lower edge in barrel style about 1⅝ yards. 7 sizes, 22 to 34 waist; 36 to 49½ hip. As on figure, the medium size requires 3¾ yards of figured 36 with 3 yards plain pongee.   20 cents each.

9579—LADIES' BLOUSE. 7 sizes, 32 to 44 bust. **9564**—SKIRT. Lower edge about 2½ yards. 7 sizes, 22 to 34 waist; 36 to 49½ hip. As shown the medium size needs 2 yards 40 for blouse, and 2⅞ yds. 40 for skirt. 20 cts. each.

Blouse—**9588**   Skirt—**9589**

Blouse—**9563**   Skirt—**9564**

Blouse—**9579**
Skirt—**9564**
Transfer Design—**10318**

9588—9589   9561—9554   9568—9575   9563—9564   9579—9564

APT SUGGESTIONS FOR YOUR SUIT

Coat—9561
Skirt—9564

9561
9564

9586
9569

9566

9579
9580

9578

Coat—9586
Skirt—9569

Blouse—9579
Skirt—9580

9578

9578—LADIES' ONE-PIECE DRESS: To be Slipped Over the Head; Barrel or Regulation Style, Convertible Collar or Open Neck. Lower edge in barrel style about 1⅝ yards. 6 sizes, 32 to 42 inches bust measure. The 36-inch size will require as illustrated on figure, 4⅜ yards of 36-inch foulard, and ⅞ yard of 36-inch satin will be needed for cuffs, belt and pipings.   Price, 25 cents.

9586—LADIES' COAT. 7 sizes, 32 to 44 bust.
9569—LADIES' TWO-PIECE SKIRT: Slightly High Waistline. The braiding design is an adaptation of Standard transfer 10310. Lower edge about 2⅛ yards. 7 sizes, 22 to 34 waist, corresponding to 36 to 49½ hip. Combined as on-figure, the medium size requires 3⅜ yards of 60-inch jersey cloth, with ¾ yard of 32-inch satin for collar.   20 cents each.

9561—LADIES' COAT. For the braiding design use Standard transfer 10086. 6 sizes, 32 to 42 inches bust measure. 9564—LADIES' TWO-PIECE GATHERED SKIRT. Lower edge in regulation style about 2½ yards. 7 sizes, 22 to 34 inches waist measure, corresponding to 36 to 49½ inches hip measure. If combined as illustrated on figure the medium size will require 5¼ yards of 48-inch cloth.   20 cents each.

9566

9579—LADIES' BLOUSE. 7 sizes, 32 to 44 inches bust measure. 9580—LADIES' FOUR-PIECE SKIRT. Lower edge measures about 2¼ yards. 8 sizes, 22 to 36 inches waist measure, corresponding to 36 to 52 inches hip measure. If combined as illustrated on figure, the medium size will require 2⅜ yards of 36-inch lawn for blouse, and 2⅝ yards of 44-inch linen for skirt.   Price, 20 cents each.

9566—LADIES' SEMI-FITTED DRESS. Lower edge about 2 yards. 6 sizes, 32 to 42 inches bust measure. The 36-inch size requires as on figure, 3¾ yards of 36-inch twilled silk for blouse and upper section of skirt, with 1½ yards of 40-inch satin for lower section of skirt, ¼ yard of 27-inch white silk for collar and ⅞ yard of 6-inch ribbon will be required for a girdle.   Price, 25 cents.

A SHORT COAT AND A LONGER ONE

Blouse—**9563**   Skirt—**9564**

Coat—**9561**   Skirt—**9559**   **9555**

Blouse—**9553**   Skirt—**9554**

Coat—**9586**   Skirt—**9442**

9563—Ladies' Chemise Blouse. 6 sizes, 32 to 42 inches bust measure. **9564**—Ladies' Skirt. Lower edge in regulation style about 2½ yards. 7 sizes, 22 to 34 inches waist measure, corresponding to 36 to 49½ inches hip measure. As illustrated on figure, the medium size will require 2⅞ yards of 36-inch pongee for blouse with 3½ yards of 36-inch figured pongee for skirt.   Price, 20 cents each.

9559—Ladies' Coat. 6 sizes, 32 to 42 inches bust measure. For braiding illustrated use transfer 10086. **9559**—Ladies' Two-Piece Skirt. Lower edge in regulation style about 2¼ yards. 7 sizes, 22 to 34 inches waist measure or to 36 to 49½ inches hip measure. As on figure, the medium size requires 5⅜ yards of 36-inch shantung, with 1¾ yards of ribbon for sash.   Price, 20 cents each.

9555—Ladies' Semi-Fitted Dress. Lower edge about 2¼ yards. 5 sizes, 32 to 40 inches bust measure. The 36-inch size requires, as on figure, 4¼ yards of 32-inch foulard for front and back of blouse and upper section of skirt, with 4½ yards of 36-inch plain foulard for sleeves, cuffs, girdle and lower section of skirt, and ¼ yard of 36-inch contrasting silk for collar.   Price, 25 cents.

9553—Ladies' Blouse. 8 sizes, 32 to 46 bust. **9554**—Ladies' Three-Piece Skirt. Clearing or Shorter Length. Lower edge about 2⅛ yards. 9 sizes, 22 to 38 waist measure, corresponding to 36 to 54 inches hip measure. As illustrated on figure, the medium size will require 2¾ yards of 36-inch lawn for blouse, and 1⅞ yards of 54-inch gabardine for skirt.   Price, 20 cents each.

9586—Ladies' Coat: 28 or 15 Inch Length at the Back. 7 sizes, 32 to 44 bust. **9442**—Ladies' Four-Piece Skirt. Lower edge about 2⅛ yards. 6 sizes, 22 to 32 inches waist measure, corresponding to 36 to 47 inches hip measure. As illustrated on figure the medium size will require 5⅞ yards of 50-inch French serge, with ¼ yard of 27-inch velvet for collar.   Price, 20 cents each.

9586
9442

9553
9554

9555

9561—9559

9563—9564

9568

9571-B

9609

9552   9568   9567

9567

9571   9571-A

9571   9571   9609

9552—LADIES' ONE-PIECE PAJAMAS: Convertible Collar or Open Neck; Long or Short Sleeves. 6 sizes from 32 to 42 inches bust measure. As illustrated on figure, the 36-inch size will require 6⅞ yards of 36-inch lawn, with 2 yards of ribbon.   Price, 20 cents.

9568—LADIES' BLOUSE: to be Slipped Over the Head and to be Worn Inside or Outside the Skirt. 6 sizes, 32 to 42 bust. As on figure, the 36-inch size will require 1¾ yards of 32-inch plain galatea, with 1 yard of 32-inch striped galatea.   Price, 20 cents.

9609—LADIES' COVERALL APRON OR HOUSE DRESS; CAP. 7 sizes, 32 to 42 bust. As shown, the 36-inch size needs 7¾ yds. of 27-inch gingham and ¾ yds. of 27-inch dotted material.   Price, 20 cents.

9571 — LADIES' ONE-PIECE NEGLIGEE AND CAP. For the embroidery design, on figure B, use Standard transfer 10297. 6 sizes, 32 to 42 bust. As on figure A, the 36-inch size needs 3⅞ yards 42, with ¾ yard 40. As on figure B, 2⅜ yds. 36.   Price, 20 cents.

9567—LADIES' DRESS. (Suitable for Maternity or General Wear.) For the scallop design, use Standard transfer pattern 10112. Lower edge about 2½ yards. 7 sizes, 32 to 44 inches bust. As on figure, the 36-inch size will require 8⅝ yds. 44, with ⅝ yd. 50. 25 cts.

9577 A

9592 A

9602

9592 A   9602   9604

9577 B

9577 A   9577 B

9604   9592 B   9592 B

9592—Girls' and Juniors' Bathing-Suit. For the braiding design on figure A use Standard transfer 10086. 7 sizes, 4 to 16 years. The 14-year size requires as on figure A, 4⅝ yards of 36-inch mohair, with 1⅜ yards of 27-inch material for underwaist; the 6-year size requires as on figure B, 2⅛ yards of 32-inch flannel, with 1⅝ yards of 32-inch striped flannel for bloomers, and bands to trim and 1 yard of 27-inch material will be needed for underwaist.   Price, 15 cents.

9602—Ladies' Bathing-Suit: to be Slipped Over the Head; Two Lengths; Collar and Shield Sleeves which may be Omitted; Bloomers; Cap. The pattern is cut in 7 sizes from 32 to 44 inches bust measure. The 36-inch size will require as illustrated on figure, 3¼ yards of 40-inch poplin for front, belt, band on cap and bloomers, with 2½ yards of 40-inch figured poplin for back and sides of dress, sleeves, collar and top of cap.   Price, 20 cents.

9577—Ladies' One-Piece Bathing-Suit: Bloomers; Cap. 7 sizes, 32 to 44 bust. The 36-inch size requires as on figure A, 4⅝ yards of 36-inch pongee, with 2 yards of 36-inch contrasting pongee; as on figure B, 5¼ yards of 36-inch surf cloth, and ⅞ yard of 6-inch ribbon will be needed for a girdle.   Price, 20 cents.

9604—Ladies' Bathing-Suit: Short Sleeves and Pockets which may be Omitted. 6 sizes, 32 to 42 inches bust measure. The 36-inch size will require as illustrated on figure, 7⅜ yards of 36-inch surf satin for bathing-suit, bloomers and cap, with ½ yard of 24 or more inch mohair for collar.   Price, 20 cents.

9581

Coat—9612   Skirt—9032

Blouse—9588   Skirt—9589

Blouse—9593   Skirt—9594

Blouse—9598   Skirt—9599

9581 — Ladies' Dress: Three-Piece Facing which may be Omitted. Lower edge about 2¾ yards. 6 sizes, 32 to 42 inches bust measure. The 36-inch size will require as illustrated on figure, 4⅛ yards of 32-inch dark galatea, with 3⅛ yards of 32-inch contrasting galatea and 3¾ yards of 32-inch striped galatea. Price, 25 cents.

9612—Ladies' Coat. 8 sizes, 32 to 46 bust. **9032**—Ladies' Two - Piece Skirt. Lower edge about 2¾ yards. 7 sizes, 22 to 34 waist, corresponding to 36 to 49½ hip. If combined as illustrated on figure, the medium size will require 6 yards of 44 - inch shepherd's check, with ⅝ yard of 48-inch cloth.   Price, 20 cents each.

9588—Ladies' Blouse. 7 sizes, 32 to 44 bust. **9589**—Ladies' One - Piece Skirt. 6 sizes, 22 to 32 waist, 36 to 47 hip. As on figure, the medium size requires 2⅛ yards of 33-inch bordered voile, with 2¼ yards of 36-inch figured voile for blouse and ⅝ yard of 36-inch net. Price, 20 cents each.

9598—Ladies' Blouse: Back Extending over the Shoulder to Form Yoke. 7 sizes, 32 to 44 bust. **9599**—Ladies' Four-Piece Skirt. Lower edge about 2¼ yards. 6 sizes, 22 to 32 waist, 36 to 47 hip.   20 cents each.

9593—Ladies' Blouse. 5 sizes, 32 to 40 inches bust measure. **9594**—Ladies' Two-Piece Skirt. Lower edge about 1¾ yards. 5 sizes, 22 to 30 inches waist measure, 36 to 44½ inches hip measure.   Price, 20 cents each.

9581

9612
9032

9588
9589

9598
9599

9593
9594

FEATURING TURKISH HEMS

9601—A

Blouse—**9593** Skirt—**9594**

Blouse—**9574** Skirt—**9575**   **9607**

9601—B

9601—LADIES' DRESS. Lower edge of dress about 2½ yards; of foundation about 1¾ yards. 6 sizes, 32 to 42 bust. As on figure A, the 36-inch size needs 6⅝ yards of 36-inch foulard, ⅜ yards of 20-inch or more filet lace, 1¼ yards of edging, ⅞ yards 32 for girdle and 2½ yards of 32 or more for foundation. As on figure B, 2¾ yards of 40-inch voile, ⅝ yard of 24-inch or more net, 2¾ yards of 44-inch novelty stripe. Price, 25 cents.

9593—LADIES' BLOUSE: to be Slipped Over the Head. 5 sizes, 32 to 40 bust. **9594**—LADIES' TWO-PIECE SKIRT, One-Piece Straight Gathered Flounce. Lower in edge puff style about 2½ yards. 5 sizes, 22 to 30 waist, or 36 to 44½ hip. As on figure the medium size needs 2¼ yards of 40-inch all-over lace, 2 yards of 18-inch lace flouncing, 3¼ yards of 36-inch silk, 2¾ yards 32 or more for foundation gores and 1½ yards of 6-inch ribbon. Price, 20 cents each.

9574—LADIES' BLOUSE. 6 sizes, 32 to 42 bust. **9575**—LADIES' TWO-PIECE SKIRT. For the braiding designs use transfer 10310. Lower edge about 2 yards. 6 sizes, 22 to 32 waist, or 36 to 47 hip. As shown the medium size needs 5 yards 36. Price, 20 cents each.

9607—LADIES' SEMI-FITTED DRESS: Clearing or Shorter Length. Lower edge about 1⅝ yards. 7 sizes from 32 to 44 bust. As illustrated on figure the 36-inch size will require 4⅜ yards of 36-inch printed silk, with 1⅞ yards of 36-inch plain silk. Price, 25 cents.

9593 9594	9601-A	9601-B	9574 9575	9607

9556

9613

9611

9597

9551

9576

9556   9590   9590   9562   9562   9613   9611   9573

9597   9551   9573

9576—LITTLE GIRLS' DRESS. 8 sizes, 1 to 8 years. The 4-year size requires, as on figure, 1⅞ yards of 36-inch lawn for dress, with 2¾ yards of edging for ruffle, and ¼ yard of 18-inch embroidery,   Price, 15 cents.

9551—LITTLE GIRLS' DRESS. For the embroidery design use Standard transfer 10347. 7 sizes, 4 to 10 years. The 8-year size will require as illustrated on figure 2¾ yards of 40-inch linen.   Price, 15 cents.

9597—GIRLS' AND JUNIORS' DRESS. 6 sizes, 6 to 16 years. The 12-year size will require, as illustrated on figure, 3 yards of 44-inch serge, with ⅝ yard of 40-inch linen for collar and cuffs.   Price, 15 cents.

9611—GIRLS' AND JUNIORS' DRESS. 9 sizes, 6 to 14 years. The 10-year size requires as illustrated on figure, 1½ yards of 32-inch plain galatea, with 2⅞ yards of 32-inch checked galatea.   Price, 15 cents.

9613—LITTLE GIRLS' DRESS. The embroidery design is an adaptation of Standard transfer 10196. 5 sizes, 4 to 12 years. The 6-year size will require as illustrated on figure, 2⅞ yards of 32-inch pongee.   Price, 15 cents.

9556—GIRLS' AND JUNIORS' COAT. 6 sizes, 4 to 14 years. The 6-year size requires as on figure. 2½ yards of 36-inch satin for coat, with ¼ yard of 18-inch or more silk for collar.   Price, 15 cents.

9562—GIRLS' AND JUNIORS' DRESS. 6 sizes, 6 to 16 years. The 14-year size will require as illustrated on figure, 1¾ yards of 36-inch cotton gabardine, with 2½ yards of 36-inch figured gabardine.   Price, 15 cents.

9590—GIRLS' AND JUNIORS' COAT IN TWO LENGTHS. 6 sizes, 6 to 16 years. The 14-year size requires as on figure, 3⅞ yards of 50-inch gabardine, with ⅜ yard of 36-inch striped silk.   Price, 15 cents.

9573—GIRLS' AND JUNIORS' DRESS. 6 sizes, 6 to 16 years. The 12-year size requires as on figure, 2¾ yards of 36-inch voile, with ¾ yard of 36-inch plain voile for sleeves, cuffs and collar.   Price, 15 cents.

9612—LADIES' COAT. 8 sizes, 32 to 46 bust. **9569**—LADIES' TWO-PIECE SKIRT. Lower edge about 2⅛ yards. 7 sizes, 22 to 34 waist, 36 to 49½ hip. As illustrated on figure, the medium size will require 5½ yards of 44-inch cheviot, with ½ yard of 36-inch velvet for collar and cuffs.
Price, 20 cents each.

9596—LADIES' COAT. 8 sizes, 32 to 46 inches bust measure. **9580**—LADIES' FOUR-PIECE SKIRT. Lower edge about 2¼ yards. 8 sizes, 22 to 36 inches waist measure, corresponding to 36 to 52 inches hip. As on figure the medium size requires 5¼ yards of 50-inch gabardine with ½ yard of 36-inch faille for collar and cuffs.
Price, 20 cents each.

9591

Coat—**9572**   Skirt—**9599**

Blouse—**9583**   Skirt—**9532**

9591—LADIES' DRESS. Lower edge about 2⅜ yards. 7 sizes, 32 to 44 inches bust measure. The 36-inch bust size requires as illustrated on figure, 3¼ yards of 44-inch light linen, with 3⅛ yards of 44-inch contrasting linen, and ⅝ yard of 36-inch dotted linen.
Price, 25 cents.

9572—LADIES' COAT. 7 sizes, 32 to 44 bust. **9599**—LADIES' SKIRT. Lower edge about 2¼ yards. 6 sizes, 22 to 32 waist, 36 to 47 hip. As on figure the medium size requires 6 yards 42 for coat, with ½ yard 50 for collar, revers and cuffs and 3½ yards 44 for skirt.
Price, 20 cents each.

9583—LADIES' BLOUSE. 6 sizes, 32 to 42 bust. **9532**—LADIES' SKIRT. Lower edge about 2¼ yards. 6 sizes, 22 to 32 waist, 36 to 47 hip. As on figure the medium size requires 3 yards of bordered voile 48, with 1⅜ yards 40 for overblouse and 1⅛ yards 36 for blouse front and back.   20 cents each.

Coat—**9612**
Skirt—**9569**

9612-9569   9591   9572-99   9583-32   9596-80

Coat—**9596**   Skirt—**9580**

9873

9743

9743

9873

9708

Blouse—9873
Skirt—9769

9873—9769

Coat—9847
Skirt—9840

9755

9847   9840   9695   9708   9861-9686

Coat—9755
Skirt—9695

Blouse—9861
Skirt—9686

9873—LADIES' BLOUSE: Open Neck in Two Depths; Long or Short One-Seam Sleeves. 7 sizes, 32 to 44 inches bust measure. **9769**—LADIES' TWO-PIECE SKIRT: Two-Piece Straight Box-Plaited Tunic in Two Outlines: Overblouse which may be Omitted. Lower edge about 2 yards. 7 sizes, 32 to 44 inches bust measure.   Price, 20 cents each.

9755—LADIES' COAT: Three-piece Cape which may be Omitted. 9 sizes, 32 to 48 inches bust measure. **9695**—LADIES' TWO-PIECE BARREL SKIRT: Slightly High Waistline; 38-Inch Length or Shorter. Lower edge about 1⅝ yards. 6 sizes, 22 to 32 inches waist measure, corresponding to 36 to 47 inches hip measure.   Price, 20 cents each.

9708—LADIES' DRESS in Moyen-Age Style: Three-Quarter Length One-Seam Sleeves; Two-Piece Straight Gathered Skirt. Lower edge about 2 yards. 7 sizes, 32 to 44 bust.   25 cents.

9743—LADIES' BLOUSE: Back Extending Over the Shoulders; Collar in Two Outlines; Long or Short One-Seam Sleeves. 9 sizes, 32 to 48 inches bust measure.   Price, 20 cents.

9873—LADIES' BLOUSE: In Regulation Style or Worn Outside the Skirt; Open Neck in Two Depths; Long or Short One-Seam Sleeves. 7 sizes, 32 to 44 inches bust measure. Price, 20 cents.

9847—LADIES' SLIGHTLY FITTED COAT. 9 sizes, 32 to 48 inches bust. **9840**—LADIES' THREE-PIECE SKIRT. Lower edge about 2 yards. 6 sizes, 22 to 32 waist, or 36 to 47 hip. 20 cts. each.

9861—LADIES' TIE-ON BLOUSE. 8 sizes, 32 to 46 inches bust. **9686**—LADIES' FOUR-PIECE SKIRT. Lower edge about 2⅝ yards. 6 sizes, 22 to 32 inches waist, or 36 to 47 hip. 20 cents each.

Blouse—9848
Hat—9852

9853

9853

9825   9862   9847   9848   9863

1863

9836

Coat—9825
Skirt—9862

Coat—9847
Hat—9852

9863

9836

9853—Ladies' Dress: to be Slipped Over the Head; Open Neck in Two Depths; Long One-Seam Sleeves in Two Styles or Short Sleeves; 38-Inch Length or Shorter. 7 sizes 32 to 44 inches bust. Lower edge about 2⅛ yards.   Price, 25 cents.

9848—Ladies' Blouse: Back Extending Over the Shoulders; Collar in Two Outlines at the Front; Long Dart-Fitted or Short Sleeves. 9 sizes, 32 to 48 bust measure. **9852**—Hats: 2 sizes, ladies and misses.   Blouse 20 cents; Hat 15 cents.

9847—Ladies' Slightly Fitted Coat: 50 or 45 Inch Length at the Back; Two-Seam Sleeves. 9 sizes, 32 to 48 bust. **9852**—Hats: in Various Styles. The pattern is cut in 2 sizes, ladies and misses. Coat Price 20 cents; Hat Price 15 cents.

9825—Ladies' Coat: in 35-Inch Length at the Back; Two Styles of Two-Seam Sleeves. 8 sizes, 32 to 46 bust. **9862**—Ladies' Skirt. Lower edge about 1¾ yards. 6 sizes, 22 to 32 waist, or 36 to 47 hip.   Price, 20 cents each.

9863—Ladies' Dress: Convertible Collar or Open Neck; Four-Piece Tunic with or without the Front and Back and with Sides Draped in Pocket Effect or in Regulation Style; Separate Two-Piece Skirt; Gathered into a One-Piece Band or Hanging Free; 38-Inch Length or Shorter. Lower edge of skirt about 2 yards.   7 sizes, 32 to 44 bust.   Price, 25 cents.

9836—Ladies' Dress: Convertible Collar or Open Neck with Large Collar; Long or Short One-Seam Flowing Sleeves or Long Dart-Fitted Sleeves; Back Panel which may be Omitted; Separate Two-Piece Skirt; Slightly High Waistline; 38-Inch Length or Shorter. Lower edge about 2 yards. 5 sizes 32 to 40 inches bust measure.   Price, 25 cents.

Coat—9825
Skirt—9830

Blouse—9856
Skirt—9851

Blouse—9839
Skirt—9840

9839
9840

9875

9838

9825

9830

9856-9851

Blouse
9861
Skirt
9867

9861—9867

9838

9875   9875

9875

9839—LADIES' BLOUSE: Back Extending Over the Shoulders; Revers which may be Omitted. 9 sizes, 32 to 48 inches bust measure. **9840**—LADIES' THREE-PIECE SKIRT: Circular Trimming Piece which may be Omitted. Lower edge about 2 yards. 6 sizes, 22 to 32 inches waist; or 36 to 47 hip. Price, 20 cents each.

9825—LADIES' COAT: in 35-Inch Length at the Back; Straight or Cutaway Closing; Two Styles of Two-Seam Sleeves. 8 sizes, 32 to 46 bust. **9830**—LADIES' SIX-PIECE SKIRT. (Overblouse not shown.) Lower edge about 2½ yards. 6 sizes, 32 to 42 bust measure.   Price, 20 cents each.

9856—LADIES' BLOUSE: Square or V Neck; Long or Short One-Seam Sleeves. 9 sizes, 32 to 48 inches bust. **9851**—LADIES' FOUR-PIECE SKIRT: One-Piece Straight Gathered Tunic which may be Omitted. Lower edge about 1¾ yards. 8 sizes, 22 to 36 waist; or 36 to 52 hip.   Price, 20 cents each.

9861—LADIES' TIE-ON BLOUSE: Convertible Collar or Open Neck; Long or Short One-Seam Sleeves. The pattern is cut in 8 sizes from 32 to 46 inches bust. **9867**—LADIES' TWO-PIECE SKIRT: Slightly High Waistline; Two-Piece Side Yokes. Lower edge about 1¾ yards. 6 sizes, 32 to 42 bust. 20 cents each.

9838—LADIES' COAT: 45 or 36-Inch Length at the Back; Standing or Convertible Collar; Two-Seam Sleeves with Slight Fulness at the Top which may be Shrunken Out. The pattern is cut in 7 sizes from 32 to 44 inches bust measure. This design has very smart and attractive lines.   Price, 20 cents.

9875—LADIES' ONE-PIECE DRAPED DRESS: to be Slipped Over the Head; Convertible Collar or Open Neck; Long Dart-Fitted or Short Sleeves. Lower edge about 2 yards. The pattern is cut in 7 sizes from 32 to 44 inches bust measure. The drapery lends grace and charm to the entire costume and makes the dress especially suitable for special occasions. As you see by the illustrations, it develops equally well, whether you use one material or a combination of materials.   Price, 25 cents.

Coat
9838
Skirt
9719

9838

9719

9868

9868 9863 9758—9867 9834—9835 9824—9865 9868 9737

Blouse—9758
Jumper Skirt—9867

Blouse—9824
Skirt—9865

9863

Blouse
9834
Skirt—9835

Coat—9868
Skirt—9737

9863—LADIES' DRESS: Four-Piece Tunic with or without the Front and Back and with Sides Draped in Pocket Effect or in Regulation Style; Separate Two-Piece Skirt; Gathered into a One-Piece Band or Hanging Free. Lower edge about 1¾ yards. 7 sizes, 32 to 44 inches bust measure.   Price, 25 cents.

9834—LADIES' BLOUSE: Long or Short One-Seam Sleeves. 6 sizes, 32 to 42 inches bust. 9835—LADIES' TWO-PIECE SKIRT: One-Piece Side Yokes; Pockets which may be Omitted; 38-Inch Length or Shorter. Lower edge about 2 yards. 9 sizes, 22 to 38 inches waist, or 36 to 54 hip.   Price, 20 cents each.

9758—LADIES' BLOUSE: Convertible Collar. 9 sizes, 32 to 48 bust. 9867—LADIES' TWO-PIECE SKIRT: Front and Back Gores in One with Jumper which may be Omitted; Two-Piece Side Yokes; 38-Inch Length or Shorter. Lower edge about 1¾ yards. 6 sizes, 32 to 42 inches bust.   Price, 20 cents each.

9824—LADIES' BLOUSE: Collar in Two Outlines at the Back may be Omitted; Long or Short One-Seam Sleeves. 7 sizes, 32 to 44 inches bust. 9865—LADIES' SIX-PIECE SKIRT: 38-Inch Length or Shorter. Lower edge about 3 yards. 7 sizes, 22 to 34 waist, or 36 to 49½ hip.   Price, 20 cents each.

9838—LADIES' COAT: 45 or 36 Inch Length at the Back; Standing or Convertible Collar; Two-Seam Sleeves. 7 sizes, 32 to 44 inches bust. 9719—LADIES' FOUR-PIECE BARREL SKIRT: Side Gores in Two Sections. Lower edge about 1¾ yards. 6 sizes, 22 to 32 waist, or 36 to 47 hip.   Price, 20 cents each.

9868—LADIES' COAT: 48 or 36 Inch Length at the Back; Standing or Convertible Collar; Two-Seam Sleeves with Slight Fulness at the Top which may be Shrunken Out. The pattern is cut in 8 sizes from 32 to 46 inches bust measure. Heavy stitching makes an attractive trimming.   Price, 20 cents.

9868—LADIES' COAT: 48 or 36 Inch Length at the Back; Standing or Convertible Collar; Two-Seam Sleeves with Slight Fulness at the Top which may be Shrunken Out. The pattern is cut in 8 sizes from 32 to 46 inches bust measure. 9737—LADIES' FIVE-PIECE SKIRT: Slightly High Waistline; Inverted Plait or Gathers at the Back; Clearing or Shorter Length. Lower edge of skirt measures about 2½ yards. The pattern is cut in 9 sizes, from 32 to 48 inches bust measure.   Price, 20 cents each.

Blouse—9272
Skirt—9830

Blouse—
9839
Skirt—
9835

Blouse—9758   Skirt—9865

Blouse—9873   Skirt—9862

Brassiere—9859   Petticoat—9314   9424

9859—Ladies' One-piece Brassiere or Lining: In Two Lengths: Closed at the Front or Back. 9 sizes, 32 to 48 inches bust measure. **9314**—Ladies' Three-Piece Petticoat: Lower edge of flounce about 2¾ yards. 9 sizes, 22 to 38 inches waist measure, or 36 to 54 inches hip. 15 cts. for Brassiere; 20 cts. for Petticoat.

9839—Ladies' Blouse: Back Extending Over the Shoulders. 9 sizes, 32 to 48 inches bust. **9835**—Ladies' Two-Piece Skirt: Slightly High Waistline; One-Piece Side Yoke; 38-Inch Length or Shorter. Lower edge about 2 yards. 9 sizes, 22 to 38 inches waist, or 36 to 54 inches hip.   Price, 20 cents each.

9873—Ladies' Blouse: In Regulation Style or Worn Outside the Skirt. 7 sizes, 32 to 44 inches bust measure. **9862**—Ladies' Skirt: 38-inch Length or Shorter. Lower edge about 1¾ yards. 6 sizes, 22 to 32 inches waist measure, corresponding to 36 to 47 inches hip measure.   Price, 20 cents each.

9424—Ladies' Nightgown: In Two Lengths; Closed to the Neck or Rolled Open or Open Neck; Applied Yoke which may be Omitted; Long or Short One-Seam Sleeves. The pattern is cut in 9 sizes, from 32 to 48 inches bust measure. This is a comfortable gown for the cool night.   Price, 20 cents.

9272—Ladies' Blouse. The pattern is cut in 8 sizes from 32 to 46 inches bust measure. **9830**—Ladies' Six-Piece Skirt: Slightly High Waistline. 38-Inch Length or Shorter. Lower edge about 2½ yards. The pattern is cut in 6 sizes from 32 to 42 inches bust measure.   Price, 20 cents each.

9758—Ladies' Blouse. Convertible Collar. 9 sizes, 32 to 48 inches bust measure. **9865**—Ladies' Six-Piece Skirt: Slightly High Waistline. Lower edge about 3 yards. The pattern is cut in 7 sizes from 22 to 34 inches waist measure corresponding to 36 to 49½ inches hip measure.   Price, 20 cents each.

9873—9862   9758—9865   9272—9830   9839—9835   9424   9859—9314

9866

9552

9353

9843

9869   9841

9866—LADIES' ENVELOPE COMBINATION UNDERGARMENT: Round Neck or Straight Outline Across the Top; Tab Extension Lapped Over or Under the Front; Straight Plaited or Gathered Side Sections. 9 sizes, 32 to 48 inches bust measure. The plaited side sections are very pretty.   Price, 20 cents.

9843—LADIES' DRESS: Plain or Scalloped Outline at the Front; Convertible Collar or Open Neck with Large Collar; Long Dart-Fitted or Short Sleeves; Three-Piece Skirt; Two-Piece Facing which may be Omitted; 38-Inch Length or Shorter. Lower edge about 2 yards. 9 sizes, 32 to 48 inches bust.   Price, 25 cents.

9841—LADIES' DRESS: Back Extending Over the Shoulders; Convertible Collar or Open Neck; Long Dart-Fitted or Short Sleeves; Three-Piece Skirt; Clearing or Shorter Length; Cap. Lower edge about 2¼ yards. 9 sizes, 32 to 48 inches bust. A practical model for the housewife as well as the nurse.   25 Cents.

9552—LADIES' ONE-PIECE PAJAMAS: Convertible Collar or Open Neck; Long or Short Sleeves. The pattern is cut in 6 sizes from 32 to 42 inches bust measure. A very comfortable sleeping-garment made of flannelette, pongee, cotton crêpe or for very best wear crêpe de Chine.   Price, 20 cents.

9353—LADIES' KIMONO: in Two Lengths; Long Shoulders; Long or Short One-Seam Sleeves. The pattern is cut in 7 sizes, from 32 to 44 inches bust measure. A very comfortable and practical garment and so simple in construction that a beginner will have no difficulty in making it.   Price, 20 cents.

9869—LADIES' BREAKFAST COAT IN MOYEN-AGE STYLE: Reversible Closing; Long Dart-Fitted or Short Sleeves; One-Piece Straight Gathered Skirt; 38-Inch Length or Shorter. The pattern is cut in 9 sizes from 32 to 48 inches bust measure. Chambray, dimity and cashmere are suitable materials for this garment. 20 cents.

9552   9866   9353   9843   9841   9869

Showing Us The Bewitching

WHAT are you going to have in your Fall wardrobe, O Miss Particular? A top-coat? That is—well, they are so smart and comfortable. A dress to wear on the street without a coat? Well, choose one of these clever designs and trim it very simply. A frock that is suitable for afternoon reception or church? The multitude of these becoming modes are enough to bewilder any one, so you will choose very carefully, if you are wise. The soft silks and satins are so attractive made up in the Moyen-Age style or any of the other styles that are spread before you. A touch of hand-embroidery and lo! you have a creation you will be proud to wear on any occasion.

Blouse—9829   Skirt—9849

9870

9853

9829—Ladies' Blouse. 6 sizes, 32 to 42 bust. **9849**—Ladies' Two-Piece Skirt: Two-Piece Tunic; 38-Inch Length or Shorter. Lower edge about 1¾ yards. 6 sizes, 22 to 32 waist, or 36 to 47 hip.   Price, 20 cents each.

9832—Ladies' Dress: Convertible Collar or Open Neck; Long Dart-Fitted or Short Sleeves; Three-Piece Skirt; Loose Front Panels which may be Omitted. Lower edge about 1¾ yards. 7 sizes, 32 to 44 inches bust measure.   25 cents.

9870—Ladies' Dress: To be Slipped Over the Head; Lower Collar in One with Chemisette; Long or Short Sleeves; Two-Piece Gathered Skirt; 38-Inch Length or Shorter. Lower edge about 2 yards. 6 sizes, 32 to 42 bust.   25 cents.

9853—Ladies' Dress: To be Slipped Over the Head; Open Neck in Two Depths; Long One-Seam Sleeves in Two Styles or Short Sleeves; 38-Inch Length or Shorter. Lower edge about 2⅛ yards. 7 sizes, 32 to 44 inches bust.   25 cents.

9843—Ladies' Dress: Plain or Scalloped Outline at the Front; Convertible Collar or Open Neck with Large Collar; Long Dart-Fitted or Short Sleeves; Three-Piece Skirt; Two-Piece Facing which may be Omitted. Lower edge about 2 yards. The pattern is cut in 9 sizes, from 32 to 48 inches bust measure. This dress will develop very effectively in serge, broadcloth, taffeta and stripes, plaids and checks. 25 cts.

9870   9829   9849   9853   9832   9843

9843   9832

Ways of the Autumn Modes

Straight lines and exclamation points! One-piece frocks and soft draperies! In either of these ways you may describe Fashion's decrees for the autumn season. From coats to dresses and back again, these rules hold good, and every one is glad, for the straight lines of the Grecian draperies are standards of beauty and now we may have them, too! Have you ever seen so great a variety in pockets and belts, in fascinating collars and cuffs? Big or little, old or young, every true daughter of Eve delights in these fascinating details of the costume. Buttons, too, are found in crowds on the smartest gown and if they are brass buttons, so much the better, for these are military times!

9762   Blouse—9848   Skirt—9851   9836

9848—LADIES' BLOUSE: Back Extending Over the Shoulders; Collar in Two Outlines at the Front; Long Dart-Fitted or Short Sleeves. 9 sizes, 32 to 48 bust. **9851**—LADIES' FOUR-PIECE SKIRT: Slightly High Waistline; One-Piece Straight Gathered Tunic which may be Omitted; 38-Inch Length or Shorter. Lower edge about 1¾ yards. 8 sizes, 22 to 36 waist, or 36 to 52 hip.   20 cents each.

9762—LADIES' DRESS: Slightly Open or Open Neck; Long Dart-Fitted or Short Sleeves; Two or Three Piece Skirt; Clearing or Shorter Length. Lower edge of skirt measures about 2⅛ yards. The pattern is cut in 9 sizes, from 32 to 48 inches bust measure.   Price, 25 cents.

9878—LADIES' DRESS: Separate Overblouse to be Slipped Over the Head and with Round or V Neck at the Back; One-Piece Straight Gathered Skirt Draped or in Regulation Style; Two-Piece Foundation Skirt. The Sleeves, Overblouse, Foundation Skirt and Train in 63-Inch Length on in Panel Style may be Omitted. Lower edge of gathered skirt about 2⅝ yards, of foundation 1¾ yards. 6 sizes, 32 to 42 bust;   25 cents.

9836—LADIES' DRESS: Convertible Collar or Open Neck with Large Collar; Long or Short One-Seam Flowing Sleeves or Long Dart-Fitted Sleeves; Separate Two-Piece Skirt; 38-Inch Length or Shorter. Lower edge about 2 yards. 5 sizes, 32 to 40 inches bust measure.   25 cents.

9878
Transfer—10318

9878

9878   9762   9848—9851   9836

YOUNG FOLKS

9860

9723

9880

9872

9876

9833

9837

9854

9881

9723—LITTLE BOYS' SUIT: Blouse in Two Styles; Removable Shield in High or Open Neck; Two Styles of Long or Short Sleeves; Yoke Facing which may be Omitted; Knickerbockers or Trousers. The pattern is cut in **7** sizes from 2 to 8 years.   Price, 15 cents.

9880—BOYS' SUIT: Epaulettes and Pockets which may be Omitted. The pattern is cut in 6 sizes from 3 to 8 years. A suit of this kind plays an important part in the happiness of the small boy for epaulettes, pockets and brass buttons give such a wonderful military effect. Suitable materials for this type of suit are khaki, serge, rep, piqué, galatea and drilling. Price, 15 cents.

9860—LITTLE GIRL'S COAT: Convertible Collar; Two-Seam Sleeves with Slight Fulness at the Top which may be Shrunken Out. The pattern is cut in 6 sizes from 2 to 12 years. Many materials are suitable for a coat of this style, among them are serge, gabardine, coatings, velveteen, fur cloth, cheviot and tweed. The convertible collar, cuffs, pockets and sash are smart features. It is very simple to make.   Price, 15 cents.

9876—CHILD'S NIGHT DRAWERS: Two Styles of One-Seam Sleeves. The pattern is cut in 8 sizes from 1 to 8 years. For chilly Fall, night drawers like these are essential. Flannelette, outing flannel and longcloth in either stripes, or checks are suitable for it. 15 Cents.

9872—GIRLS' AND JUNIORS' DRESS: High or Open Neck; Long Dart-Fitted or Short Sleeves. The pattern is cut in 11 sizes from 6 to 16 years. An attractive dress is this for the growing girl. The belt slipped through the slash in the back is unusual and smart. The design will develop effectively if serge, gabardine, chambray or galatea are used.   Price, 15 cents.

9881—BOYS' MILITARY SUIT, with Two Styles Puttee. The pattern is cut in 9 sizes from 6 to 14 years. This military suit will be appreciated by many boys. The puttees are very smart and good-looking and the cap and pockets are attractive.   Price, 20 cents.

9833—LITTLE GIRLS' AND JUNIORS' BATHROBE: Body in One with Long Sleeves. The pattern is cut in 8 sizes from 2 to 16 years. No matter how little she may be, a bathrobe is essential. This one is simple in construction because the body and sleeve are in one. It is also comfortable. Flannels, eiderdown and turkish towelling are suitable.   Price, 15 cents.

9854—GIRLS' AND JUNIORS' DRESS: High or Open Neck; Long or Short Sleeves. The pattern is cut in 11 sizes from 6 to 16 years. This dress has very attractive lines. The arrangement of the sash is unusual and smart. Serge, and chambray are suitable. Price, 15 cents.

9837—LITTLE GIRLS' AND JUNIORS' COMBINATION UNDERGARMENT: Round or Square Neck; Drawers in Regulation or Curved Outline or in Knickerbocker Style. 8 sizes, 2 to 16 years. This is a very pretty combination and can be developed very daintily. If desired, they may be caught up at the sides by a tiny bow of satin ribbon. By omitting the lace and ribbon they are extremely practical for every day.   15 cents.

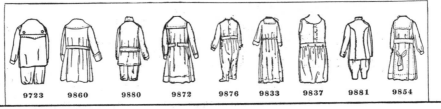

9723   9860   9880   9872   9876   9833   9837   9881   9854

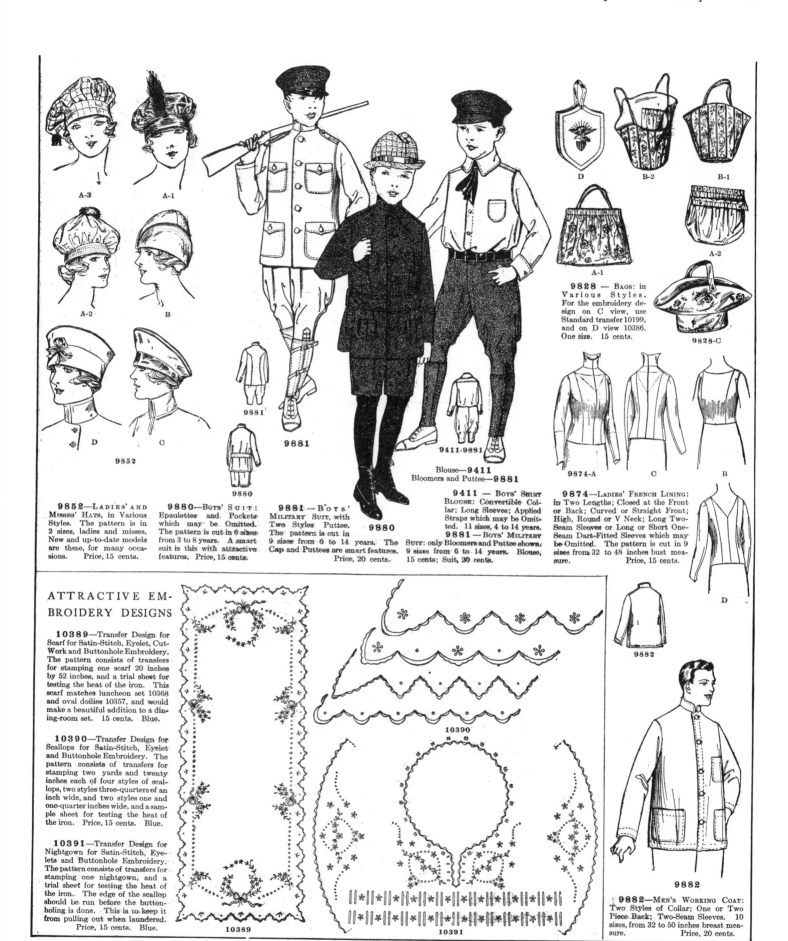

9852—LADIES' AND MISSES' HATS, in Various Styles. The pattern is in 2 sizes, ladies and misses. New and up-to-date models are these, for many occasions. Price, 15 cents.

9880—BOYS' SUIT: Epaulettes and Pockets which may be Omitted. The pattern is cut in 6 sizes from 3 to 8 years. A smart suit is this with attractive features. Price, 15 cents.

9881—BOYS' MILITARY SUIT, with Two Styles Puttee. The pattern is cut in 9 sizes from 6 to 14 years. The Cap and Puttees are smart features. Price, 20 cents.

Blouse—**9411**
Bloomers and Puttee—**9881**

9411 — BOYS' SHIRT BLOUSE: Convertible Collar; Long Sleeves; Applied Straps which may be Omitted. 11 sizes, 4 to 14 years. **9881** — BOYS' MILITARY SUIT: only Bloomers and Puttee shown. 9 sizes from 6 to 14 years. Blouse, 15 cents; Suit, 20 cents.

9828 — BAGS: in Various Styles. For the embroidery design on C view, use Standard transfer 10199, and on D view 10386. One size. 15 cents.

9874—LADIES' FRENCH LINING: in Two Lengths; Closed at the Front or Back; Curved or Straight Front; High, Round or V Neck; Long Two-Seam Sleeves or Long or Short One-Seam Dart-Fitted Sleeves which may be Omitted. The pattern is cut in 9 sizes from 32 to 48 inches bust measure. Price, 15 cents.

ATTRACTIVE EMBROIDERY DESIGNS

10389—Transfer Design for Scarf for Satin-Stitch, Eyelet, Cut-Work and Buttonhole Embroidery. The pattern consists of transfers for stamping one scarf 20 inches by 52 inches, and a trial sheet for testing the heat of the iron. This scarf matches luncheon set 10368 and oval doilies 10357, and would make a beautiful addition to a dining-room set. 15 cents. Blue.

10390—Transfer Design for Scallops for Satin-Stitch, Eyelet and Buttonhole Embroidery. The pattern consists of transfers for stamping two yards and twenty inches each of four styles of scallops, two styles three-quarters of an inch wide, and two styles one and one-quarter inches wide, and a sample sheet for testing the heat of the iron. Price, 15 cents. Blue.

10391—Transfer Design for Nightgown for Satin-Stitch, Eyelets and Buttonhole Embroidery. The pattern consists of transfers for stamping one nightgown, and a trial sheet for testing the heat of the iron. The edge of the scallop should be run before the buttonholing is done. This is to keep it from pulling out when laundered. Price, 15 cents. Blue.

9882—MEN'S WORKING COAT: Two Styles of Collar; One or Two Piece Back; Two-Seam Sleeves. 10 sizes, from 32 to 50 inches breast measure. Price, 20 cents.

It's not so much
WHAT we wear
that counts, as
HOW we wear it!

Facts and Fancies of Fall Fashions

"THE time has come," Dame Fashion says,
"To speak of many things;
Of hats and veils and bags and furs
Of Autumn's offerings.
And why the silhouette's so straight,
And what October brings."

Indeed, we will be only too glad to do so for we want to know these very things, do we not? I hope the sketches on this page will give you as pleasant thrills as they have me. They are such a delightful way to learn the latest style in little things. Take the saucy person at the foot of the page with hairpins sticking out of her head in a most alarming manner. She is an ornament in any family: her headdress(?) is of gold net and she complacently allows your hairpins a safe-abiding place till you may have need of them.

POWDER-puffs are now developing individuality at a great rate. The coy one, here, decided that cane knitting-bags should not be allowed to corner all the alluring uncertainty of feminine millinery. Speaking of knitting brings up a really important question: Are you knitting for yourself or for the soldiers and sailors? If for yourself you may go into silent raptures over this stunning knitted skating set. The sweater with its deep V-neck has a belt effect of Roman colors, done in knitting and purling and the tam-o'shanter matches it. I think she holds her scarf behind her to tease you, but it has the Roman stripes on the ends. If you are making sweaters, socks and scarfs for "the service" the Red Cross knitting-bag will prove most convenient and satisfactory. The cross arm of the cross runs around the entire bag. Another bag for quite a different use is the theater bag of bronze gold net with large white daisies growing in reckless profusion over it. The ribbon is that wonderful shade of bronze gold that shades from the yellow centers of the daisies to green bronze gold. There is ample room for the opera-glass, handkerchief, powder puff, tiny mirror, purse and front-door key. The dainty handkerchiefs below have tiny red, white and blue threads pulled through the linen; and the monograms are in white on a blue background.

ONE may always see interesting sights at the theater, off the stage as well as on! The two ladies in the center at the top of the page were in a box. The one on the right wore a charming hat of interwoven ribbons with a trimming of field flowers, so appropriate to the harvest season. Her dainty collar-and-cuff set were of Georgette crêpe, tucked almost to the edge, and then left free, forming a ruffle. The edge itself was a tiny gold cord. On her left, one first noticed the tall Russian hat, bright with the glowing colors of the Orient. The long tassel was of iridescent beads, in which gold predominated. The flowers of her odd corsage were of blue with gold leaves, making a charming spot of color against the white of her fur cape.

At the extreme right is a lady stepping into her waiting car. The night was chilly and so she drew her wonderful scarf more closely around her throat. Between the bands of the ermine was white chiffon, and the tails were used only on the rolling collar and scarf ends. Of course, such a wrap was all she needed to keep her warm! The filmy veil over the large hat in the left-hand corner has beauteous butterflies, winging their way around the lower edge. Polka-dot foulard collars are the latest decree of Dame Fashion for the serge walking costume.

OH, THE stores are full of them, those delectable trifles that ensnare the stoutest heart. From every side they peek at one, glimpses of the next aisle display further charms, and so one lingers and adds a collar here and a bag there to one's collection of unnecessary necessities. Does one really need them? Ah, that is not the question. They seem absolutely necessary to one's pursuit of happiness, and that is all one knows. Filmy laces, enchanting colors—what matters the form, really, so long as one enjoys them? A bottomless purse would be needed to satisfy one's every whim, for they are all so fascinating, one naturally wants them all, all the smart accessories that add so much distinction, as every clever woman knows.

Would you be fascinating and individual? Ah, that is easy if you first know yourself. Study your mirror, find out whether long lines are becoming to you, and if not, what is. Colors, too, must be carefully considered. Remember that it's the little things in dress that count, the trifles the careless woman overlooks. Shoes run over at the heels, dingy collars and untidy hair have spoiled many an otherwise perfect effect. It's the missing button here and the torn lace there that detracts more from your general appearance than you will care to admit. Be an aristocrat of dress.

FROCKS TO BRIGHTEN WINTER DAYS

Blouse—**1032**
Skirt—**9835**

1030
Transfer—**10310**

Blouse—**1041**   Skirt—**9690**

1008

Guimpe—**9471**   Jumper Skirt—**1026**

1032—LADIES' BLOUSE: in Two Lengths; to be Slipped Over the Head. 6 sizes, 32 to 42 inches bust measure. **9835**—LADIES' TWO-PIECE SKIRT: Slightly High Waistline. Lower edge about 2 yards. 9 sizes, 22 to 38 inches waist measure, corresponding to 36 to 54 inches hip measure.   Price, 20 cents each.

1030—LADIES' DRESS: High or Open Neck; Long Dart-Fitted or Short Sleeves; Revers which may be Omitted; Two-Piece Gathered Tunic in Two Outlines; Two-Piece Skirt; 38-Inch Length or Shorter. Lower edge about 1⅞ yards. The pattern is cut in 9 sizes from 32 to 48 inches bust measure.   Price, 25 cents.

1008—LADIES' DRESS: Back Extending Over the Shoulders; High or Open Neck; Long or Short One-Seam Sleeves or Long Dart-Fitted Sleeves; Two-Piece Skirt; 38-Inch Length or Shorter. Lower edge about 2 yards. The pattern is cut in 5 sizes from 32 to 40 inches bust measure.   Price, 25 cents.

9471—LADIES' GUIMPE. 9 sizes, 32 to 48 inches bust measure.
1026—LADIES' TWO-PIECE SKIRT; Overblouse which may be Omitted; Drapery or Three-Piece Belt; 38-Inch Length or Shorter. Lower edge about 1¾ yards. The pattern is cut in 7 sizes from 32 to 44 inches bust measure.   Guimpe 15 cents; Skirt 20 cents.

1041—LADIES' RUSSIAN BLOUSE. The pattern is cut in 6 sizes from 32 to 42 inches bust measure. **9690**—LADIES' ONE-PIECE STRAIGHT TUCKED SKIRT. Lower edge about 2¼ yards. 6 sizes, 22 to 32 inches waist measure, corresponding to 36 to 47 inches hip measure.   Price, 20 cents each.

1041

1030   9690   1032   9835   1008   9471
                                      1026

STANDARD FASHIONS

3

PUBLISHED BY STANDARD FASHION COMPANY
12-16 Vandam Street, New York City.
BRANCHES:

SAN FRANCISCO	609 MISSION S1.
ST. LOUIS,	1629 WASHINGTON AVE.
TORONTO ONT.,	472 WELLINGTON ST., W.
CHICAGO,	205 WEST MONROE ST.
BOSTON,	105 CHAUNCY ST.
ATLANTA	79-89 MARIETTA ST.
WINNIPEG, MANITOBA,	WOODS WESTERN BUILDING

Copyright 1917, by Standard Fashion Company in the
United States and Great Britain

DECEMBER 1917

Guimpe—9471
Jumper Skirt—1024

1042

Blouse—9729
Jumper Skirt—1014

Blouse—1032   Skirt—9695

1032—LADIES' BLOUSE: in Two Lengths; to be Slipped Over the Head, Back Extending Over the Shoulders. 6 sizes, 32 to 42 inches bust measure. **9695**—LADIES' SKIRT: Lower edge about 1⅝ yards. 6 sizes, 22 to 32 inches waist measure or 36 to 47 inches hip.   Price, 20 cents each.

9729—LADIES' BLOUSE. 7 sizes, 32 to 44 inches bust measure. **1014**—LADIES' FOUR-PIECE SKIRT; Jumper which may be Omitted: Lower edge measures about 1¾ yards.   The pattern is cut in 7 sizes, from 32 to 44 inches bust measure.   Price, 20 cents each.

1042—LADIES' COAT, in Moyen-Age Style: 50 or 45 or 38 Inch Length at the Back; Convertible Collar; Two Styles of Two-Seam Sleeves with Slight Fulness at the Top which may be Shrunken Out. 7 sizes, 32 to 44 inches bust measure.   Price 20 cents.

9471—LADIES' GUIMPE. 9 sizes, 32 to 48 inches bust measure. **1024**—LADIES' TWO-PIECE SKIRT: Separate Tie-On Overblouse which may be Omitted. Lower edge about 1⅞ yards. 7 sizes, 32 to 44 inches bust measure.   Guimpe 15 cents; Skirt 20 cents.

1047—LADIES' COAT: 45 or 32 Inch Length at the Back; Convertible or Notched Collar; Two Styles of Two-Seam Sleeves with Slight Fulness at the Top which may be Shrunken Out. 7 sizes, 32 to 44 inches bust measure.   Price, 20 cents.

1008—LADIES' DRESS: Back Extending Over the Shoulders; High or Open Neck; Long or Short One-Seam Sleeves or Long Dart-Fitted Sleeves; Two-Piece Skirt. Lower edge about 2 yards. 5 sizes, 32 to 40 inches bust measure.   Price, 25 cents.

1008   1047

For back views see page 15

FIRST AID TO WINTER

1006

1004

9800

1006

9791

1006—LADIES' COAT: 45 or 38 Inch Length at the Back; Convertible or Standing Collar; Two-Seam Sleeves with Slight Fulness at the Top which may be Shrunken Out; Three-Piece Skirt; Three-Piece Facing which may be Omitted. The pattern is cut in 6 sizes, from 32 to 42 inches bust measure. This is an unusually smart coat and the fact that it may be used for a top coat or a suit coat makes it especially desirable. The lines are on the redingote style which are youthful and are very becoming to most figures. The opening at the sides with the buttons and button holes is a very popular feature this season. Price, 20 cents.

1004—LADIES' COAT DRESS: Convertible Collar; Long Dart-Fitted or Short Sleeves; Two Styles of Pocket; Loose Straps which may be Omitted; 38-Inch Length or Shorter. Lower edge about 2 yards. The pattern is cut in 6 sizes, from 32 to 42 inches bust measure. Here is a dress that makes you decide just how you want your new one made. The convertible collar is one of the most popular features of the season's dresses and the pockets give a very smart outline. The loose straps and the yoke are two attractive features and the youthful lines help to make it unusually charming. Satin, taffeta, serge, or gabardine are suitable materials. Price, 25 cents.

9800—LADIES' COAT: 50 or 30 Inch Length at the Back; Convertible Collar; One-Seam Flowing Sleeves or Two-Seam Sleeves with Slight Fulness at the Top which may be Shrunken Out; Pockets and Three-Piece Cape which may be Omitted. The pattern is cut in 7 sizes, from 32 to 44 inches bust measure. This smart coat can shut out the winds of the winter and make the wearer cozy and happy. It would be handsome in velveteen or plush and serviceable in mixed material serge, corduroy or cloth. Price, 20 cents.

1006—LADIES' COAT: 45 or 38 Inch Length at the Back; Convertible or Standing Collar; Two-Seam Sleeves with Slight Fulness at the Top which may be Shrunken Out; Three-Piece Skirt; Three-Piece Facing which may be Omitted. The pattern is cut in 6 sizes, from 32 to 42 inches bust measure This smart top-coat is just the thing for a cold winter day. The use of the fur gives it the final note of elegance and makes it cozy and becoming. The collar may be worn standing but it is also attractive when it is left open. The rows of stitching at the bottom of the coat are an attractive feature that adds interest. Novelty buttons may be used. Price, 20 cents.

9791—LADIES' BOX-PLAITED COAT: 50 or 34 Inch Length at the Back; Two Styles of Convertible Collar; Two-Seam Sleeves with Slight Fulness at the Top which may be Shrunken Out; Applied Yoke which may be Omitted. The pattern is cut in 7 sizes, from 32 to 44 inches bust measure. The scarf of this coat serves the double purpose of making the wearer comfortable and look very charming. The youthful lines of the coat are also becoming to many types of figures. The spacious pockets are very attractive. Price, 20 cents.

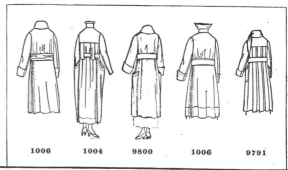

1006　**1004**　**9800**　**1006**　**9791**

DRESSES WE ALL LOVE

1020

Blouse—1040 Skirt—1026

1030

1046

1033

1020—LADIES' COAT DRESS in Moyen-Age Style; Convertible Collar; Long Dart-Fitted or Short Sleeves; Body Fronts in One with Fronts of Five-Piece Skirt; 38-inch Length or Shorter. Lower edge about 3 yards. The pattern is cut in 7 sizes, from 32 to 44 inches bust measure. What could be smarter, and yet so practical? You would like this dress made of serge, duvetyn, taffeta or satin. Price, 25 cents.

1040—LADIES' BLOUSE: High or Open Neck; Two Styles of Long One-Seam Sleeves or Short Sleeves. The pattern is cut in 7 sizes, from 32 to 44 inches bust measure.

1026—LADIES' TWO-PIECE SKIRT: Slightly High Waistline; Overblouse which may be Omitted; Drapery or Three-Piece Belt; 38-Inch Length or Shorter. Lower edge about 1¾ yards. 7 sizes from 32 to 44 inches bust measure. Price, 20 cents each.

1030—LADIES' DRESS: High or Open Neck; Long Dart-Fitted or Short Sleeves; Revers which may be Omitted; Two-Piece Gathered Tunic in Two Outlines; Two-Piece Skirt; 38-Inch Length or Shorter. Lower edge about 1⅞ yards. 9 sizes from 32 to 48 inches bust measure. This is just the kind of dress that gives you genuine service and pleasure. The collar and revers are becoming and the little vest does its part. The tunic is very graceful. Satin, taffeta, crêpe de Chine or Georgette are suitable materials for this charming dress. Price, 25 cents.

1033—LADIES' DRESS: Convertible Collar or Open Neck; Long or Short One-Seam Sleeves or Long Dart-Fitted Sleeves; Separate Two-Piece Gathered Skirt; Slightly High Waistline; 38-Inch Length or Shorter. Lower edge about 2¼ yards. The pattern is cut in 6 sizes, from 32 to 42 inches bust measure. Extremely smart and distinctive is this charming costume. Price, 25 cents.

1046—LADIES' DRESS: Convertible Collar or Open Neck; Long or Short One-Seam Sleeves or Long Dart-Fitted Sleeves; Separate Tie-on Overblouse; Three-Piece Gathered Tunic; Two-Piece Skirt; 38-Inch Length or Shorter. Lower edge about 1¾ yards. 6 sizes, from 32 to 42 inches bust measure. This dress is just the kind that most women like to wear for it is both becoming and smart. 25 cts.

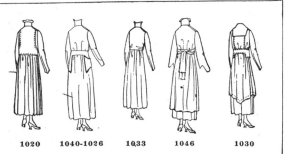

1020   1040-1026   1033   1046   1030

1023

1004

Back view of Cover

1029

Blouse—1032
Skirt—1037

1029   1023

1033

Blouse—1052
Skirt—9781

Blouse—1005
Skirt—1021

1032   1037   1033   1052—9781   1005—1021

1029—Ladies' Coat: 48 or 38 Inch Length at the Back; Convertible Collar; Two-Seam Sleeves with Slight Fulness at the Top which may be Shrunken Out; Loose Back and Sash which may be Omitted; Three-Piece Gathered Skirt. The pattern is cut in 7 sizes from 32 to 44 inches bust measure. Price, 20 cents.

1033—Ladies' Dress: Convertible Collar or Open Neck; Long or Short One-Seam Gathered Sleeves or Long Dart-Fitted Sleeves; Separate Two-Piece Gathered Skirt; Slightly High Waistline; Drapery which may be Omitted; 38-Inch Length or Shorter. Lower edge about 2¼ yards. The pattern is cut in 6 sizes from 32 to 42 inches bust measure. Price, 25 cents.

1005—Ladies' Blouse. The pattern is cut in 6 sizes from 32 to 42 inches bust measure.
1021—Ladies' Two or Four Piece Skirt: Two-Piece Belt and One-Piece Straight Gathered Side Tunics which may be Omitted. Lower edge about 1¾ yards. 6 sizes, 22 to 32 inches waist measure corresponding to 36 to 47 inches hip measure. Price, 20 cents each.

1023—Ladies' Dress: Convertible Collar; Separate Overblouse with or without the Panel; Long or Short One-Seam Sleeves or Long Dart-Fitted Sleeves; Three-Piece Gathered Tunic; Two-Piece Skirt; 38-Inch Length or Shorter. Lower edge about 1¾ yards. The pattern is cut in 7 sizes from 32 to 44 inches bust measure. Broadcloth and satin are excellent for this design. Price, 25 cents.

1004—Ladies' Coat Dress: Convertible Collar; Long Dart-Fitted or Short Sleeves; Two Styles of Pocket; Loose Straps which may be Omitted; 38-Inch Length or Shorter. Lower edge about 2 yards. The pattern is cut in 6 sizes from 32 to 42 inches bust measure. Serge is an excellent material for the development of this dress. Price, 25 cents.

1032—Ladies' Blouse: in Two Lengths; to be Slipped Over the Head. The pattern is cut in 6 sizes from 32 to 42 inches bust measure.
1037—Ladies' Four-Piece Skirt: High Waistline; Overblouse which may be Omitted. Lower edge about 2½ yards. The pattern is cut in 5 sizes from 32 to 40 inches bust measure. Price, 20 cents each.

1052—Ladies' Blouse: High or Open Neck; Back Extending Over the Shoulders; One-Piece Camisole which may be Omitted. 8 sizes, 32 to 46 inches bust measure. **9781**—Ladies' Two-Piece Skirt: Slightly High Waistline; Jumper and Pockets which may be Omitted. Lower edge about 2⅝ yards. 9 sizes, 32 to 48 inches bust measure. Price, 20 cents each.

Dressing-Sack—**9776**
Skirt—**9198**

1036

9703
Transfer—4290

Transfer—
10374

9287

1036   9776   9198   1002   9703   9287

1002

1000   1034

1034

1000

9776—Ladies' Kimono or Dressing-Sack: Collar in Two Outlines; Long or Short One-Seam Sleeves. 9 sizes, 32 to 48 inches bust measure. **9198** — Ladies' Three - Piece Skirt: Clearing or Shorter Length. Lower edge about 2 yards. 9 sizes, 22 to 38 inches waist measure, corresponding to 36 to 54 inches hip measure.   Price, 20 cents each.

9287—Ladies' Surplice Dressing-Sack: Three-Quarter Length One-Seam Sleeves; Four-Piece Peplum. For embroidery design illustrated on the figure use Standard transfer pattern 10374. The pattern is cut in 8 sizes from 32 to 46 inches bust measure. French flannel will make up attractively with scallops outlining the edges.   Price, 20 cents.

1036—Ladies' Five - Gored Slightly Fitted Princess Slip: Closed at the Front or Back; Round Neck or Straight Outline Across the Top; Straight Gathered or Circular Flounce which may be Omitted. Lower edge of gathered flounce measures about 2⅜ yards. The pattern is cut in 6 sizes from 32 to 42 inches bust measure.   Price, 20 cents.

9703—Ladies' Nightgown: Convertible Collar or Open Neck; Long One-Seam Sleeves or Short Sleeves. For the embroidery design illustrated use Standard transfer pattern 4290. The pattern is cut in 9 sizes from 32 to 48 inches bust measure. This nightgown is very comfortable and is nice for practical wear, and is also very dainty.   Price, 20 cents.

1002—Ladies' Undergarment: Camisole with Round Neck or Straight Outline Across the Top; Drawers in Two Outlines at the Lower Edge. The pattern is cut in 4 sizes from 32 to 38 inches bust measure. Here is a very dainty undergarment. The lower part in plain or pointed outline gives one a nice choice.   Price, 20 cents.

1034—Ladies' Semi-Princess Undergarment: Two-Piece Corset Cover and Two-Piece Petticoat Worn Together or Separately; One-Piece Straight Gathered Flounce which may be Omitted. Lower edge of flounce about 2¼ yards. The pattern is cut in 7 sizes from 32 to 44 inches bust measure. Nainsook or crêpe de Chine may be used for the making.   Price, 20 cents.

1000—Ladies' .One - Piece Combination Undergarment: Buttoned on the Shoulders; Round Neck or Straight Outline Across the Top. For the embroidery design illustrated use Standard transfer pattern 10383 and 10155 for the scallop design. 6 sizes, from 32 to 42 inches bust measure. This undergarment is very attractive and simple to make. Price, 20 cents.

Coat—1042   Skirt—1050   Blouse—1041   Skirt—1053   Blouse—1028   Skirt—1031   Blouse—1040   Skirt—1024   1018
Transfer—10393

1042—Ladies' Coat in Moyen-Age Style: 50 or 45 or 38 Inch Length at the Back; Convertible Collar; Two Styles of Two-Seam Sleeves with Slight Fulness at the Top which may be Shrunken Out. The pattern is cut in 7 sizes from 32 to 44 inches bust measure. **1050**—Ladies' Two-Piece Skirt: Slightly High Waistline; Separate Overblouse and Four-Piece Panel Tunic which may be Omitted; 38-Inch Length or Shorter. Lower edge about 1⅝ yards. 7 sizes, 32 to 44 inches bust measure.

1041—Ladies' Russian Blouse: Longer Length in Two Outlines or Shorter Length; High or Open Neck; Long Dart-Fitted or Short Sleeves; Applied Straps which may be Omitted. Use transfer 10057 for Band at bottom of Blouse. The pattern is cut in 6 sizes from 32 to 42 inches bust measure. **1053**—Ladies' Four-Piece Skirt: Slightly High Waistline; Overblouse which may be Omitted; 38-Inch Length or Shorter. Lower edge about 2⅜ yards. 7 sizes from 32 to 44 inches bust measure. Price, 20 cents each.

1028—Ladies' Blouse: Convertible Collar or Open Neck; Long Two-Piece Sleeves or Long Dart-Fitted or Short Sleeves. 9 sizes, 32 to 48 inches bust measure. **1031**—Ladies' Two-Piece Gathered Skirt: Overblouse which may be Omitted. Use transfer 10399 for banding at bottom of skirt. Lower edge about 1¾ yards. 6 sizes, 32 to 42 inches bust measure. Price, 20 cents each.

1018—Ladeis' Dress in Moyen-Age Style: Back Extending Over the Shoulders; High or Open Neck; Long Dart-Fitted or Short Sleeves; Two-Piece Gathered Skirt; 38-Inch Length or Shorter. Lower edge about 2 yards. The pattern is cut in 7 sizes from 32 to 44 inches bust measure. For a woman of taste and distinction this dress has very appealing qualities. The surplice closing and sash give a remarkably graceful line. The embroidery on the pockets adds interest and richness. Price, 25 cents.

1040—Ladies' Blouse: High or Open Neck; Two Styles of Long One-Seam Sleeves or Short Sleeves. (May be Attached to a Skirt or Worn Separately.) The pattern is cut in 7 sizes from 32 to 44 inches bust measure. **1024**—Ladies' Two-Piece Skirt: Slightly High Waistline; Two-Piece Trimming Band in Two Styles and Separate Tie-On Overblouse which may be Omitted; 38-Inch Length or Shorter. Lower edge about 1⅞ yards. The pattern is cut in 7 sizes from 32 to 44 inches bust measure. Price, 20 cents each.

1042   1050   1041   1053   1028—31   1040—24   1018

Guimpe—8284
Jumper Skirt—1031

1055

1055

Blouse—1039 Skirt—9362

Blouse—1007 Skirt—9636

IN HER HOLIDAY ATTIRE

8284—1031   1055   1055   1039—9362   1007—9636

8284—Ladies' Guimpe: in Two Lengths; High or Open Neck; Long One-Seam Dart-Fitted or Short Sleeves, or Long or Three-Quarter Length Bishop Sleeves; Collar and Sleeves may be Omitted. The pattern is cut in 9 sizes from 32 to 48 inches bust measure. **1031**—Ladies' Two-Piece Gathered Skirt: Slightly High Waistline; Overblouse which may be Omitted; 38-Inch Length or Shorter. Lower edge about 1¾ yards. 6 sizes from 32 to 42 inches bust measure. Guimpe, 15 cents; skirt, 20 cents.

1055—Ladies' Empire Evening Dress: Two-Piece Straight Gathered Skirt; Two-Piece Gathered Tunic and Train in 63-Inch Length or Panel which may be Omitted; 38-Inch Length or Shorter. Lower edge about 2 yards. The pattern is cut in 5 sizes from 32 to 40 inches bust measure. When evening comes lovely woman will find herself ever so lovelier in this charming Empire gown. The handsomeness of the dress depends on the material used and the train may be left off for less formal occasions. Price, 25 cents.

1007—Ladies' Blouse: Back Extending Over the Shoulders; High or Open Neck; Long or Short One-Seam Sleeves. The pattern is cut in 7 sizes from 32 to 44 inches bust measure. **9636**—Ladies' Two-Piece Draped Skirt: Slightly High Waistline; Two-Piece Yoke; Clearing or Shorter Length. (May be Attached to a Blouse or Worn Separately.) Lower edge about 1¾ yards. The pattern is cut in 6 sizes from 22 to 32 inches waist measure, corresponding to 36 to 47 inches hip measure. Price, 20 cents each.

1039—Ladies' Blouse: Back Extending Over the Shoulders; High or Open Neck; Long or Short One-Seam Sleeves. The embroidery design is an adaptation of transfer 10377. 7 sizes, 32 to 44 inches bust measure. **9362**—Ladies' Two-Piece Gathered Skirt: in Tunic or Full-Length; Slightly High or Regulation Waistline; Two-Piece Foundation Skirt; Clearing or Shorter Length. Lower edge of foundation skirt about 1¾ yards. 8 sizes, 22 to 36 inches waist measure, or 36 to 52 inches hip measure. 20 cents each.

1025

1015

1038

1016

1017

1022

1003

1022

1012

1017   1022

1025   1015

*1022   1012   1003

1038   1016

1003—Girls' Coat: Closed to the Neck with Cape Collar or Rolled Open without Cape Collar; Two-Seam Sleeves; One-Piece Straight Gathered Skirt. 5 sizes, 6 to 14 years.   Price, 15 cents.

1017—Girls' Coat: Body in One with Long Sleeves; Convertible Collar; Body Fronts in One with Fronts of Three-Piece Gathered Skirt. 5 sizes, from 6 to 14 years.   Price, 15 cents.

1025—Little Girls' Dress: High or Open Neck; Long or Short Sleeves; Straight Gathered Skirt. The pattern is cut in 9 sizes, from 2 to 10 years. A dainty party dress for the little one.   Price, 15 cents.

1015—Girls' Dress: Long or Short One-Seam Sleeves or Long Dart-Fitted Sleeves; Overblouse which may be Omitted; Two-Piece Skirt. 9 sizes, from 6 to 14 years.   Price, 15 cents.

1022—Little Girls' Dress: High or Open Neck; Long or Short Sleeves. The pattern is cut in 9 sizes, from 2 to 10 years. Serge or linen will make a serviceable dress, using this smart design.   15 cents.

1012—Girls' and Juniors' Dress: to be Slipped Over the Head; Convertible Collar or Open Neck; Long Dart-Fitted or Short Sleeves. 11 sizes, from 6 to 16 years.   Price, 15 cents.

1038—Girls' and Juniors' Dress: Back Extending Over the Shoulders to Form a Yoke; Separate Blouse; Convertible Collar; Four-Piece Skirt Attached to the Overblouse. 9 sizes, 6 to 14 years. 15 cents.

1016—Little Girls' Dress: Collar in Two Outlines at the Front; Two-Piece Straight Skirt with the Front in One with Bib which may be Omitted. 9 sizes, from 4 to 12 years.   Price, 15 cents.

9827

Blouse—1056
Knickerbockers—2742

1016

1013

Blouse—1056   Trousers—1057

1011

1015

1025

1048
Transfer—10372

9827   1056   2742

1013   1016

1056—Boys' Blouse: with Adjustable Waistband. The pattern is cut in 9 sizes from 4 to 12 years. **1057** —Boys' Trousers. The pattern is cut in 7 sizes from 8 to 14 years.   Price, 15 cents each.

1056—Boys' Blouse: with Adjustable Waistband. The pattern is cut in 9 sizes from 4 to 12 years. **2742**—Little Boys' Knickerbockers. 7 sizes, from 2 to 8 years.   Price, 15 cents each.

9827—Little Girls' Dress: High or Open Neck; Long or Short Sleeves; Bloomers. The pattern is cut in 11 sizes from 2 to 12 years. A very smart school dress for a nice little girl.   Price, 15 cents.

1013—Girls' and Little Girls' Coat: in Two Lengths; Convertible Collar; Two-Seam Sleeves with Slight Fulness at the Top which may be Shrunken out. 6 sizes, 4 to 14 years.   Price, 15 cents.

1025—Little Girls' Dress: High or Open Neck; Long or Short Sleeves; Straight Gathered Skirt. 9 sizes, 2 to 10 years.   Price, 15 cents.

1048—Girls' and Juniors' Dress: Convertible Collar or Open Neck; Long Dart-Fitted or Short Sleeves. 11 sizes, 6 to 16 years.   Price, 15 cents.

1015—Girls' Dress: High or Open Neck; Overblouse which may be Omitted; Two-Piece Skirt. 9 sizes, 6 to 14 years.   Price, 15 cents.

1011—Girls' and Juniors' Dress: Convertible Collar or Open Neck with Large Collar. 11 sizes, 6 to 16 years.   Price, 15 cents.

1016—Little Girls' Dress: Two-Piece Straight Skirt with the Front in One with Bib which may be Omitted. 9 sizes, 4 to 12 years.   Price, 15 cents.

1025   1015   1048

1011   1056   1057

Bag—1107

1241–42

Blouse—1241   Jumper Skirt—1242

1264

Guimpe—9471
Jumper Skirt—1249

9471
1249

1262
1251

Blouse—1262
Jumper Skirt—1251

1123   1268   1262

1241—LADIES' BLOUSE. 7 sizes, 32 to 44 inches bust measure. **1242**—LADIES' THREE-PIECE SKIRT; Overblouse with Back Extending Over the Front to Form a Yoke which may be Omitted. Lower edge about 1¾ yards. 6 sizes, 32 to 42 bust. **1107**—HAND-BAG. One size. Blouse and Skirt, 20 cts. each; Bag, 15 cts.

1123—LADIES' BLOUSE: Back Extending Over the Shoulders; Two Styles of Collar; Long or Short One-Seam Gathered Sleeves or Long Dart Fitted Sleeves; Blouse Facing and Three-Piece Tunic which may be Omitted. The pattern is cut in 9 sizes, 32 to 48 inches bust measure.   Price, 20 cents.

1268—LADIES' BLOUSE; Long or Short One-Seam Sleeves; Plaited Jabot Sections, and Frill which may be Omitted. (May be attached to a Skirt or worn Separately.) For embroidery design illustrated, use Standard transfer 10167. The pattern is cut in 7 sizes, from 32 to 44 inches bust measure.   Price, 20 cents.

1262—LADIES' BLOUSE: to be Slipped Over the Head and Worn Inside or Outside the Skirt; Collar in Two Outlines; Long or Three-Quarter Length One-Seam Flowing Sleeves. For the scallop design use Standard transfer 10062. The pattern is cut in 5 sizes from 32 to 40 inches bust measure.   20 cents.

1264—LADIES' BOLERO DRESS: High or Open Neck; Long Dart-Fitted or Short Sleeves; Vest which may be Omitted; Two-Piece Skirt; One-Piece Straight Gathered Side Tunics which may be Omitted; 38-Inch Length or Shorter. Lower edge about 1¾ yards. 6 sizes, 32 to 42 inches bust measure. Price, 25 cents.

9471—LADIES' GUIMPE. 9 sizes, 32 to 48 bust. **1249**—LADIES' TWO-PIECE STRAIGHT GATH-ERED YOKE SKIRT; Overblouse and One-Piece Straight Gathered Side Tunics which may be Omitted. Lower edge about 1⅝ yards. 6 sizes, 32 to 42 bust measure.   Guimpe 15 cents; Skirt 20 cents.

1262—LADIES' BLOUSE; Collar in Two Outlines. The pattern is cut in 5 sizes, from 32 to 40 inches bust measure. **1251**—LADIES' TWO-PIECE STRAIGHT GATHERED SKIRT; Overblouse which may be Omitted. Lower edge about 1¾ yards. 6 sizes, 32 to 42 inches bust. 20 cents each.

1238-A

1238-A

Blouse—1246
Jumper-Skirt—1243

1245

Coat—1252
Skirt—1249

1252

1249

Coat—1252
Skirt—1126

1252

1126

1246-1243

1238-B   1238-B   1245

1246—LADIES' BLOUSE: Convertible Collar or Open Neck with Large Collar. The pattern is cut in 7 sizes from 32 to 44 inches bust measure. **1243**—LADIES' THREE-PIECE SKIRT; Overblouse which may be Omitted. Lower edge about 1¾ yards. The pattern is cut in 6 sizes from 32 to 42 inches bust. 20 cents each.

1252—LADIES' COAT: 36 or 28 Inch Length at the Back. The pattern is cut in 6 sizes from 32 to 42 inches bust measure. **1126**—LADIES' TWO-PIECE SKIRT; (Jumper not illustrated). Lower edge about 1⅝ yards. 7 sizes, 32 to 44 inches bust measure. A smart coat and skirt combination is shown here.
Coat, 25 cents; Skirt 20 cents.

1252—LADIES' COAT. The pattern is cut in 6 sizes from 32 to 42 inches bust measure. **1249**—LADIES' TWO-PIECE STRAIGHT GATHERED YOKE SKIRT; (Overblouse and One-Piece Straight Gathered Side Tunics not illustrated). Lower edge about 1⅝ yards. 6 sizes, 32 to 42 bust. Coat, 25 cents; Skirt, 20 cents.

1245—LADIES' DRESS in MOYEN-AGE STYLE: Long or Short One-Seam Sleeves; Two-Piece Side Tunics; Facings which may be Omitted; Separate Two-Piece Skirt; Slightly High Waistline. For braiding design use Standard transfer 10310. Lower edge about 1¾ yards. 6 sizes, 32 to 42 inches bust.   Price, 25 cents.

1238—LADIES' DRESS: Back Extending Over the Shoulders; High or Open Neck; Long Dart-Fitted or Short Sleeves; Two-Piece Gathered Skirt; 38-Inch Length or Shorter. For the embroidery design illustrated on figure A, use Standard transfer pattern No. 10407. Lower edge about 1¾ yards. 6 sizes 32 to 42 ins. bust measure. 25 cents.

DESIGNS SHOWING NEW MODELS FOR SPRING

1278—LADIES' DRESS: Back Extending Over the Shoulders; High or Open Neck; Long or Short One-Seam Gathered Sleeve or Long Dart-Fitted Sleeves; Applied Front and Back Skirt Sections which may be Omitted; 38-Inch Length or Shorter. Lower edge about 2⅛ yards. The pattern is cut in 6 sizes from 32 to 42 inches bust measure. This smart dress has a very fashionable collar.   Price, 25 cents.

1276—LADIES' BLOUSE: Collar in Two Styles; Shoulder Yoke in One with Long or Short Sleeves. 5 sizes from 32 to 40 inches bust measure. **1275—** LADIES' TWO-PIECE STRAIGHT GATHERED SKIRT: Hanging Free or Gathered into a Two-Piece Straight Band; Three-Piece Belt in Two Outlines at the Front. Lower edge of band about 1¼ yards. 7 sizes, 22 to 34 waist corresponding to 35 to 48½ hip. 20 cts. each.

1245
Transfer 10399

Blouse—1262
Skirt—1288

Coat—1258
Skirt—1287

1245—LADIES' DRESS: in Moyen-Age Style; Long or Short One-Seam Sleeves; Two-Piece Side Tunic; Facings which may be Omitted; Separate Two-Piece Skirt; Slightly High Waistline; 38-Inch Length or Shorter. For the embroidery design illustrated, use transfer 10399. Lower edge about 1¾ yards. 6 sizes, 32 to 42 inches bust.   Price, 25 cents.

1262—LADIES' BLOUSE: to be Slipped Over the Head and Worn Inside or Outside the Skirt; Long or Three-Quarter Length One-Seam Flowing Sleeves. 5 sizes from 32 to 40 inches bust measure. **1288—**LADIES' THREE-PIECE SKIRT: High Waistline; Overblouse is Omitted. Lower edge about 1½ yards. 5 sizes, 32 to 40 inches bust.   20 cents each.

1286—LADIES' BLOUSE: to be Slipped Over the Head; Long or Short Raglan Sleeves. 5 sizes, 32 to 40 inches bust measure. **1251—**LADIES' TWO-PIECE STRAIGHT GATHERED SKIRT; Slightly High Waistline; Bag and Overblouse which may be Omitted. Lower edge about 1¾ yards. 6 sizes, 32 to 42 inches bust measure.   Price, 20 cents each.

1258—LADIES' COAT: 30 or 24 Inch Length at the Back; Two-Seam Sleeves with Slight Fulness at the Top which may be Shrunken Out; Sleeves and Pockets which may be Omitted. 6 sizes, 32 to 42 inches bust measure. **1287—**LADIES' TWO-PIECE SKIRT: Slightly High Waistline; Collar in Two Outlines; One-Piece Apron Tunic; Overblouse is Omitted. Lower edge measures about 1⅝ yards. 5 sizes, from 32 to 40 inches bust measure. Coat, 25 cents; Skirt 20 cents.

1245   1262   1288   1278   1286
                                      1251

Blouse—1286
Skirt—1251
Transfer—10393

1278   Blouse—1276
         Suspender Skirt—1275

1276   1258   1287
1275

THE NEW SUITS AND DRESSES

1078—Ladies' Guimpe in Two Lengths or Blouse. 9 sizes, 32 to 48 inches bust measure.
1281—Ladies' Four-Piece Skirt: Front and Back Gores in One with Bands; Overblouse which may be Omitted. For the embroidery use Standard Transfer 10372. Lower edge about 1¾ yards. 6 sizes, 32 to 42 inches bust.   Price, 20 cents each.

1261—Ladies' Dress: High Neck or Open Neck with Tucker and Draped Collar; Long Dart-Fitted or Short Sleeves; One-Piece Straight Gathered Skirt or Tunic in Regulation or Bustle Style; Two-Piece Foundation Skirt which may be Omitted. Lower edge of foundation skirt about 1¾ yards. 5 sizes, 32 to 40 inches bust measure. Price, 25 cents.

Blouse—**1241**
Jumper Skirt—**1243**

1241
1243

1241—Ladies' Blouse: Back Extending Over the Shoulders; High or Open Neck; Long or Short One-Seam Gathered Sleeves or Long Dart-Fitted Sleeves. (May be Attached to a Skirt or Worn Separately.) 7 sizes, 32 to 44 inches bust measure. **1243**—Ladies' Three-Piece Skirt: Slightly High Waistline; Overblouse which may be Omitted. Lower edge about 1¾ yards. 6 sizes, 32 to 42 inches bust. Price, 20 cents each.

1261   1078
           1281

Blouse—**1078**
Jumper Skirt—**1281**

1261

Coat—**1269**
Skirt—**1126**

Sleeveless Coat—**1258**
Blouse—**1077**
Skirt—**1281**

1258—Ladies' Coat, with or without Sleeves: 30 or 24 Inch Length at the Back. 6 sizes, 32 to 42 inches bust measure. **1077**—Ladies' Blouse. 9 sizes, 32 to 48 bust. **1281**—Ladies' Four-Piece Skirt: Front and Back Gores in One with Bands; Overblouse not illustrated. Lower edge about 1¾ yards. 6 sizes, 32 to 42 inches bust measure. Coat, 25 cents; Skirt and Blouse 20 cents each.

1269—Ladies' Coat: 27-Inch Length at the Back; Pointed or Straight Outline at the Front; Collar in Two Outlines. The pattern is cut in 7 sizes, from 32 to 44 inches bust measure. **1126**—Ladies' Two-Piece Skirt: Jumper not illustrated. Lower edge about 1⅝ yards. 7 sizes, 32 to 44 inches bust measure.   Coat, 25 cents; Skirt, 20 cents.

1280—Ladies' Coat: 34 or 26-Inch Length at the Back. 6 sizes, 32 to 42 inches bust measure. **1275**—Ladies' Two-Piece Straight Gathered Skirt: Slightly High Waistline; Three-Piece Belt in Two Outlines at the Front. Lower edge of skirt about 1¾ yards. 7 sizes, 22 to 34 ins. waist or 35 to 48½ inches. hip.   Coat, 25 cents; Skirt, 20 cents.

Coat—**1280**
Skirt—**1275**

1280   1269   1258

1275   1126   1077   1281

1236

Bolero
1263

1236

1230

1246

Bolero—**1263**
Blouse—**1217**

1236 — LADIES'
BLOUSE: Convertible Col-
lar; Long or Short One-
Seam Sleeves; Revers which
may be Omitted. (May
be Attached to a Skirt or
Worn Separately.) The
pattern is cut in 8 sizes
from 32 to 46 inches bust
measure. A very attrac-
tive blouse. 20 cents.

1263—LADIES' BOLE-
ROS: Long Dart-Fitted
Sleeves or Long or Three-
Quarter Length One-Seam
Flowing Sleeves which may
be Omitted. The pattern
is cut in 6 sizes from 32 to
42 inches bust measure.
1217—LADIES' BLOUSE
OR GUIMPE. 9 sizes, 32 to
48 bust. 20 cents each.

1252—LADIES' COAT:
36 or 28 Inch Length at the
Back. 6 sizes, 32 to 42
inches bust measure.
1248 — LADIES' TWO-
PIECE STRAIGHT SKIRT.
The Overblouse is Omitted.
Lower edge about 1¾
yards. 6 sizes, 32 to 42 bust.
Coat, Price, 25 cents; Skirt,
Price, 20 cents.

1246 — LADIES
BLOUSE: Convertible Col-
lar or Open Neck with
Large Collar: Long or
Short One-Seam Gathered
Sleeves or Long Dart-Fitted
Sleeves. (May be Attached
to a Skirt or Worn Separ-
ately.) The pattern is cut
in 7 sizes from 32 to 44
bust. Price, 20 cents.

1230 — L A D I E S'
BLOUSE: High or Open
Neck; Long or Short One-
Seam Sleeves; Applied
Straps which may be Omit-
ted. (May be Attached
to a Skirt or Worn Separ-
ately). The pattern is cut
in 7 sizes from 32 to 44
inches bust measure. Lin-
en may be used. 20 cents.

1221—LADIES' DRESS:
High or Open Neck; Long
Dart-Fitted or Short
Sleeves; Two-Piece Gath-
ered Tunic which may be
Omitted; One-Piece
Straight Gathered Skirt.
Lower edge about 1¾
yards. 5 sizes, from 32 to
40 inches bust measure.
Price, 25 cents.

1244

1244—LADIES' BLOUSE: Back
Extending Over the Shoulders; Long
or Short One-Seam Gathered Sleeves
or Long Dart-Fitted Sleeves. (May
be Attached to a Skirt or Worn Separately.) The pattern is cut in 8
sizes from 32 to 46 inches bust measure.
Price, 20 cents.

1244

1263
1217

1263   1252   1248   Coat—1252   Skirt—1248   1221   1230   1221   1246

1253

9485

9715

1273

9715

1282

9485—Ladies' Dress-
ing-Sack: High or Open
Neck; Long or Short One-
Seam Sleeves; Three-Piece
Peplum in Two Outlines at
the Lower Edge. The pat-
tern is cut in 9 sizes from 32
to 48 inches bust measure.
Dimity and lawn are suit-
able materials for this simple dressing-sack.   15 cts.

9715—Ladies' House
Dress: Convertible Collar
or Open Neck with Large
Collar; Long or Short One-
Seam Sleeves; Two-Piece
Skirt; Clearing or Shorter
Length. Cap. Lower edge
about 2¼ yards. The pattern
is cut in 9 sizes from 32 to 48
inches bust measure.
           Price, 25 cents.

1259—Ladies' Apron:
in Two Lengths; to be
Slipped Over the Head;
Pockets in Two Styles. The
pattern is cut in 3 sizes,
small, medium and large.
The construction of this
apron is very unusual having pockets in two styles.
It is easy to put on or take
off.   Price, 20 cents.

1282—Ladies' Combination
Undergarment.   The pattern is
cut in 5 sizes from 32 to 40 inches
bust measure. A combination
which needs to be adjusted only
when put on or when taken off
speaks for itself as to comfort and
simplicity.   Price, 20 cents.

1273—Ladies' Night-
gown; Frills which may be
Omitted. The pattern is
cut in 5 sizes from 32 to 40
inches bust measure. Sim-
plicity in underwear is always a desirable thing and
this gown is one of the best
types requiring little or no
trimming. A model simple
to make. Price, 20 cents.

1253 — Ladies' Com-
bination Undergarment:
Corset-Cover and Drawers
Worn Together or Separately.
5 sizes 32 to 40 inches bust
measure. A surplice com-
bination is favored by many
women. This one is simple
in construction, having the
drawers in envelope style.
           Price, 20 cents.

1272—Ladies' Paja-
mas or Lounging Robe:
One-Piece Jacket to be
Slipped Over the Head. The
pattern is cut in 5 sizes from
32 to 40 inches bust mea-
sure. This garment may be
used as pajamas or as a
lounging robe in one's bou-
doir. It is excellent in
style.   Price, 20 cents.

9715   1259   1259   9485   1282   1272   1253   1272   1273

1278   **1247**   **1264-B**

THE ETON HOLDS FIRST PLACE

1278—LADIES' DRESS: Back Extending Over the Shoulders; High or Open Neck; Long or Short One-Seam Gathered Sleeves or Long-Dart Fitted Sleeves; Applied Front and Back Skirt Sections which may be Omitted; 38-Inch Length or Shorter. Lower edge about 2⅛ yards. The pattern is cut in 6 sizes, from 32 to 42 inches bust measure. A smart and simple dress.   25 cents.

1247—LADIES' DRESS: Back Extending Over the Shoulders; Deep Armhole; Three-Quarter Length or Short One-Seam Flowing Sleeve or Long Dart-Fitted Sleeves; Two-Piece Gathered Skirt; 38-Inch Length or Shorter. Lower edge about 1¾ yards. The pattern is cut in 7 sizes from 32 to 44 inches bust measure. Foulard is an excellent material for this dress.   Price, 25 cents.

1264—LADIES' BOLERO DRESS: High or Open Neck; Long Dart-Fitted or Short Sleeves; Vest and One-Piece Straight Gathered Side Tunics which may be Omitted; Two-Piece Skirt; 38-Inch Length or Shorter. Lower edge measures about 1¾ yards. The pattern is cut in 6 sizes from 32 to 42 inches bust measure. This design is an excellent one for street wear.   Price, 25 cents.

1078—LADIES' GUIMPE IN TWO LENGTHS OR BLOUSE. 9 sizes, 32 to 48 inches bust measure.
1248—LADIES' TWO-PIECE STRAIGHT SKIRT: Two-Piece Side Yokes; Overblouse and Loose Front and Back Panels which may be Omitted. Use Transfer pattern 10399 for the embroidery design. Lower edge about 1¾ yards. The pattern is cut in 6 sizes, from 32 to 42 bust.   20 cts. each.

1278   1264-A

1264-A

Guimpe—1078
Jumper Skirt—1248

1078
1248

1264 B   1247

1240

1261   1270   9553
1232

1240   1270   1261

FIVE NEW AND SMART DESIGNS

1240—Ladies' Dress: High or Open Neck; Long Dart-Fitted or Short Sleeves; One-Piece Gathered Tunic; Separate Two-Piece Skirt; Slightly High Waistline; 38-Inch Length or Shorter. Lower edge about 1¾ yards. The pattern is cut in 5 sizes from 32 to 40 inches bust measure. This dress has unusually attractive lines. The slightly high waistline is a good feature. 25 cents.

1271—Ladies' Sleeve-less Jacket: Collar which may be Omitted. 6 sizes, 32 to 42 inches bust measure. **9904** — Ladies' Tucked or Gathered Blouse. 9 sizes, 32 to 48 inches bust measure. **9554** — La-dies' Three-Piece Skirt. Lower edge about 2⅛ yards. 9 sizes, 22 to 38 inches waist measure, corresponding to 36 to 54 inches hip measure. A very smart combination. Price, 20 cents each.

1270—Ladies' Dress: to be Slipped Over the Head; Back Extending Over the Shoulders; Two Styles of Collar; Long Dart-Fitted or Short Sleeves; 38-Inch Length or Shorter. Lower edge about 2⅜ yards. The pattern is cut in 5 sizes from 32 to 40 inches bust measure. This dress made of a combination of materials is very fashionable but if desired it may be made all of one material. Price, 25 cents.

1261—Ladies' Dress: High Neck or Open Neck with Tucker and Draped Collar; Long Dart-Fitted or Short Sleeves; One-Piece Straight Gathered Skirt or Tunic in Regulation or Bustle Style; Two-Piece Foundation Skirt which may be Omitted; 38-Inch Length or Shorter. Lower edge about 1¾ yards. The pattern is cut in 5 sizes from 32 to 40 inches bust measure. 25 cents.

9553—Ladies' Blouse: Rolled Open with Large Collar. 8 sizes, 32 to 46 inches bust measure. **1232** — Ladies' Two-Piece Straight Gathered or Shirred Skirt: Slightly High Waistline; Overblouse and Two-Piece Facing which may be Omitted. For the braiding design use Standard transfer 10310. Lower edge about 1⅞ yards. The pattern is cut in 5 sizes from 32 to 40 bust. 20 cts. each.

1271
9904

9554

Sleeveless Jacket
1271
Blouse—9904
Skirt—9554

Blouse
9553
Jumper Skirt
1232

1277-A
Transfer—10310

1291

Coat—1291
Skirt—9903

1235

1277-A

1284
Transfer—10406

1290

1291   1291   9903   1277-A

1290   1284   1235   1277-B

1291—Misses' and Small Women's Coat: in Two Lengths; Convertible Collar; Deep Armhole; One-Seam Sleeves. The pattern is cut in 4 sizes, 14 to 20 years. A very smart coat that may be used in full length as a coverall or in shorter length as part of a suit.   Price, 25 cents.

1291—Misses' and Small Women's Coat: in Two Lengths. 4 sizes, 14 to 20 years. **9903**—Misses' and Small Women's Three-Piece Skirt: Overblouse which may be Omitted. Lower edge about 2⅛ yards. 4 sizes, from 14 to 20 years. Price—Coat 25 Cents; Skirt 15 cents.

1277—Misses' and Small Women's Empire Dress: Long or Short One-Seam Sleeves or Long Dart-Fitted Sleeves; Bolero in Two Outlines; Two-Piece Straight Gathered Skirt. Lower edge about 2 yards. 4 sizes, 14 to 20 years.   Price, 25 cents.

1235—Misses' and Small Women's Dress: High, Round or Square Neck; Long or Short One-Seam Sleeves or Long Dart-Fitted Sleeves; Tunic in Two Lengths; One-Piece Skirt. Lower edge about 1⅝ yards. 4 sizes, 14 to 20 years.   Price, 25 cents.

1284—Misses' and Small Women's Dress: Collar in Two Styles; Long Dart-Fitted or Short Sleeves; Bolero Closed at the Left Side which may be Omitted; Two-Piece Skirt. Lower edge about 1½ yards. 4 sizes, 14 to 20 years.   Price, 25 cents.

1290—Misses' and Small Women's Pajamas or Lounging Robe: Long or Short One-Seam Sleeves which may be Omitted. The pattern is cut in 4 sizes from 14 to 20 years. A most attractive as well as comfortable garment is shown here.   Price, 15 cents.

1149

1260

1267

1231

1234

1257

1285

1233

1293

1285 — Girls' and Juniors' Dress: Long or Short Sleeves. The pattern is cut in 9 sizes from 8 to 16 years. A very attractive dress for the young girl is shown here. Linen, chambray and galatea are suitable materials.   Price, 15 cents.

1257 — Girls' and Juniors' Dress: High or Open Neck; Long Dart-Fitted Sleeves or Short Straight Sleeves; Straight Gathered Skirt. The pattern is cut in 11 sizes from 6 to 16 years. A smart and simple dress for the girl.   Price, 15 cents.

1233 — Little Girls' Dress: High or Open Neck; Long or Short Sleeves; Separate Bolero which may be Omitted; One-Piece Straight Gathered Skirt. The pattern is cut in 9 sizes from 4 to 12 years. Gingham is suitable.   Price, 15 cents.

1293 — Little Boys' Suit: Blouse to be Slipped Over the Head; Two Styles of Collar; Long or Short One-Seam Sleeves; Trousers. The pattern is cut in 5 sizes from 2 to 6 years. Galatea is an excellent material.   Price, 15 cents.

1149 — Child's Coat: High or Open Neck; Two-Seam Sleeves with Slight Fulness at the Top which may be Shrunken Out. The pattern is cut in 4 sizes from 2 to 8 years. Taffeta is an excellent material for this coat.   Price, 15 cents.

1260 — Girls' and Juniors' Empire Dress: High or Open Neck; Long or Short Sleeves; Bolero which may be Omitted; Straight Gathered Skirt. The pattern is cut in 9 sizes from 8 to 16 years. Voile may be used.   Price, 15 cents.

1267 — Girls' and Juniors' Dress: Body in One with Long or Short Sleeves; Overblouse which may be Omitted; One-Piece Straight Gathered Skirt. The pattern is cut in 9 sizes, from 8 to 16 years. A smart design.   Price, 15 cents.

1234 — Child's Rompers in Knickerbocker or Regulation Style; High or Open Neck; Long or Short Sleeves. The pattern is cut in 4 sizes from 1 to 4 years. Gingham and chambray are excellent materials.   Price, 15 cents.

1231 — Little Girls' Dress: to be Slipped Over the Head; Long or Short Sleeves. For the scallop design illustrated on the figure, use Standard transfer pattern 10155. The pattern is cut in 9 sizes from 2 to 10 years. Linen is suggested.   Price, 15 cents.

1255

1255—Girls' and Juniors' Dress: High or Open Neck; Long or Short Sleeves. The pattern is cut in 11 sizes from 6 to 16 years. A very smart and attractive dress is shown here. It is suitable for afternoon wear. Price, 15 cents.

1237   1274   1071   1080   1260   1255

1239   1293   1229

1237—Little Girls' Dress: High or Open Neck; Long or Short Sleeves; Straight Gathered Skirt. The pattern is cut in 9 sizes from 2 to 10 years. A smart and simple model suitable for afternoon wear. Price, 15 cents.

1274—Girls' Coat: Side Body in One with Long Sleeves; Convertible Collar. The pattern is cut in 5 sizes from 6 to 14 years. An attractive coat for the growing girl is shown here. It is simple to make. Price, 20 cents.

1071—Child's Dress: High or Open Neck; Long or Short Sleeves. The pattern is cut in 5 sizes from ½ to 4 years. A smart and dainty dress for the little girl. Batiste, nainsook, lawn and linen are suitable. Price, 15 cents.

1239—Little Girls' Dress: High or Open Neck; Long or Short Sleeves. The pattern is cut in 9 sizes from 2 to 10 years. Linen, rep, piqué, gingham and chambray are excellent materials for this design. Price, 15 cents.

1260—Girls' and Juniors' Empire Dress: High or Open Neck; Long or Short Sleeves; Bolero which may be Omitted; Straight Gathered Skirt. The pattern is cut in 9 sizes from 8 to 16 years. A suitable dress for school. Price, 15 cents.

1080—Girls' and Little Girls' Dress: to be Slipped Over the Head; Body in One with Short Sleeves; Separate Guimpe with Long Sleeves. For the scallop design use Standard transfer 10225. 11 sizes, 4 to 14 years. Price, 15 cents.

1293—Little Boys' Suit: Blouse to be Slipped Over the Head; Two Styles of Collar; Long or Short One-Seam Sleeves; Trousers. The pattern is cut in 5 sizes from 2 to 6 years. A smart suit for the small boy. Price, 15 cents.

1229—Child's Kimono in Two Length: High or Open Neck; Long Dart-Fitted or Short Flowing Sleeves. The pattern is cut in 6 sizes, 1 to 10 years. Figured cotton crêpe is excellent for this child's kimono. Price, 15 cents.

Dress—1366

Blouse—1360
Jumper Skirt—1367

1369

1366   1369

1365

1360
1367   1365

1361
1189   1362
1367

Blouse—1361
Skirt—1189

Blouse—1362
Skirt—1367

1366—LADIES' DRESS: High or Open Neck; Long One-Seam Dart-Fitted of Short Sleeves or Long Two-Seam Sleeves; Vest in Two Styles; Two-Piece Gathered Skirt; 38-Inch Length or Shorter. For the embroidery design use Standard transfer pattern 10416. Lower edge about 1⅝ yards. The pattern is cut in 7 sizes from 32 to 44 inches bust measure.   Price, 25 cents.

1362—LADIES' BLOUSE: High or Open Neck; Long Dart-Fitted or Short Sleeves; One-Piece Straight Gathered Peplum which may be Omitted. 6 sizes from 32 to 42 inches bust measure. **1367** —LADIES' THREE-PIECE SKIRT: Slightly High Waistline. Overblouse Omitted; 38-Inch Length or Shorter; Lower edge about 1⅝ yards. 7 sizes, 32 to 44 inches bust measure.   20 cents each.

1369—LADIES' DRESS: Back Extending Over the Shoulders to Form a Yoke; Square or V Neck; Long or Short One-Seam Sleeves; 38-Inch Length or Shorter. Lower edge about 2⅛ yards. The pattern is cut in 6 sizes from 32 to 42 inches bust measure. This design is attractive and very easy to make.   Gingham, chambray, poplin and linen are suitable.   Price, 20 cents.

1360—LADIES' BLOUSE: High or Open Neck; Long or Short One-Seam Sleeves or Long Dart-Fitted Sleeves. 6 sizes, 32 to 42 inches bust measure.   **1367**—LADIES' THREE-PIECE SKIRT: Slightly High Waistline; Overblouse and Panel which may be Omitted. For braiding design use Standard transfer 10086. Lower edge about 1⅝ yards. 7 sizes, 32 to 44 bust.   20 cents each.

1365—LADIES' DRESS: Back Extending Over the Shoulders; Long Dart-Fitted or Short Sleeves; Two-Piece Gathered Skirt; 38-Inch Length or Shorter. Lower edge about 1¾ yards. The pattern is cut in 7 sizes from 32 to 44 inches bust measure. This dress is very smart for either morning or afternoon wear. The double collar is a novel feature of the dress.   Price, 25 cents.

1361—LADIES' BLOUSE: Collar in Two Outlines; Long Dart-Fitted or Short Sleeves; Cuff Facing which may be Omitted. 9 sizes, 32 to 48 inches bust measure. **1189**—LADIES' TWO-PIECE SKIRT: with Short Side Sections; Slightly High Waistline. Lower edge about 1¾ yards. 6 sizes, 22 to 32 inches waist measure corresponding, to 35 to 46 inches hip measure.   20 cents each.

1372

1372

1208

1373

1276
1189

1168

1377

1361
1367

Blouse—1361
Skirt—1367

1204

Coat—1377
Skirt—1204

Coat—1373   Skirt—1168   Coat—1208   Blouse—1276
Skirt—1189

Blouse—1329
Jumper Skirt
1367

1329
1367

1208—LADIES' COAT. 5 sizes, 32 to 40 bust. **1276**—
LADIES' BLOUSE. 5 sizes, 32 to 40 bust. **1189**—LADIES' TWO-
PIECE SKIRT. Lower edge about 1¾ yards. 6 sizes, 22 to 32
waist; 35 to 46 hip. Coat 25 cts.; Blouse and Skirt 20 cts. each.

1373—LADIES' COAT. 9 sizes, 32 to 48 inches bust measure.
1168—LADIES' TWO-PIECE SKIRT: Overblouse omitted here.
Lower edge about 1¾ yards. 6 sizes, 32 to 42 inches bust
measure.   Price, Coat 25 cents; Skirt 20 cents.

1377—LADIES' COAT. 7 sizes, 32 to 44 inches bust measure.
1204—LADIES' FOUR-PIECE SKIRT. Lower edge about 1⅝
yards. 9 sizes, 22 to 38 waist, corresponding to 35 to 53 inches
hip measure.   Price, Coat 25 cents; Skirt 20 cents.

1361—LADIES' BLOUSE. 9 sizes, 32 to 48 inches bust measure. **1367**—LADIES' THREE-PIECE SKIRT: Overblouse Omitted here. Lower edge about 1⅝ yards. The pattern is cut in 7
sizes, from 32 to 44 inches bust measure. Price, 20 cents each.

1372—LADIES' BLOUSE: to be Slipped Over the Head; Long
One-Seam Gathered Sleeves or Long Dart-Fitted or Short Sleeves.
The pattern is cut in 6 sizes from 32 to 42 inches bust measure.
A very smart blouse.   Price, 20 cents.

1329—LADIES' BLOUSE OR
GUIMPE: High Neck or Open
Neck in Various Outlines.
8 sizes, 32 to 46 inches bust
measure. **1367**—LADIES'
THREE-PIECE SKIRT: Slightly
High Waistline; Overblouse
and Panel Back which may be
Omitted. Lower edge about
1⅝ yards. 7 sizes, 32 to 44
inches bust measure
        Price, 20 cents each.

1395

Blouse—1401
Skirt—1390

Blouse—1396
Skirt—1096

1406   1389

1398

Blouse—9452
Skirt—1388

1389—LADIES' DRESS: Three-Quarter Length
One-Seam Sleeves or Long Dart-Fitted Sleeves;
Three-Piece Gathered Skirt; Bolero and Three-Piece
Facing which may be Omitted. Lower edge about
1⅝ yards. 6 sizes, 32 to 42 inches bust mea-
sure.   Price, 25 cents.

1406—LADIES' COAT: 50 or 45 Inch Length at
the Back; Convertible Collar; Two-Seam Sleeves
with Slight Fulness at the Top which may be
Shrunken out; Five-Piece Skirt. The pattern is cut
in 6 sizes from 32 to 42 inches bust measure. A
simple and attractive coat.   Price, 25 cents.

1401—LADIES' BLOUSE: High or Open Neck.
The pattern is cut in 7 sizes, from 32 to 44 inches
bust measure. **1390**—LADIES' TWO-PIECE SKIRT;
Soft Plaits or Gathers at the Top; Overblouse Omitted here. Lower edge about 1⅝ yards. 6 sizes, 32
to 42 inches bust measure. Price, 20 cents each.

1396—LADIES' TUCKED BLOUSE. The pattern
is cut in 7 sizes from 32 to 44 inches bust measure.
1096—LADIES' TWO-PIECE GATHERED SKIRT.
Lower edge about 2 yards. 7 sizes, 22 to 34 inches
waist measure, corresponding to 36 to 49½ inches
hip measure.   Price, 20 cents each.

1395—LADIES' COAT: 50 or
45 Inch Length at the Back;
Convertible Collar; Body Front
and Back in One with Skirt;
Two-Seam Sleeves with Slight
Fulness at the Top which may be
Shrunken Out. The pattern is
cut in 7 sizes from 32 to 44
inches bust measure. A very
smart coat is shown here.
Price, 25 cents.

1398—LADIES' DRESS: in
Moyen-Age Style; Long or Short
One-Seam Sleeves or Long Dart-
Fitted Sleeves; Three - Piece
Straight Gathered Tunic; Two-
Piece Straight Gathered Skirt.
For embroidery design use trans-
fer 10406. Lower edge about
1½ yards. The pattern is cut in
5 sizes from 32 to 40 inches bust
measure.   Price, 25 cents.

9452—LADIES' TUCKED
BLOUSE. 5 sizes, 32 to 40 inches
bust measure. For the scallop
design use Standard transfer
10123. **1388**—LADIES' TWO-
PIECE STRAIGHT GATHERED
TUCKED SKIRT. Lower edge
about 1¾ yards. 7 sizes, 22 to
34 inches waist, corresponding to
35 to 48½ inches hip measure.
Price, 20 cents each.

9452   1398   1395   1401   1396   1406   1389
1388   1390   1096

1414

Blouse—1401
Jumper Skirt—1411

1383

1409

1417

Guimpe—1329
Overblouse and Skirt—1390

Blouse—1397
Skirt—1411

1414—LADIES' DRESS: Two Depths of Open Neck; Long Dart-Fitted or Short Sleeves; Separate Bolero; Two-Piece Gathered Tunic in Two Outlines; Two-Piece Gathered Skirt. Lower edge about 1⅝ yards. The pattern is cut in 7 sizes from 32 to 44 inches bust measure. Price, 25 cents.

1401—LADIES' BLOUSE: Long Dart-Fitted or Short Sleeves. 7 sizes, 32 to 44 inches bust measure. **1411**—LADIES' ONE OR TWO PIECE GATHERED SKIRT: Overblouse Omitted here. Lower edge about 1⅜ yards. 7 sizes, 32 to 44 inches bust measure. Price, 20 cents each.

1383—LADIES' DRESS: Back Extending Over the Shoulders; Collar in Two Styles; Long or Short One-Seam Sleeves; Slightly High Waistline; Two-Piece Skirt; 38-Inch Length or Shorter. Lower edge about 1⅝ yards. 9 sizes, 32 to 48 inches bust measure. Price, 25 cents.

1409—LADIES' DRESS: High or Open Neck; Long Dart-Fitted or Short Sleeves; Vest in Two Outlines; One-Piece Straight Gathered Peplum; Two-Piece Skirt; 38-Inch Length or Shorter. Lower edge about 1⅝ yards. 5 sizes, 32 to 40 inches bust measure. Price, 25 cents.

1417—LADIES' DRESS: in Regulation Style or Gathered into a Two-Piece Band; To be Slipped Over the Head; Convertible Collar or Open Neck; Three-Quarter Length Flowing Sleeves; Tunic which may be Omitted. Lower edge about 1⅝ yards. 5 sizes, 32 to 40 inches bust measure. Price, 25 cents.

1329—LADIES' BLOUSE OR GUIMPE. 8 sizes, 32 to 46 inches bust measure. **1390**—LADIES' TWO-PIECE SKIRT, with or without the Tuck; Soft Plaits or Gathers at the Top; Collar and Overblouse which may be Omitted. Lower edge about 1⅝ yds. 6 sizes, 32 to 42 inches bust measure. Price, 20 cents each.

1397—LADIES' BLOUSE; Back Extending Over the Shoulders. For the scallop design use transfer 10123. 8 sizes, 32 to 46 inches bust measure. **1411**—LADIES' ONE OR TWO PIECE GATHERED SKIRT: Overblouse Omitted here. Lower edge about 1⅜ yards. 7 sizes, 32 to 44 inches bust. 20 cents each.

1414
1401 1411
1409
1383
1329 1390
1397 1411
1417

JUNE CALLS FOR

A NEW VARIATION

IN THE

SUMMER FROCK AND

THE GARDEN DRESS

1359—Ladies' Blouse. 5 sizes, 32 to 40 inches bust measure. **1275**—Ladies' Two - Piece Straight Skirt. Lower edge of skirt about 1¾ yards. 7 sizes, 22 to 34 waist, corresponding to 35 to 48½ hip. Price, 20 cents each.

1386—Ladies' Dress: Back Extending Over the Shoulders to Form a Yoke; Two-Piece Skirt. Lower edge about 1½ yards. The pattern is cut in 6 sizes from 32 to 42 inches bust measure. A smart design.   Price, 25 cents.

1381—Ladies' Dress: Long or Short One-Seam Gathered Sleeves; Four-Piece Straight Skirt; Applied Straps and Trimming Bands which may be Omitted. Lower edge about 1½ yards. 7 sizes, 32 to 44 inches bust measure. Price, 25 cents.

1391—Ladies' House-Dress or Negligee: to be Slipped Over the Head; Body in One with Short Sleeves; Collar and Pockets in Two Outlines; Cap. Lower edge about 2¼ yards. 6 sizes, 32 to 42 inches bust.   Price, 20 cents.

1329—Ladies' Blouse or Guimpe. 8 sizes, 32 to 46 inches bust measure. **1380**—Ladies' Four - Piece Skirt and Overblouse. Lower edge about 1¾ yards. 7 sizes from 32 to 44 inches bust measure.   Price, 20 cents each.

1372—Ladies' Blouse. 6 sizes 32 to 42 inches bust measure. **1380**—Ladies' Four - Piece Skirt; Overblouse Omitted here. Lower edge about 1¾ yards. 7 sizes, 32 to 44 inches bust measure.   Price, 20 cents each.

1365—Ladies' Dress: Back Extending Over the Shoulders; Long Dart-Fitted or Short Sleeves; Two-Piece Gathered Skirt. Lower edge about 1¾ yards. The pattern is cut in 7 sizes, 32 to 44 inches bust measure.   Price, 25 cents.

The Designer
STYLES ARE
REPRODUCED BY
Standard Patterns

Blouse **1359**
Skirt **1275**

Dress
1381

1391

Blouse
1372
Skirt
1380

1386

Blouse—**1329**
Jumper Skirt—**1380**

1365

1365   1372–1380   1391   1386   1359–1275   1381   1329–1380

1190—Ladies' Negligee or Dressing-Sack: High or Open Neck; Long or Short One-Seam Straight Sleeves or Flowing Sleeves. The pattern is cut in 7 sizes, 32 to 44 inches bust measure. Cotton crepe is excellent.   Price, 20 cents.

1273 — Ladies' Nightgown: Frills which may be Omitted. 5 sizes, 32 to 40 inches bust measure. This is a very dainty nightgown. It is simple in construction and very comfortable. Nainsook and long-cloth are suitable. Price, 20 cents.

1369—Ladies' House-Dress; Back Extending Over the Shoulders to Form a Yoke; Square or V Neck; Long or Short One-Seam Sleeves. Lower edge about 2⅛ yards. 6 sizes, from 32 to 42 inches bust measure.   Price, 20 cents.

9571—Ladies' One-Piece Negligee: to be Slipped Over the Head; Two Lengths; One-Piece Cap. The pattern is cut in 6 sizes from 32 to 42 inches bust measure. A simple and attractive negligee. Cap not illustrated.   20 cents.

1034—Ladies' Semi-Princess Undergarment. Lower edge of petticoat about 1⅞ yards; of flounce about 2¼ yards. The pattern is cut in 7 sizes, from 32 to 44 inches bust measure. A very simple design.   Price, 20 cents.

1368—Ladies' Envelope Combination Undergarment: Two Outlines at the Lower Edge. For embroidery design illustrated, use Standard transfer 10252. The pattern is cut in 5 sizes from 32 to 40 inches bust measure.   20 cents.

1416 — Ladies' Combination Undergarment: Two Outlines at the Lower Edge. 5 sizes, 32 to 40 inches bust measure. Suitable materials for this undergarment are long-cloth, cambric, dimity, crêpe and nainsook.   Price, 20 cents.

1364—Ladies' Apron and Cap. The pattern is cut in 3 sizes, Small, Medium and Large. **1369**—Ladies' House-Dress. Lower edge about 2⅛ yards. 6 sizes from 32 to 40 inches bust measure. An unusual apron.   20 cents each.

1386

Blouse—1217
Jumper Skirt—1390

Blouse—1329
Jumper Skirt—1404

1398

1386—Ladies' Dress: Back Extending Over the Shoulders to Form a Yoke; Collar in Two Styles; Long Dart-Fitted or Short Sleeves; Bolero which may be Omitted; Two-Piece Skirt. Lower edge about 1½ yards. 6 sizes 32 to 42 inches bust. Price, 25 cents.

1398—Ladies' Dress; in Moyen-Age Style; Long or Short One-Seam Sleeves or Long Dart-Fitted Sleeve; Three-Piece Straight Gathered Tunic; Two-Piece Straight Gathered Skirt. Lower edge about 1½ yards. 5 sizes, 32 to 40 inches bust. Price, 25 cents.

1396—Ladies' Tucked Blouse. 7 sizes, 32 to 44 inches bust measure. **1404**—Ladies' Two-Piece Gathered Skirt: Overblouse Omitted here. Lower edge about 1½ yards. The pattern is cut in 7 sizes from 32 to 44 inches bust measure. Price, 20 cents each.

1217—Ladies' Blouse or Guimpe: High Neck or Open Neck. 9 sizes 32 to 48 inches bust measure. **1390**—Ladies' Two-Piece Skirt and Overblouse. Lower edge about 1⅝ yards. 6 sizes 32 to 42 inches bust measure. Price, 20 cents each.

1329—Ladies' Blouse or Guimpe. 8 sizes, 32 to 46 inches bust measure. **1404**—Ladies' Two-Piece Gathered Skirt and Overblouse. Lower edge about 1½ yards. The pattern is cut in 7 sizes from 32 to 44 inches bust measure. Price, 20 cents each.

1397—Ladies' Blouse. 8 sizes, 32 to 46 inches bust measure. **1393**—Ladies' Two or Three-Piece Skirt. Lower edge about 1½ yards. 6 sizes, 22 to 32 inches waist measure corresponding to 35 to 46 inches hip measure. Price, 20 cents each.

1386

1217
1390

1329
1404

1396
1404

1398

1397
1393

Blouse—1397 Skirt—1393

Blouse—1396 Skirt 1404

Blouse **1359**
Skirt **1202**

Blouse—**1362**
Skirt—**1126**

Sleeveless Coat
1377
Dress—**9843**   **1366**

'Coat—**1373**
Skirt—**1371**

Blouse—**1217**
Jumper Skirt
1371

1362—Ladies' Blouse. 6 sizes, 32 to
42 inches bust measure. **1126**—Ladies'
Two-Piece Skirt: Jumper Omitted here.
For banding design use transfer 10413. Lower
edge about 1⅝ yards. 7 sizes, 32 to 44 inches
bust measure.   Price, 20 cents each.

1359—Ladies' Blouse. 5 sizes, 32 to 40
inches bust measure. **1202**—Ladies' Two-
Piece Skirt. Lower edge measures about 1¾
yds. 9 sizes from 22 to 38 inches waist measure,
corresponding to 35 to 53 inches hip measure.
Price, 20 cents each.

1217—Ladies' Blouse or Guimpe. 9
sizes, 32 to 48 inches bust measure. **1371**—
Ladies' Three-Piece Gathered Skirt and
Overblouse. Lower edge about 1½ yards.
The pattern is cut in 7 sizes from 32 to 44
inches bust measure. Price, 20 cents each.

1366—Ladies' Dress: High or Open
Neck; Long One-Seam Dart-Fitted or Short
Sleeves or Long Two-Seam Sleeves; Vest in
Two Styles; Two-Piece Gathered Skirt. Low-
er edge about 1⅝ yards. 7 sizes, 32 to 44
inches bust measure.   Price, 25 cents.

1377—Ladies' Sleeveless Coat: 30 or
22 Inch Length at the Back. The pattern is
cut in 7 sizes from 32 to 44 inches bust
measure. **9843** — Ladies' Dress: Three-
Piece Skirt. Lower edge about 2 yards. 9
sizes, 32 to 48 bust.   25 cents each.

1373—Ladies' Coat. The pattern is cut
in 9 sizes, 32 to 48 inches bust measure.
1371—Ladies' Three-Piece Gathered
Skirt. Overblouse Omitted here. Lower
edge about 1½ yards. 7 sizes, 32 to 44 inches
bust.   Coat 25 cents; Skirt 20 Cents.

1217
1371   **1371**   **1373**   **1359**
1202   **1362**
1126   **1377**   **9843**   **1366**

1255

1379-A

1385

1379-B

1370

1374

Cap—8787
Coat—1405

1376

1363

1370—LITTLE GIRLS' DRESS: High or Open Neck; Long or Short Sleeves; Bolero Fronts which may be Omitted; Bloomers. 9 sizes, 2 to 10 years. This is a very becoming play dress for the little girl.   Price, 15 cents.

1385—LITTLE GIRLS' DRESS: to be Slipped Over the Head; High or Open Neck; Long or Short Sleeves; The pattern is cut in 9 sizes from 2 to 10 years. A very simple dress for the little girl.   Price, 15 cents.

1374—LITTLE GIRLS' DRESS: High or Open Neck; Long or Short Sleeves; Trimming Pieces which may be Omitted; Bloomers. The pattern is cut in 9 sizes from 2 to 10 years. A very smart design is shown here.   Price, 15 cents.

1376—GIRLS' DRESS: Collar in Two Styles; Long or Short Sleeves; One-Piece Straight Gathered Tunic which may be Omitted; One-Piece Straight Gathered Skirt. 9 sizes, 6 to 14 years.   Price, 15 cents.

8787—CHILD'S CAP. 4 sizes, 2 to 8 years.
1405—BOYS' COAT: In Two Lengths. For the emblem illustrated use Standard transfer 10015. The pattern is cut in 4 sizes from 2 to 8 years.   Price, 15 cents each.

1379—GIRLS' DRESS: Blouse to be Slipped Over the Head; High or Open Neck; Long or Short Sleeves; Straight Plaited or Gathered Skirt Attached to the Underbody. 9 sizes, 6 to 14 years.   Price, 15 cents.

1363—GIRLS' DRESS: to be Slipped Over the Head; High or Open Neck; Long or Short Sleeves; Two-Piece Trimming Band which may be Omitted. The pattern is cut in 9 sizes, from 6 to 14 years.   Price, 15 cents.

1255—GIRLS' AND JUNIORS' DRESS: High or Open Neck; Long or Short Sleeves. For the scallop design illustrated use Standard transfer 10155. The pattern is cut in 11 sizes from 6 to 16 years.   Price, 15 cents.

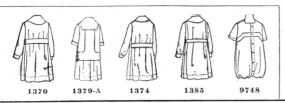

1370   1379-A   1374   1385   9748

9748—CHILD'S ROMPERS: High, Round or Square Neck; Long or Short Sleeves; Two Styles of Belt. 4 sizes, from ½ to 3 years. Unusually comfortable rompers are these. The square neck and short sleeves are very cool for summer. The belt is attractive. Gingham, rep, chambray and galatea are suitable.   Price, 15 cents.

1405   1379-B   1376   1255   1363

WARM, languid days may distress us, but a tiny breeze has whispered to me of the rest, and wonderful bathing in the cool ocean. Our interests are awakened and we think back as to just where our last season's bathing-suit is and we speculate as to whether or not we can make it do for this season. This, of course, is only speculation, for when we see the new smart suits, the old one is scorned. This season Fashion offers us new material, new styles and smart additions to the beach costume. Let me take you through the shops and show you these things.

ONE of the first things we see are the popular bathing stockings called hosettes. They are in all the bright colors which blend so well with the sky, the sands and the ocean. One pretty pair of hosettes were open-work in red-and-white plaid with plain white tops. When worn with the black-and-white-checked slippers and a black taffeta suit the effect is very stunning. Bathing hats are extremely important, and the three models below are very new and becoming. The upper hat was made of blue rubber with a deep white band fitting the head rather snugly. The trimming-piece is a wide piece of white rubber wired into the form of a question-mark giving the effect of a flattened feather. The cap directly below is of rubberized white satin with a gray-and-white band and gray rosette. The tied cap is black.

1382 A   1382 B   1343   1349

1343—LITTLE GIRLS' ONE-PIECE BATHING-SUIT: Buttoned on the Shoulders; Cap. 5 sizes, 4 to 12 years. This is an attractive bathing-suit for the small girl. It is very easy to make. Poplin, mohair, serge and jersey are suitable materials.   Price, 15 cents.

1382—LADIES' BATHING-SUIT in Moyen-Age Style; Shield Sleeve and Bolero may be Omitted; Straight Gathered Skirt in Two Lengths; Cap; Pantalettes in Two Styles. The pattern is cut in 6 sizes from 32 to 42 inches bust measure.   Price, 25 cents.

1349—LADIES' BATHING-SUIT: Back Extending Over the Shoulders; Shield Sleeve and Trimming Piece which may be Omitted; Breeches in Two Styles at the Knee; Cap. The pattern is cut in 5 sizes, 32 to 40 inches bust measure.   Price, 25 cents.

1382   1382   1349   1343

AT THE beach one will need protection from the sun while knitting for our men in service. Nothing would be better than this black-and-white-striped satin parasol and knitting-bag of checked and plain material. The odd joining of the white silk to the black-and-white silk is very unique and smart. This bag is large and roomy and will carry even your light lunch when planning to spend a morning at the beach. The knotted bathing-cap has simplicity of adjustment for its main feature, and combined with this, it stays "put."

THE parasol below is very dainty and pretty and adds a wonderful color. It is made of black-and-white satin and a deep piece of yellow ribbon shirred at the edge. The dull black handle is finished with a mushroom top. Polka-dots are seen in all places and in all forms, and they are very proper when seen on these hosettes and bathing-slippers.

Blouse **1461**
Overblouse and Skirt **1471**

1472

1485

Coat **1486**
Skirt **1478**

Blouse **1329**
Overblouse and Skirt **1478**

1461—LADIES' BLOUSE OR GUIMPE. The pattern is cut in 9 sizes from 32 to 48 inches bust measure. **1471**—LADIES' THREE-PIECE SKIRT AND OVERBLOUSE. Lower edge about 1¾ yards. 9 sizes, 32 to 48 inches bust. Price, 20 cents each.

1472—LADIES' DRESS: Body in One with Three-Quarter Length or Shorter Flowing Sleeves; Convertible Collar or Open Neck; Tie-On Bib which may be Omitted. Lower edge about 2⅜ yards. 7 sizes, 32 to 44 inches bust. Price, 25 cents.

1500—LADIES' BLOUSE. 9 sizes, 32 to 48 inches bust measure. **1478**—LADIES' TWO-PIECE SKIRT. (Overblouse included in pattern but not shown here.) Lower edge about 1⅝ yards. 5 sizes, 32 to 40 bust. Price, 20 cents each.

1486—LADIES' COAT. 6 sizes, 32 to 42 inches bust measure. **1478**—LADIES' TWO-PIECE SKIRT. (Overblouse included in pattern but not shown here.) Lower edge about 1⅝ yards. 5 sizes, 32 to 40 inches bust measure. Coat 25 cents; Skirt 20 cents.

1078—LADIES' GUIMPE. The pattern is cut in 9 sizes from 32 to 48 inches bust measure. **1473**—LADIES' TWO-PIECE SKIRT AND OVERBLOUSE. Lower edge about 1⅝ yards. 7 sizes 32 to 44 inches bust measure. Price, 20 cents each.

DESIGNS FOR AUGUST WEAR

1485—LADIES' DRESS: Long or Short Sleeves; Collar and Separate Overblouse in Two Outlines; Back Extending Over the Shoulders; Three-Piece Skirt; 38-Inch Length or Shorter. Lower edge about 1⅝ yards. The pattern is cut in 6 sizes from 32 to 42 inches bust measure.
Price, 25 cents.

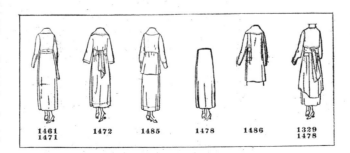

| 1461 1471 | 1472 | 1485 | 1478 | 1486 | 1329 1478 |

1329—LADIES' BLOUSE OR GUIMPE. 8 sizes, 32 to 46 inches bust measure. **1478**—LADIES' SKIRT WITH TUNIC AND OVERBLOUSE. Lower edge about 1⅝ yards. 5 sizes, 32 to 40 inches bust measure. Price, 20 cents each.

1490—LADIES' DRESS: Collar in Two Outlines; Long or Short One-Seam Gathered Sleeves or Long Dart-Fitted Sleeves; Two-Piece Straight Gathered Skirt. Lower edge about 1¾ yards. 7 sizes, 32 to 44 inches bust measure. Price, 25 cents.

1494—LADIES' DRESS: Back Extending Over the Shoulders; Two Styles of Collar; Long or Short One-Seam Gathered Sleeves or Long Dart-Fitted Sleeves; Two-Piece Gathered Skirt. Lower edge about 1¾ yards. 9 sizes, 32 to 48 bust. 25 cents.

1493—LADIES' SLIP-ON BLOUSE. 5 sizes, 32 to 40 bust. **1334**—LADIES' STRAIGHT GATHERED SKIRT. (Overblouse included in pattern but not shown here.) Lower edge about 2 yards. 5 sizes, 32 to 40 inches bust. Price, 20 cents each.

1318—LADIES' DRESS: to be Slipped Over the Head; Back Extending Over the Shoulders; Two Styles of Collar; Long Dart-Fitted Sleeve or Three-Quarter Length Flowing Sleeve. Lower edge about 2⅛ yards. 5 sizes, 32 to 40 bust. Price, 25 cents.

Blouse—**1493**
Skirt—**1334**

For descriptions see opposite page

1490

Blouse—**1500**
Skirt—**1478**

1494   **1493**   **1078**
          1334   **1473**

1490

1485   **1318**   **1500**
                      1478

1494   Guimpe—**1078** Jumper Skirt—**1473**   **1485**   **1318**
                                                                          Scallop—**10155**

Blouse—1500
Skirt—1189

Blouse—1470
Skirt—1275

1507

Blouse—1510
Skirt—1511

1505   1509

FOR THE FASTIDIOUS WOMAN
SIMPLE SMART DESIGNS

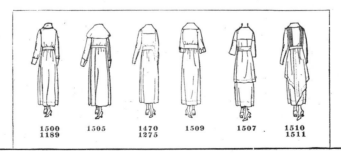

| 1500 | 1505 | 1470 | 1509 | 1507 | 1510 |
| 1189 | | 1275 | | | 1511 |

1500—Ladies' Blouse: Back Extending Over the Shoulders; Two Styles of Collar; Vest Facing which may be Omitted. The pattern is cut in 9 sizes from 32 to 48 inches bust measure. **1189**—Ladies' Two-Piece Skirt: with Short Side Sections· Slightly High Waistline. Lower edge about 1¾ yards. 6 sizes, 22 to 32 waist, corresponding to 35 to 46 hip measure.   Price, 20 cents each.

1505—Ladies' Empire Coat: 50 or 38 Inch Length at the Back; Two Styles of Collar; Two-Seam Sleeves with Slight Fulness at the Top which may be Shrunken Out; Three-Piece Gathered Skirt. The pattern is cut in 6 sizes from 32 to 42 inches bust measure. This is an exceptionally attractive coat. In the shorter length it makes a smart suit coat.   Price, 25 cents.

1470—Ladies' Shirt-Blouse: High or Open Neck or Neckband for Wear with Separate Collars. 9 sizes, 32 to 48 inches bust measure. **1275**—Ladies' Two-Piece Straight Gathered Skirt: Three-Piece Belt in Two Outlines at the Front. Lower edge of skirt about 1¾ yards. 7 sizes, 22 to 34 inches waist measure, corresponding to 35 to 48½ inches hip measure. Price, 20 cents each.

1510—Ladies' Tucked Blouse: Square or V Neck. The pattern is cut in 6 sizes from 32 to 42 inches bust measure. **1511**—Ladies' Two-Piece Skirt. (Overblouse included in pattern but not shown here:) Two-Piece Tunic in Two Outlines at the Lower Edge. Lower edge about 1½ yards. The pattern is cut in 6 sizes from 32 to 42 inches bust measure.   Price, 20 cents each.

1507—Ladies' Dress: Blouse to be Slipped Over the Head; Collar which may be Omitted; Long Dart-Fitted Sleeves or Long or Three-Quarter Length One-Seam Sleeves in Two Sections; Separate Two-Piece Skirt; Slightly High Waistline; 38-Inch Length or Shorter. Lower edge about 1⅝ yards. The pattern is cut in 6 sizes from 32 to 42 inches bust measure.   Price, 25 cents.

1509—Ladies' Dress: Round or V Neck; Long Dart-Fitted Raglan Sleeves or Short Sleeves; Two-Piece Gathered Skirt; 38-Inch Length or Shorter. Lower edge about 1½ yards. The pattern is cut in 6 sizes from 32 to 42 inches bust measure. This dress is good for general wear. Linen, crash, gingham, pongee and jersey are suitable materials.   Price, 25 cents.

Guimpe—**1078**
Overblouse and Skirt
1511

Blouse—**1501**
Skirt—**1511**

Blouse—**1510**
Skirt—**1513**
Transfer—**10418**

1512—A

1512—B

Blouse—**1470** Skirt—**1202**

WOOL CONSERVATION DESIGNS
NEW TUNICS AND COLLARS

1078—LADIES' GUIMPE, in Two Lengths, or Blouse: Long Dart-Fitted Sleeves which may be Omitted. The pattern is cut in 9 sizes from 32 to 48 inches bust measure. **1511**—LADIES' TWO-PIECE SKIRT: and Overblouse which may be Omitted; Two-Piece Tunic in Two Outlines at the Lower Edge. For the scallop design use Standard Transfer 10123. Lower edge about 1½ yards. 6 sizes from 32 to 42 inches bust measure. Price, 20 cents each.

1501—LADIES' BLOUSE: Reversible Closing; Collar in Two Outlines. The pattern is cut in 5 sizes from 32 to 40 inches bust measure. **1511**—LADIES' TWO-PIECE SKIRT: Slightly High Waistline; (Overblouse included in pattern but not shown here.) Two-Piece Tunic in Two Outlines at the Lower Edge. Lower edge about 1½ yards. The pattern is cut in 6 sizes from 32 to 42 inches bust measure. Price, 20 cents each.

1510—LADIES' TUCKED BLOUSE: Square or V Neck; Long One-Seam Gathered Sleeves; Jabot which may be Omitted. 6 sizes, 32 to 42 inches bust measure. **1513**—LADIES' TWO-PIECE SKIRT: (Overblouse included in pattern but not shown here.) Two-Piece Gathered Tunic with or without the Back which may be used as a Cape; 38-Inch Length or Shorter. Lower edge about 1⅝ yards. 6 sizes 32 to 42 inches bust measure. 20 cents each.

1470—LADIES' SHIRT-BLOUSE: High or Open Neck or Neckband for Wear with Separate Collars. The pattern is cut in 9 sizes from 32 to 48 inches bust measure. **1202**—LADIES' TWO-PIECE SKIRT: Two-Piece Belt which may be Omitted; 38-inch Length or Shorter. Lower edge measures about 1¾ yards. The pattern is cut in 9 sizes from 22 to 38 inches waist measure, corresponding to 35 to 53 inches hip measure. Price, 20 cents each.

1512—LADIES' DRESS: Full Vest which may be Omitted; Large Collar or Bib in One with Collar; Long Dart-Fitted or Short Sleeves; Straight Gathered Tunic in Two Lengths; Two-Piece Straight Gathered Skirt; 38-Inch Length or Shorter. Lower edge about 1⅝ yards. The pattern is cut in 6 sizes from 32 to 42 inches bust measure. A smart design is shown here for general or more dressy wear. Pongee or silk are suitable. Price, 25 cents.

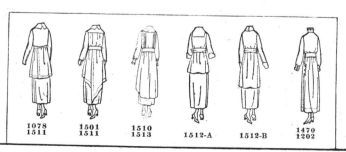

| 1078 | 1501 | 1510 | 1512-A | 1512-B | 1470 |
| 1511 | 1511 | 1513 | | | 1202 |

FASHIONS are always new and interesting. This month our summer styles are cool and ensure real comfort for the warm August days. The designs shown here are simple to make and very charming in their youthfulness. Do not hesitate in the matter of getting these sheer dresses. Purchase a Standard Pattern and be your own dressmaker.

Smock—1465
Breeches—6321

9665

1125

9665

1481

1494

1502

1496

1503

1494—Ladies' Dress: Back Extending Over the Shoulders; Two Styles of Collar; Long or Short One-Seam Gathered Sleeves. Two-Piece Gathered Skirt. Lower edge about 1¾ yards. 9 sizes, 32 to 48 inches bust measure.   Price, 25 cents.

1496—Ladies' Envelope Combination Undergarment: Round or Square Neck; Two Outlines at the Lower Edge. The pattern is cut in 9 sizes from 32 to 48 inches bust measure. Crêpe de Chine and nainsook are suitable. Price, 20 Cts.

1502—Ladies' Apron: in Two Lengths; Body in One with Short Sleeves; Round or V Neck; Cap. The pattern is cut in 7 sizes from 32 to 44 inches bust measure. This good looking apron is simple to make. Gingham and chambray are suitable.   Price, 20 cents.

1503—Ladies' Combination Undergarment: Two Outlines at the Lower Edge; Round Neck or Straight Band; Short Sleeves which may be Omitted. The pattern is cut in 9 sizes from 32 to 48 inches bust measure.   Price, 20 cents.

1481—Ladies' Corset-Cover: Round or V Neck; Two Styles of Sleeves which may be Omitted. The pattern is cut in 9 sizes from 32 to 48 inches bust measure. This design may be used as a brassiere, or a separate lining.   Price, 15 cents.

1472—Ladies' Dress or Negligee: Body in One with Three-Quarter Length of Shorter Flowing Sleeves; Convertible Collar or Open Neck; Tie-On Bib which may be Omitted. (Suitable for Maternity or General Wear). Lower edge about 2⅜ yards. 7 sizes, 32 to 44 bust. 25 cents.

1469—Ladies' Corset Cover or Brassiere: Peplum which may be Omitted. 9 sizes, 32 to 48 inches bust measure. **1489**—Ladies' Pettibockers: Plaited or Gathered Ruffles which may be Omitted. 9 sizes, 22 to 38 inches waist measure. Corset Cover, 15 cents; Pettibockers, 20 cents.

Corset Cover **1469**   Pettibockers **1489**

1469 1489   1481   1494   1502

The Designer
STYLES ARE REPRODUCED BY
Standard Patterns

1496   1503   1472

1472

Blouse—1493
Skirt—1111

Blouse—1500
Skirt—1488

1495

Blouse—1501
Skirt—1100

Blouse—1497
Skirt—1334

TUNICS AND TUCKS FEATURES OF THIS SEASON

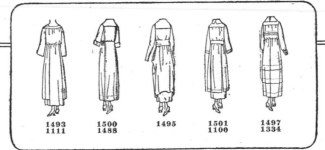

1493
1111

1500
1488

1495

1501
1100

1497
1334

1493—LADIES' SLIP-ON BLOUSE: with or without the Tucks; Long One-Seam Gathered Sleeves or Three-Quarter Length Flowing Sleeves. 5 sizes, 32 to 40 inches bust measure. **1111**—LADIES' FOUR-PIECE GATHERED SKIRT: Straight Side Panels which may be Omitted. Lower edge about 2 yards. 7 sizes, 22 to 34 inches waist measure, corresponding to 36 to 49¼ inches hip.   Price, 20 cents each.

1500—LADIES' BLOUSE: Back Extending Over the Shoulders; Two Styles of Collar; Long or Short One-Seam Gathered Sleeves; Vest Facing which may be Omitted. 9 sizes, 32 to 48 inches bust. **1488**—LADIES' FOUR-PIECE SKIRT: Slightly High Waistline; (Overblouse Included in Pattern but not shown here). 38-inch Length or Shorter. Lower edge about 1⅞ yards. 7 sizes, 32 to 44 bust. 20 cents each.

1495—LADIES' DRESS: Round or V Neck; Long Dart-Fitted or Short Sleeves; Slightly High Waistline; One-Piece Straight Tunic Draped or in Regulation Style; Two-Piece Straight Gathered Skirt; 38-Inch Length or Shorter. Lower edge about 1⅝ yards. The pattern is cut in 6 sizes from 32 to 42 inches bust measure. This attractive dress has an unusually graceful tunic. The round neck and dart-fitted sleeves are style features.   Price, 25 cents.

1497—LADIES' SLIP-ON BLOUSE: with or without the Tucks; Long or Short One-Seam Gathered Sleeve. 6 sizes, 32 to 42 inches bust measure. **1334** — LADIES' ONE-PIECE STRAIGHT GATHERED SKIRT, with Two or Three Tucks; (Overblouse Included in Pattern but not shown here). Lower edge about 2 yards. The pattern is cut in 5 sizes, from 32 to 40 inches bust measure.   Price, 20 cents each.

1501—LADIES' BLOUSE: Reversible Closing; Long One-Seam Gathered or Three-Quarter Length Flowing Sleeves. 5 sizes, 32 to 40 inches bust. **1100**—LADIES' TWO-PIECE SKIRT: Four-Piece Panel Tunic; in Bustle or Regulation Style which may be Omitted. For the braiding design use Standard transfer 10418. Lower edge about 1⅝ yards. 7 sizes, 22 to 34 inches waist or 36 to 49½ inches hip.   Price, 20 cents each.

1509   1495   1507   Coat 1505   Cape and Skirt 1513

SIMPLE AND ATTRACTIVE MODELS

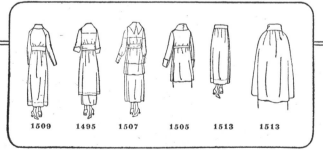

1509   1495   1507   1505   1513   1513

1509—LADIES' DRESS: Round or V Neck; Long Dart-Fitted Raglan Sleeves or Short Sleeves; Two-Piece Gathered Skirt; 38-Inch Length or Shorter. For the Braiding design use Standard transfer 10421. Lower edge about 1½ yards. The pattern is cut in 6 sizes from 32 to 42 inches bust measure. The collar is an unusually attractive feature of this dress. The dress is easy to make.   Price, 25 cents.

1495—LADIES' DRESS: Round or V-Neck; Long Dart-Fitted or Short Sleeves; Slightly High Waistline; One-Piece Straight Tunic Draped or in Regulation Style; Two-Piece Straight Gathered Skirt; 38-Inch Length or Shorter. Lower edge about 1⅝ yards. The pattern is cut in 6 sizes from 32 to 42 inches bust measure. This dress is very good for afternoon wear. Crêpe de Chine and pongee are suitable.   25 cents.

1507—LADIES' DRESS: Blouse to be Slipped Over the Head; Collar which may be Omitted; Long Dart-Fitted Sleeves or Long or Three-Quarter Length One-Seam Sleeves in Two Sections; Separate Two-Piece Skirt; Slightly High Waistline; 38-Inch Length or Shorter. Lower edge about 1⅝ yards. The pattern is cut in 6 sizes from 32 to 42 inches bust measure. This dress developed in a combination of material is very attractive. Silk, satin, and crêpe de Chine are suitable materials.   25 cents.

1513—LADIES' TWO-PIECE SKIRT: High Waistline (Overblouse included in pattern but not shown here); Two-Piece Gathered Tunic with or without the Back which may be Used as a Cape; 38-Inch Length or Shorter. Lower edge about 1⅝ yards. 6 sizes, 32 to 42 inches bust measure. The back tunic of this skirt makes an attractive cape as shown in the illustration above.   Price, 20 cents.

1505—LADIES' EMPIRE COAT: 50 or 38 Inch Length at the Back; Two Styles of Collar; Two-Seam Sleeves with Slight Fulness at the Top which may be Shrunken Out; Three-Piece Gathered Skirt. The pattern is cut in 6 sizes from 32 to 42 inches bust measure. This design makes a smart suit or top coat. It is very becoming and has attractive collar and cuffs. It is easy to make.   Price, 25 cents.

Sleeveless Coat **1482**
Dress **1350**

1498

1403

1350

1508

1353

1335

1378

Dress **1498**
Transfer **10123**

SUITABLE DESIGNS FOR THE GROWING GIRL AND THE YOUNGER SET

8338—LITTLE BOYS' SUIT: High or Square Neck; Long or Short Sleeves; Plain Trousers. 6 sizes, 2 to 7 years. This little boy's suit is very comfortable and cool for either the beach or country. Made of two materials as illustrated, it is very smart. Gingham and chambray are suitable.   Price, 15 cents.

1484—LITTLE GIRLS' AND JUNIORS' PETTICOAT: in Two Styles; Round or Square Neck. The pattern is cut in 8 sizes from 2 to 16 years. This is a necessary garment for the little girl. The neck outlines which may be either square or round are both very good. Nainsook, lawn, batiste, and silk are suitable materials. 15 cents.

1506—BOYS' SUIT: Two-Seam Sleeves; Knickerbockers or Trousers. The pattern is cut in 7 sizes from 8 to 14 years. This is the kind of suit that every little boy loves to wear. The notched collar and pockets are style features. Serge, gabardine, suitings, flannel, duck and drilling are suitable materials.   Price, 20 cents.

1491—CHILD'S SMOCKED OR GATHERED DRESS: High or Open Neck; Long or Short Sleeves. The pattern is cut in 7 sizes from ½ to 6 years. This little dress is very dainty and pretty. The skirt is gathered to the yoke making the dress very becoming. Batiste, lawn and silk are suitable.   Price, 15 cents.

1477—LITTLE GIRLS' DRESS: High or Open Neck; Long or Short Sleeves; Straight Plaited Skirt, Tie-On Panel in Two Lengths which may be Omitted. For the Braiding design illustrated use Standard transfer pattern 10410. The pattern is cut in 9 sizes from 4 to 12 years.   Price, 15 cents.

1499—GIRLS' DRESS: Collar in Two Outlines; Long Dart-Fitted or Short Sleeves. The pattern is cut in 9 sizes from 6 to 14 years. This is a very practical and becoming dress for a girl. The yoke and plaits are style features. Pongee, linen and gingham are suitable materials for it.   Price, 15 cents.

1376—GIRLS' DRESS: Collar in Two Styles; Long or Short Sleeves; One-Piece Straight Gathered Tunic which may be Omitted; One-Piece Straight Gathered Skirt. The pattern is cut in 9 sizes from 6 to 14 years. This design is suitable for embroidery flouncing and batiste.   Price, 15 cents.

1479—LITTLE GIRLS' DRESS: High or Open Neck; Long or Short One-Seam Sleeves; Applied Straps which may be Omitted; Bloomers. The pattern is cut in 9 sizes from 2 to 10 years. This is a very smart-looking dress for afternoon wear. The applied straps add to its attractiveness.   Price, 15 cents.

8338   1484   1491   1499   1506

1476—GIRLS' AND JUNIORS' DRESS, to be Slipped Over the Head; Collar in Two Outlines; Long or Short One-Seam Sleeves; Overblouse and Two-Piece Facing which may be Omitted. The pattern is cut in 9 sizes from 8 to 16 years. This design is especially suitable for combination of materials. It is very easy to make. Gingham, chambray and linen are suitable.   Price, 15 cents.

1476   1477   1479   1376

BLOUSES NOW IMPORTANT

1520

1527

1419

1515

9904

9780
1529

Blouse—9780
Skirt—1529

1524

9904—LADIES' TUCKED OR GATHERED BLOUSE: Back Extending Over the Shoulders; Convertible Collar or Standing Collar with Jabot; Long, Dart-Fitted or Short Sleeves. (May be Attached to a Skirt or Worn Separately.) The pattern is cut in 9 sizes from 32 to 48 inches bust measure. A blouse of unusual charm.   Price, 20 cents.

1520—LADIES' BLOUSE: Back Extending Over the Shoulders; Convertible Collar or Open Neck; Long One-Seam Gathered or Short Sleeves or Long Dart-Fitted Sleeves. (May be Attached to a skirt or Worn Separately. The pattern is cut in 9 sizes from 32 to 48 inches bust measure. A very smart blouse is shown here.   Price, 20 cents.

1527—LADIES' BLOUSE: Back Extending Over the Shoulders; Two Styles of Collar; Long One-Seam Gathered or Short Sleeves or Long Dart-Fitted Sleeves. (May be Attached to a Skirt or Worn Separately). The pattern is cut in 9 sizes from 32 to 48 inches bust measure. Linen is a suitable material for the making of this blouse.   Price, 20 cents.

9780—LADIES' BLOUSE: Back Extending Over the Shoulders; Convertible Collar or Open Neck; Long or Short One-Seam Gathered Sleeves or Long Plain Sleeves. (May be Attached to a Skirt or Worn Separately.) 9 sizes, 32 to 48 inches bust measure. **1529**—LADIES' TWO-PIECE SKIRT: Slightly High Waistline; 38-Inch Length or Shorter (May be Attached to a Blouse or Worn Separately). Lower edge about 1½ yards. 9 sizes, 22 to 38 inches wasit, 35 to 53 inches hip.   Price, 20 cents each.

1524—LADIES' BLOUSE: Back Extending Over the Shoulders; High Neck with Collar in Two Outlines or Open Neck; Long One-Seam Gathered or Short Sleeves or Long Dart-Fitted Sleeves. (May be Attached to a Skirt or Worn Separately.) The pattern is cut in 9 sizes from 32 to 48 inches bust measure. A smart and attractive blouse.   Price, 20 cents.

1419—LADIES' BLOUSE: Back Extending Over the Shoulders to Form a Yoke; Tie-On Vest which may be Omitted; Long or Short One-Seam Gathered Sleeves or Long Dart-Fitted Sleeves. (May be Attached to a Skirt or Worn Separately.) For the embroidery design use Standard transfer 10425. 8 sizes, 32 to 46 inches bust measure.   Price, 20 cents.

1515—LADIES' SLIP-ON BASQUE BLOUSE in Two Lengths; Round or V-Neck, Long Three-Quarter Length or Shorter One-Seam Sleeve. The pattern is cut in 7 sizes from 32 to 44 inches bust measure. This blouse is very becoming to most women. The collar and cuffs are style features. It is very easy to make. Batiste and lawn are suitable.   Price, 20 cents.

1524   1515   1419   1527   9904   1520

WIN THE WAR BY WEARING THESE DESIGNS

Blouse—1524 Skirt—1526   Blouse—1515 Skirt—1202   Blouse—1172 Skirt—1514   Dress—1305   Coat—1522 Skirt—1444
Transfer—10418

1524—Ladies' Blouse. 9 sizes, 32 to 48 bust.
1526—Ladies' Four-Piece Straight Skirt. Lower edge about 1⅜ yards. 7 sizes, 22 to 34 waist, corresponding to 35 to 48½ hip.   Price, 20 cents each.

1515—Ladies' Slip-On Basque Blouse. 7 sizes, 32 to 44 bust. **1202**—Ladies' Two-Piece Skirt. Lower edge about 1¾ yards. 9 sizes, 22 to 38 waist, 35 to 53 hip.   Price, 20 cents each.

1172—Ladies' Blouse. 8 sizes, 32 to 46 bust. **1514**—Ladies' Two-Piece Straight Gathered Skirt. Lower edge about 1½ yards. 8 sizes, 22 to 36 waist, 35 to 51 hip.   Price, 20 cents each.

1305—Ladies' Dress: Two Styles of Collar; Side Body in One with Long Dart-Fitted or Short Sleeves. Lower edge about 2⅛ yards . 5 sizes from 32 to 40 inches bust measure.   Price, 25 cents.

1522—Ladies' Coat. 6 sizes, 32 to 42 bust. **1444**—Ladies' Two-Piece Skirt; (Overblouse included in this pattern.) Lower edge about 1⅝ yards. 9 sizes, 32 to 48 bust.   Coat 25 cts.—Skirt 20 cts.

STANDARD FASHIONS
SEPTEMBER, 1918
PUBLISHED BY STANDARD FASHION COMPANY

12-16 Vandam Street, New York City

─── BRANCHES ───

SAN FRANCISCO,	609 MISSION STREET
ST. LOUIS,	1207 WASHINGTON AVE.
TORONTO, ONTARIO,	472 WELLINGTON STREET, W.
CHICAGO,	2231-2249 SOUTH PARK AVE.
BOSTON,	105 CHAUNCY STREET
ATLANTA,	79-89 MARIETTA STREET
WINNIPEG, MANITOBA,	WOODS WESTERN BUILDING

1515   1522
1202   1444
1524   1172   1305
1526   1514

STYLES ANY WOMAN CAN MAKE

Coat—1535
Skirt—1514

1541   Transfer 10421

1538   Blouse 1540—Skirt 1550

1538—LADIES' DRESS: Back Extending Over the Shoulders; Collar in Two Outlines; Long One-Seam Gathered or Short Sleeves or Long Dart-Fitted Sleeves; Full Tucker and Three-Piece Gathered Peplum which may be Omitted; Separate Two-Piece Straight Gathered Skirt; Slightly High Waistline.   Lower edge about 1½ yards.   **7 sizes, 32 to 44 bust.**   Price, 25 cents.

1541—LADIES' COAT DRESS: Convertible Collar or Open Neck; Long Dart-Fitted or Short Sleeves; Panel Back in Two Lengths which may be Omitted; 38-Inch Length or Shorter.   For the braiding design use Standard transfer 10421.   Lower edge about 1¾ yards. The pattern is cut in 8 sizes from 32 to 46 inches bust measure.   Price 25 cents.

Blouse **1547**—Skirt **1526**   Blouse **1540**—Skirt **1533**

1540—LADIES' BLOUSE: to be Slipped Over the Head; Body in One with Upper Part of Sleeves; Two Styles of Lower Part which may be Omitted; Collar in Two Outlines.   6 sizes, 32 to 42 inches bust measure.   **1533**—LADIES' THREE-PIECE SKIRT: Slightly High Waistline.   Lower edge about 2 yards.   9 sizes, 22 to 38 inches waist or 35 to 53 hip.   Price, 20 cents each.

1547—LADIES' BLOUSE: Back Extending Over the Shoulders; Collar in Two Outlines; Long One-Seam Gathered or Short Sleeves or Long Dart-Fitted Sleeves.   9 sizes, 32 to 48 inches bust measure.   **1526**—LADIES' FOUR-PIECE STRAIGHT SKIRT: Slightly High Waistline.   Lower edge about 1¾ yards. 7 sizes, 22 to 34 inches waist or 35 to 48½ inches hip.   Price, 20 cents each.

1540—LADIES' BLOUSE: to be Slipped Over the Head; Body in One with Upper Part of Sleeves; Two Styles of Lower Part which may be Omitted.   6 sizes, 32 to 42 inches bust measure.   **1550**—LADIES' THREE-PIECE SKIRT: Slightly High Waistline.   Lower edge about 1½ yards.   9 sizes, 22 to 38 inches waist measure, corresponding to 35 to 53 inches hip measure.   20 cents each.

1535—LADIES' COAT: 50 or 45 or 36 Inch Length at the Back; Three or Four Piece Back; Two Styles of Collar; Two-Seam Sleeves.   9 sizes, 32 to 48 inches bust measure.   **1514**—LADIES' TWO-PIECE STRAIGHT GATHERED SKIRT.   Lower edge about 1½ yards.   8 sizes, 22 to 36 inches waist measure, corresponding to 35 to 51 inches hip measure.   Coat, 25 cents; Skirt, 20 cents.

1535   1514

1541   1538   1540   1547   1540
                 1550   1526   1533

FROCKS WITH CHARM
A SMART COAT

Blouse—1530
Skirt—1393

1549

1555

1561

1557

1554

1549—Ladies' Princess Dress: to be Slipped Over the Head; High Round or V Neck; Long Dart-Fitted or Short Sleeves; 38-Inch Length or Shorter. Lower edge about 1¾ yards. The pattern is cut in 7 sizes from 32 to 44 inches bust measure. A very smart dress is shown here. The plaited collar is a novel feature. Price, 25 cents.

1530—Ladies' Blouse: Back Extending Over the Shoulders; Three-Quarter Length One-Seam Sleeves; Collar in Two Lengths. 6 sizes, 32 to 42 inches bust measure. **1393**—Ladies' Two or Three Piece Skirt. Lower edge about 1½ yards. 6 sizes, 22 to 32 inches waist measure, corresponding to 35 to 46 inches hip measure. Price, 20 cents each.

1555—Ladies' Dress: to be Slipped Over the Head; Round or Square Neck; Long Dart-Fitted Sleeves or Three-Quarter Length Flowing Sleeves; Tunic in Two Lengths which may be Omitted; 38-Inch Length or Shorter. Lower edge about 1¾ yards. The pattern is cut in 7 sizes from 32 to 44 inches bust measure. Price, 25 cents.

1557—Ladies' Dress: High, Square or V Neck; Long Dart-Fitted Sleeves or Three-Quarter Length Flowing Sleeves; Draped Overblouse; Two-Piece Skirt; Back Panel which may be Omitted. For the braiding design illustrated on the figure, use Standard transfer pattern 10421. Lower edge about 1⅜ yards. 9 sizes, 32 to 48 bust. Price, 25 cents.

1561—Ladies' Coat: Two Styles at the Lower Edge; 50 or 32 Inch Length at the Back; Two Styles of Convertible Collar; Deep Armhole; Two-Seam Sleeves. The pattern is cut in 7 sizes from 32 to 44 inches bust measure. This coat is very attractive. It is loose-fitting and does not crush the dress underneath. It is simple to make. Price, 25 cents.

1554—Ladies' Dress: Two Styles of Open Neck; Long Dart-Fitted or Short Sleeves; One-Piece Straight Gathered Skirt or Tunic or Two-Piece Skirt; 38-Inch Length or Shorter. Lower edge about 1¾ yards. The pattern is cut in 9 sizes from 32 to 48 inches bust measure. The simplicity of this dress is its style feature. Price, 25 cents.

1549   1530-1393   1555   1561   1557   1554

1555

1553

1538

1549

Blouse—1560 Skirt—1533

1562

DISTINCTIVE MODELS FOR THE MISS
BUTTONS AND BRAID IMPORTANT TRIMMINGS

1549—LADIES' PRINCESS DRESS: to be Slipped Over the Head; High, Round or V Neck; Long Dart-Fitted or Short Sleeves; 38-Inch Length or Shorter. Lower edge about 1¾ yards. The pattern is cut in 7 sizes from 32 to 44 inches bust measure. This dress made on the Princess style is very becoming. The panel back and front gives a youthful line. The long collar is very becoming.   Price, 25 cents.

1555—LADIES' DRESS: to be Slipped Over the Head; Round or Square Neck; Long Dart-Fitted Sleeves or Three-Quarter Length Flowing Sleeves; Tunic in Two Lengths which may be Omitted; 38-Inch Length or Shorter. Lower edge about 1¾ yards. The pattern is cut in 7 sizes from 32 to 44 inches bust measure. This smart dress is made on straight youthful lines. It lends itself nicely to a combination of materials. It is very simple to make. Serge, gabardine and silk are suitable. Price, 25 cents.

1553—LADIES' DRESS: Round or Square Neck; Two Styles of Collar; Long Dart-Fitted Sleeves with or without the Cuff Facing; Sash which may be Omitted; Two-Piece Skirt with Soft Plaits at the Top; 38-Inch Length or Shorter. For the braiding design, use Standard transfer 10410. Lower edge about 1¼ yards. The pattern is cut in 6 sizes from 32 to 42 inches bust measure.   Price, 25 cents.

1538—LADIES' DRESS: Back Extending Over the Shoulders; Collar in Two Outlines; Long One-Seam Gathered or Short Sleeves or Long Dart-Fitted Sleeves; Full Tucker and Three-Piece Gathered Peplum which may be Omitted; Separate Two-Piece Straight Gathered Skirt; Slightly High Waistline; 38-Inch Length or Shorter. Lower edge about 1½ yard. 7 sizes, 32 to 44 inches bust.   Price, 25 cents.

1562—LADIES' DRESS: High, Round or Square Neck; Long Dart-Fitted or Short Sleeves; Revers and Straight Gathered Side Tunics which may be Omitted; Six-Piece Skirt; 38-Inch Length or Shorter. Lower edge about 1¾ yards. 9 sizes, 32 to 48 inches bust measure. This design makes an attractive afternoon dress. The revers are pretty. Serge, gabardine and silk are suitable materials. Price, 25 cents.

1560—LADIES' SLIP-ON BLOUSE: to be Worn Inside or Outside the Skirt; Collarless, Round or V Neck; Long Shoulders; Long or Short One-Seam Flowing Sleeves or Long Dart-Fitted Sleeves. 7 sizes, 32 to 44 inches bust. **1533**—LADIES' THREE-PIECE SKIRT: Slightly High Waistline; 38-Inch Length or Shorter. (May be Attached to a Blouse or Worn Separately). Lower edge about 2 yards. 9 sizes, 22 to 38 inches bust, corresponding to 35 to 53 inches hip.   Price, 20 cents each.

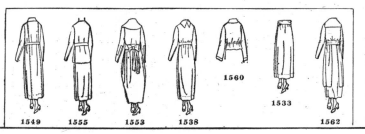

1549   1555   1553   1538

1560

1533

1562

STYLES FOR AT HOME HOURS

1446—LADIES' SHIRT-WAIST DRESS: Back Extending Over the Shoulders; High or Open Neck or Neckband for Wear with Separate Collars; Long One-Seam Sleeves with French or Regulation Cuffs or Short Sleeves; Five-Piece Skirt; Inverted Plait or Gathers at the Back; 38-Inch Length or Shorter. Lower edge about 2¼ yards. 9 sizes, 32 to 48 inches bust measure.   Price, 25 cents.

1081—LADIES' NEGLIGÉE OR DRESSING-SACK: High or Open Neck; Long or Short One-Seam Sleeves in Two Styles at the Lower edge; Cap. 8 sizes, 32 to 46 inches bust measure. This design is very becoming as a dressing-sack or negligée. The long collar is an attractive style feature. The ruffled edge makes a pretty trimming. Crêpe, cotton voile and silk mull are suitable.   Price, 20 cents.

1541—LADIES' COAT DRESS: Convertible Collar or Open Neck; Long Dart-Fitted or Short Sleeves; Panel Back in Two Lengths which may be Omitted; 38-Inch Length or Shorter. Lower edge about 1¾ yards. The pattern is cut in 8 sizes from 32 to 46 inches bust measure. A coat dress like this is very practical and becoming. The side sections are good for combination of material.   Price, 25 cents.

8947—LADIES' ONE-PIECE UNDERBLOUSE OR CORSET COVER: Straight Upper Edge; Shoulder Pieces or Straps; Peplum which may be Omitted. 8 sizes, 32 to 46 inches bust measure. This underblouse or corset cover may be made of nainsook, batiste, lawn, silk mull or crêpe de Chine. It requires very little material and is easily and quickly made.   Price, 15 cents.

1554—LADIES' HOUSE-DRESS: Two Styles of Open Neck; Long Dart-Fitted or Short Sleeves; One-Piece Straight Gathered Skirt or Tunic or Two-Piece Skirt; 38-Inch Length or Shorter. Lower edge about 1¾ yards. The pattern is cut in 9 sizes from 32 to 48 inches bust measure. The house dress is very smart and neat-looking. The collar and pockets are style features.   Price, 25 cents.

1548—LADIES' COMBINATION UNDERGARMENT; Corset-Cover and Envelope Drawers; Tab Extension Lapped Over or Under the Front; Two Outlines at the Lower Edge. The pattern is cut in 9 sizes from 32 to 48 inches bust measure. This undergarment is a very comfortable one. It is simple to make and has no fulness at the waist. It has a choice of outlines at the lower edge. Nainsook, batiste, lawn, dimity and crêpe de Chine are suitable materials.   Price, 20 cents.

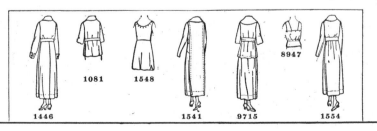

9715—LADIES' HOUSE DRESS: Convertible Collar or Open Neck with Large Collar; Long or Short One-Seam Sleeves; Two-Piece Skirt; Clearing or Shorter Length; Cap. Lower edge about 2¼ yards. 9 sizes, 32 to 48 inches bust measure. This house dress is very comfortable and attractive looking. The outline of the collar is very unusual and smart. The convertible collar is good for the cold weather. The two-piece skirt has just the right fulness and requires little work.   Price, 25 cents.

Blouse—**1560**
Skirt—**1542**

Coat—**1546**
Skirt—**1536**

1541

Blouse—**1530**
Skirt—**1202**

Coat—**1561**
Skirt—**1556**

SUITS AND DRESSES THAT SPEAK OF FALL

1560—LADIES' SLIP-ON BLOUSE; Long Shoulders; Long Dart-Fitted Sleeves. 7 sizes, 32 to 44 inches bust measure. **1542**—LADIES' SIX-PIECE SKIRT: Slightly High Waistline. For braiding design, use transfer 10421. Lower edge about 1⅝ yards. 9 sizes, 22 to 38 inches waist measure, corresponding to 35 to 53 hip.   Price, 20 cents each.

1546—LADIES' COAT: 34-Inch Length at the Back. 7 sizes, 32 to 44 inches bust measure. **1536**—LADIES' TWO-PIECE STRAIGHT SKIRT; Two-Piece Straight Tunic with Soft Plaits or Gathers at the Top which may be Omitted. Lower edge about 1⅜ yards. 8 sizes, 22 to 36 waist, or 35 to 51 hip.   Coat 25 cents; Skirt 20 cents.

1541—LADIES' COAT DRESS: Convertible Collar or Open Neck; Long Dart-Fitted or Short Sleeves; Panel Back in Two Lengths which may be Omitted; 38-Inch Length or Shorter. Lower edge about 1¾ yards. The pattern is cut in 8 sizes from 32 to 46 inches bust measure. A very smart dress is shown here.   Price, 25 cents.

1530—LADIES' BLOUSE: Back Extending Over the Shoulders; Long or Three-Quarter Length One-Seam Sleeves. 6 sizes, 32 to 42 inches bust. **1202**—LADIES' TWO-PIECE SKIRT. Lower edge about 1¾ yards. 9 sizes, 22 to 38 inches waist measure corresponding to 35 to 53 inches hip measure.   Price, 20 cents each.

1560
1542   1536   1546   1202   1530   1541   1556   1561

1561—LADIES' COAT: Two Styles at the Lower Edge; 50 or 32 Inch Length at the Back; Two Styles or Convertible Collar; Deep Armhole; Two-Seam Sleeves. 7 sizes, 32 to 44 inches bust measure. **1556**—LADIES' TWO-PIECE STRAIGHT GATHERED SKIRT. Lower edge about 1¼ yards. 9 sizes, 22 to 38 waist, corresponding to 35 to 53 hip. Coat 25 cents; Skirt 20 cents.

*N*OW that autumn is here reconstruction on our wardrobe has begun in earnest. Every possible piece of cloth is going to tell a story of real work, patriotically done. How proud we will be of the clothes we now wear.

Few of you realize that slight alterations change a dress in such a way that our appearance is generally improved fifty per cent. Remodeling your dresses is not the problem you once thought it was. The fuller skirts and blouses are just the thing for recutting the newer styles which are much narrower.

The straight narrow skirt now popular is the simplest thing to make and gives one a smart appearance. The coats of suits are long and straight. All extra pieces of trimming are being eliminated. Collars are of medium size and the extremely large pockets are not seen.

Blouse—1560
Skirt—1536

1535

Blouse—1530
Skirt—1556

Coat—1546
Skirt—1550

Coat—1522   Skirt—1529

FALL DAYS FAVOR THESE STYLES

1535—Ladies' Coat: 50 or 45 or 36 Inch Length at the Back; Three or Four-Piece Back; Two Styles of Collar; Two-Seam Sleeves with Slight Fulness at the Top which may be Shrunken Out. The pattern is cut in 9 sizes from 32 to 48 inches bust measure. A very smart coat is shown in the above illustration.   Price 25 cents.

1560—Ladies' Slip-On Blouse. 7 sizes, 32 to 44 inches bust measure. **1536**—Ladies' Two-Piece Straight Skirt with Soft Plaits at the Top. Lower edge about 1⅜ yards. 8 sizes, 22 to 36 inches waist measure, corresponding from 35 to 51 inches hip measure. For braiding design use Standard transfer 10421.   Price, 20 cents each.

1522—Ladies' Coat: 45 or 36-Inch Length at the Back; Scarf and Large Collar Worn Together or Separately; Two-Seam Sleeves with Slight Fulness at the Top which may be Shrunken Out. 6 sizes, 32 to 42 bust. **1529**—Ladies' Two-Piece Skirt: Slightly High Waistline. Lower edge about 1½ yards. 9 sizes, 22 to 38 inches waist or 35 to 53 inches hip measure.
Coat 25 cents; Skirt 20 cts.

1546—Ladies' Coat: 34-Inch Length at the Back; Two-Seam Sleeves with Slight Fulness at the Top which may be Shrunken Out. 7 sizes, 32 to 44 inches bust measure. **1550** Ladies' Three-Piece Skirt. Lower edge about 1½ yards. 9 sizes, 22 to 38 inches waist measure, corresponding from 35 to 53 inches hip measure.   Coat 25 cents; Skirt 20 cents.

1530—Ladies' Blouse: Back Extending Over the Shoulders; Collar in Two Lengths and Three-Piece Gathered Peplum which may be Omitted. 6 sizes, 32 to 42 bust. **1556**—Ladies' Two-Piece Straight Gathered Skirt: Panel Back which may be Omitted. Lower edge about 1¼ yards. 9 sizes, 22 to 38 waist, 35 to 53 hip. 20 cents each.

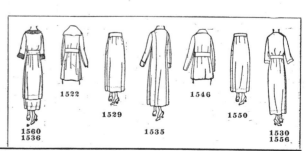

1522   1529   1535   1546   1550
1560 1536   1530 1556

1519   1521   1523   1516   1531   1534   1525

1519—GIRLS' AND JUNIORS' BOX-PLAITED DRESS, to be Slipped Over the Head; High or Open Neck; Yoke Facing which may be Omitted; Long or Short Sleeves; Bloomers. The pattern is cut in 11 sizes from 6 to 16 years.   Price, 15 cents.

1521—LITTLE GIRLS' DRESS: In Two Lengths; High or Open Neck; Long or Short Sleeves; Bloomers. For the Smocking design use Standard transfer 10423. The pattern is cut in 9 sizes from 2 to 10 years.   Price, 15 cents.

1523—LITTLE GIRLS' APRON: Plaited or Gathered at the Front: High or Open Neck; Long or Short Sleeves which may be Omitted; Bloomers. 7 sizes: 2 to 8 years. Chambray and gingham are excellent materials.   Price, 15 cents.

1516—LITTLE GIRLS' COAT: Convertible Collar; Two-Seam Sleeves with Slight Fulness at the Top which may be Shrunken Out. 6 sizes, 2 to 12 years. A smart and attractive coat is illustrated here.   Price, 15 cents.

1518—LITTLE GIRLS' BOX-PLAITED DRESS: Two Styles of Collar; Long or Short Sleeves; Bloomers. 11 sizes: 2 to 12 years. A smart and simple dress is shown here. Linen and gingham are suitable.   Price, 15 cents.

MODELS THAT CONSERVE MATERIAL

1525—GIRLS' AND JUNIORS' SMOCKED OR GATHERED DRESS: To be Slipped Over the Head; Two Lengths; Slightly Open or Open Neck; Bloomers. Smocking design transfer 10423. The pattern is cut in 11 sizes from 6 to 16 yrs. Price, 15 cts.

1534—LITTLE GIRLS' DRESS: In Two Lengths; High or Open Neck; Long or Short Sleeves; Bloomers. The pattern is cut in 9 sizes from 2 to 10 years. Gingham and chambray are suitable materials for this design.   Price, 15 cents.

1531—GIRLS' AND JUNIORS' SUIT: Convertible Collar; Two-Seam Sleeves with Slight Fulness at the Top which may be Shrunken Out; One-Piece Straight Skirt with Suspenders. 5 sizes from 8 to 16 years.   Price, 20 cents.

1551—GIRLS' AND LITTLE GIRLS' DRESS: Body in One with Long or Short Sleeves; Straight Gathered Skirt. The pattern is cut in 11 sizes, from 4 to 14 years. Voile is an excellent material for this dress.   Price, 15 cents.

1519   1521   1523   1516   1518   1518   1551   1551   1534   1531   1525

DESIGNED FOR GIRLS
SUITED TO THEIR NEEDS

1534—LITTLE GIRLS' DRESS: in Two Lengths; High or Open Neck; Long or Short Sleeves; Bloomers. The pattern is cut in 9 sizes from 2 to 10 years. For the scallop design use Standard transfer 10155.   Price, 15 cents.

1563—GIRLS' AND JUNIORS' PAJAMAS: in Two Styles; Body and Upper Part of Sleeve in One, the Lower Part of Sleeves which may be Omitted; Round or V Neck. 7 sizes, 4 to 16 years.   Price, 15 cents.

1525—GIRLS' AND JUNIORS' SMOCKED OR GATHERED DRESS: to be Slipped Over the Head; Two Lengths; Slightly Open or Open Neck; Long or Short Sleeves; Bloomers. The pattern is cut in 11 sizes from 6 to 16 years.   15 cents.

1521—LITTLE GIRLS' DRESS: in Two Lengths; High or Open Neck; Long or Short Sleeves; Bloomers. The pattern is cut in 9 sizes from 2 to 10 years. Chambray and gingham are excellent materials.   Price, 15 cents.

1516—LITTLE GIRLS' COAT: Convertible Collar; Two-Seam Sleeves with Slight Fulness at the Top which may be Shrunken Out. The pattern is cut in 6 sizes from 2 to 12 years. A smart and simple coat.   Price, 15 cents.

1537—GIRLS' DRESS: in Moyen-Age Style; to be Slipped Over the Head; High or Open Neck; Long or Short Sleeves; Tunic which may be Omitted; One-Piece Gathered Skirt. 9 sizes, 6 to 14 years.   Price, 15 cents.

1552—LITTLE GIRLS' AND JUNIORS' NIGHTGOWN: High or Open Neck; Long or Short Sleeves. 8 sizes from 2 to 16 years. Nainsook, long-cloth and flannelet are among the materials suitable for this design.   Price, 15 cents.

1543—GIRLS' AND JUNIORS' DRESS: to be Slipped Over the Head; High or Open Neck; Long Dart-Fitted or Short Sleeves; Bloomers. The pattern is cut in 11 sizes from 6 to 16 years.   Price, 15 cents.

1518—LITTLE GIRLS' BOX-PLAITED DRESS: Two Styles of Collar; Long or Short Sleeves; Bloomers. The pattern is cut in 11 sizes from 2 to 12 years. Linen and galatea are suitable materials for this dress.   Price, 15 cents.

BLOUSES FEATURING SIMPLICITY AND SMARTNESS

1753—Ladies' Blouse: Square or V Neck; Collar in Two Styles; Long Dart-Fitted or Three-Quarter Length Sleeve or Long One-Seam Gathered Sleeve. (May be Attached to a Skirt or Worn Separately.) 7 sizes 32 to 44 inches bust measure. The construction of this blouse gives one an opportunity to use a combination of materials.   Price, 25 cents.

1722—Ladies' Blouse: Convertible Collar or Open Neck; Long One-Seam Sleeve or Long Dart-Fitted or Short Sleeve. (May be Attached to a Skirt or Worn Separately.) For the scallop design illustrated on Jabot of figure, use Standard transfer pattern 10413. This pattern is cut in 9 sizes from 32 to 48 inches bust measure. The collar and jabot make this blouse very pretty.   Price, 20 cents.

1743—Ladies' Slip-On Blouse: Closed on the Shoulders and to be Worn Inside or Outside the Skirt; Round or Square Neck; Long Dart-Fitted or Short Sleeve or Long One-Seam Gathered Sleeve. This pattern is cut in 7 sizes from 32 to 44 bust measure. The yoke and frill with tucks on either side are features of this blouse.   Price, 25 cents.

1745—Ladies' Shirt Blouse: Convertible Collar or Open Neck or Neckband for Wear with Separate Collars; Long One-Seam Sleeve with Cuff in Two Styles or Short Sleeve or Long Dart-Fitted Sleeve. The pattern is cut in 9 sizes from 32 to 48 inches bust measure. This blouse has many possibilities. The pointed collar shown in the illustration is attractive while the convertible one is more tailored. 25 cents.

1749—Ladies' Blouse: Two Styles of Open Neck; Long Shoulders; Long or Short One-Seam Flowing Sleeves or Long Dart-Fitted Sleeve. (May be Attached to a Skirt or Worn Separately. This pattern is cut in 6 sizes from 32 to 42 inches bust measure. The collar and the panel front and back are most attractive features of this blouse.   Price, 25 cents.

1747—Ladies' Tucked or Gathered Slip-On Blouse: To be Worn Inside or Outside the Skirt; Long One-Seam Gathered or Short Sleeves or Long Dart-Fitted Sleeve. This pattern is cut in 7 sizes from 32 to 44 inches bust measure. A tucked blouse such as this is one of the most attractive blouses worn this season. The collar and cuffs of contrasting material make it very pretty.   Price, 25 cents.

1746—Ladies' Bouse or Guimpe: High, Square or V Neck; long One-Seam Flowing Sleeve or Long Dart-Fitted Sleeve which may be Omitted. This pattern is cut in 9 sizes from 32 to 48 inches bust measure. The high collar and pointed cuffs are smart. As a guimpe it is very serviceable and suitable to wear with jumper shirts. Taffeta, satin, linen and combinations of materials are suitable.   Price, 25 cents.

1753

1753

1749

1749

1746

1746

1747

1745

1745

1747   1746

1747

1746

1722

1743   1746

1743   1746   1747   1722

THE MID-WINTER
STYLES
ARE VERY SMART

1755
1593

Blouse—**1755**
Skirt—**1593**

1755—LADIES'
BLOUSE: High or
Open Neck; Long
or Three - Quarter
Length Flowing
Sleeve or Long
Dart-Fitted Sleeve.
This pattern is cut
in 8 sizes from 32 to
46 bust. **1593**—
LADIES' TWO-PIECE
SKIRT. Lower
edge about 1¾
yards. 9 sizes, 22
to 38 inches waist,
or 35 to 53 inches
hip measure.
Blouse, 25 cents;
Skirt, 20 cents.

1761—LADIES'
NORFOLK COAT:
34 or 28-Inch
Length at the
Back; Notched or
Shawl Collar or
Collarless. 7 sizes,
from 32 to 44 bust.
1757—LADIES'
FOUR-PIECE
SKIRT: Slot Seam
at the Front and
Back. Lower edge
about 1⅝ yards.
9 sizes, 22 to 38
waist, or 35 to 53
hip measure.
25 cents each.

Coat—**1761**
Skirt—**1757**

1761

1757

1762

1762 — LADIES'
DRESS:
Three-Quarter Length One-
Seam Flowing Sleeves or Long
Dart-Fitted Sleeves; One-Piece
Plaited or Gathered Straight
Skirt. 9 sizes, from 32 to 48
bust.   Price, 25 cents.

1768

1583

Coat—**1768**
Skirt—**1583**

1768—LADIES' COAT: 8
sizes, 32 to 46 bust. **1583**—
LADIES' SKIRT. Lower edge
about 1½ yards. 8 sizes, 22 to
36 waist; 35 to 51 hip measure.
Coat, Price, 25 cents; Skirt,
Price, 20 cents.

1768

1750

1750

1750—LADIES' DRESS: Long One-
Seam Flowing Sleeve or Long Dart-
Fitted Sleeve; Two-Piece Straight Gathered Tunic; Overblouse and Tunic Front
may be Omitted; Two-Piece Skirt. 7
sizes, 32 to 44 bust.   Price, 25 cents.

1743
1649

Blouse—**1743**
Skirt—**1649**
Transfer—**10437**

1743—LADIES' SLIP-ON BLOUSE:
Use Standard transfer pattern 10437. 7
sizes, 32 to 44 inches bust. **1649**—
LADIES' SKIRT. Lower edge about 1¾
yard. 7 sizes, 22 to 34 waist, or 35 to 48½
hip. Blouse, 25 cents; Skirt, 20 cents.

Dress
1775
Transfer
4216

1764

1780

Blouse—**1766**
Skirt—**1779**

Blouse—**1721**
Overblouse Skirt—**1758**
Transfer—**10407**

Tam **1680**
Muff **1676**
Coat **1761**
Skirt **1757**

SIMPLE STYLES MAKE FOR SMART DRESSES OR SUITS

1764   1780   1775   1766
1779   1721
1758   1761   1757

1764—LADIES' SLIP-ON DRESS: Convertible Collar; Vest with Round or Square Neck; Long Dart-Fitted Sleeves or Three-Quarter Length or Shorter One-Seam Flowing Sleeve; 37-Inch Length or Shorter. Lower edge about 1¾ yards. 8 sizes 32 to 46 inches bust measure. An attractive combination of material is shown here. Price, 25 cts.

1775—LADIES' DRESS: Side Body in One with Long or Three-Quarter Length One-Seam Sleeves; Round or Square Neck; Blouse Front in One with Front of Three-Piece Tunic in Two Lengths; Two-Piece Skirt; 37-Inch Length or Shorter. Lower edge about 1⅝ yards. 6 sizes, 32 to 42 inches bust measure. Price, 25 cents.

1780—LADIES' SLIP-ON DRESS: Closed on the Shoulders; Collarless or Open Neck; Long or Three-Quarter Length One-Seam Sleeves or Long Dart-Fitted Sleeves; 37-Inch Length or Shorter. Lower edge of skirt measures about 1⅝ yards. This pattern is cut in 7 sizes from 32 to 44 inches bust measure.   Price, 25 cents.

1680—TAM. 3 sizes, ladies', misses' and girls. **1676**—MUFF. 2 sizes, ladies' and misses'. **1761**—LADIES' NORFOLK COAT. 7 sizes, 32 to 44 bust. **1757**—LADIES' FOUR-PIECE SKIRT: Lower edge about 1⅝ yards. 9 sizes, 22 to 38 waist, or 35 to 53 hip. Tam, Price, 15 cents; Muff, 20 cents; Coat and Skirt, 25 cents each.

1721—LADIES' BLOUSE: Body in One with Long Dart-Fitted or Short Sleeve; High, Square or V Neck. 7 sizes, 32 to 44 inches bust. **1758**—LADIES' TWO-PIECE SKIRT: Two-Piece Yoke in One with Panels; Overblouse. Lower edge about 1⅝ yards. 6 sizes, from 32 to 42 inches bust measure. Blouse 20 cents; Skirt 25 cents.

1766—LADIES' SLIP-ON BOX-PLAITED BLOUSE: Closed on the Shoulders and to be worn Inside or Outside the Skirt. 6 sizes, 32 to 42 inches bust. **1779**—LADIES' FOUR-PIECE PLAITED SKIRT: Belt in One with Front and Back Gores. Lower edge about 2½ yards. 7 sizes, 32 to 44 inches bust.   Price, 25 cents each.

1783

1775

Dress 1783
Transfer 4216

1787

1783

Muff—1676
Dress—1787

JANUARY CALLS FORTH FURS
WARM DRESSES AND SUITS

1783   1775   1783   1783   1787

1783—Ladies' Slip-On Dress: Closed on the Shoulders; Collarless, Round or Square Neck; Long or Three-Quarter Length One-Seam Flowing Sleeve or Long Dart-Fitted Sleeve; Panels which may be Omitted or the Front Panels Cut Off to Simulate a Collar; 37-Inch Length or Shorter. Lower edge about 1¾ yards. This pattern is cut in 7 sizes from 32 to 44 inches bust measure.   Price, 25 cents.

1775—Ladies' Dress: Side Body in One with Long or Three-Quarter Length One-Seam Sleeves. Round or Square Neck; Collar in Two Outlines; Blouse Front in One with Front of Three-Piece Tunic in Two Lengths; Two-Piece Skirt; 37-Inch Length or Shorter. Lower edge about 1⅝ yards. This pattern is cut in 6 sizes from 32 to 42 inches bust measure.   Price, 25 cents.

FASHIONS for this time of the year continue on their straight and narrow paths. Dresses are simple affairs, boldly flaunting the fact that they are minus of much trimming. Braid, fringe and fur are popular for trimming. Fur is not essential, for there are many substitutes, such as fur cloth pile fabrics; and in some cases wool and silk floss can be camouflaged quite wonderfully.

1676—Ladies' and Misses' Cape: Scarf; Muff. The pattern is cut in 2 sizes, ladies and misses. This charming set is just what is needed for the cold winds of January. And now when we are conserving in all things what better way than in the matter of furs, for they have increased greatly in the last year.   Price, 20 cents.

1787—Ladies' Dress: High or Open Neck; Long or Three-Quarter Length One-Seam Flowing Sleeve or Long Dart-Fitted Sleeve; Panels and Vest which may be Omitted; 37-Inch Length or Shorter. Lower edge about 1⅝ yards. This pattern is cut in 6 sizes from 32 to 42 inches bust measure. This smart simple dress has the narrow lines of the season and its own individuality.   Price, 25 cents.

THE colors that we see now are brown in all its warm shades, henna or terra cotta, dark green and navy blue. Wool velours and many of the shoddy materials are exceedingly smart. The small amount of material needed in present designs permits us to have some new dresses. But we are still making over many of our last season's dresses in order to conserve wool.

Blouse—1755
Skirt—1441

Skirt-Blouse—1745
Skirt—1757

Coat—1768   Skirt—1452

Blouse—9593
Skirt—1791
Transfer—10086

1750

Coat—1786
Skirt—1471

THE SLIM SILHOUETTE AND LONGER SKIRT ARE STILL POPULAR

1755—LADIES' BLOUSE: High or Open Neck; Long or Three-Quarter Length Flowing Sleeve or Long Dart-Fitted Sleeves. 8 sizes, 32 to 46 bust. **1441**—LADIES' ONE-PIECE STRAIGHT GATHERED SKIRT. Lower edge about 1⅝ yards. 8 sizes, 22 to 36 inches waist measure, corresponding to 35 to 51 inches hip measure. A simple and neat combination is shown. Blouse, 25 cents; Skirt, 20 cents.

1745—LADIES' SHIRT-BLOUSE: Long One-Seam Sleeve with Cuff in Two Styles or Short Sleeve or Long Dart-Fitted Sleeves. 9 sizes, 32 to 48 inches bust measure. **1757**—LADIES' FOUR-PIECE SKIRT: Slot Seam at the Front and Back. Lower edge about 1⅝ yards. The pattern is cut in 9 sizes, 22 to 38 inches waist, corresponding to 35 to 53 inches hip. Price, 25 cents each.

1768—LADIES' COAT: 34 or 28 Inch Length at the Back; Convertible or Shawl Collar; Two-Seam Sleeves with Slight Fulness at the Top which may be Shrunken Out. 8 sizes, 32 to 46 inches bust. **1452**—LADIES' TWO-PIECE SKIRT. Lower edge about 2 yards. The pattern is cut in 9 sizes from 32 to 48 inches bust measure. A smart coat suit is shown. Coat, Price 25 cents; Skirt, 20 cents.

1786—LADIES' COAT: 36-Inch Length at the Back; Two Styles of Collar; Two-Seam Sleeves with Slight Fulness at the Top which may be Shrunken Out. The pattern is cut in 7 sizes from 32 to 44 inches bust. **1471**—LADIES' THREE-PIECE SKIRT: Lower edge about 1¾ yards. The pattern is cut in 9 sizes from 32 to 48 inches bust measure. Coat Price, 25 cents; Skirt Price, 20 cents.

1750—LADIES' DRESS: High or Open Neck; Long One-Seam Flowing Sleeve or Long Dart-Fitted Sleeves; Slightly High Waistline; Two-Piece Straight Gathered Tunic; Overblouse and Tunic Front which may be Omitted; Two-Piece Straight Skirt; 37-Inch Length or Shorter. Lower edge measures about 1½ yards. This pattern is cut in 7 sizes from 32 to 44 inches bust. Price, 25 cents.

9593—LADIES' BLOUSE: to be Slipped Over the Head. 5 sizes, 32 to 40 inches bust measure. **1791**—LADIES' SKIRT: Slightly High Waistline; Two-Piece Yoke with Front in One with Skirt Front; One-Piece Straight Gathered Skirt Section; One-Piece Tunic. Lower edge about 1⅝ yards. 7 sizes, 22 to 34 inches waist, to 35 to 48½ inches hip measure. Blouse, 20 cents; Skirt, 25 cents.

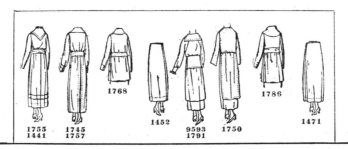

1755
1441

1745
1757

1768

1452

9593
1791

1750

1786

1471

FOR THE BOUDOIR AND KITCHEN

1119—LADIES' NEGLIGEE OR DRESSING-SACK: Body in One with Short Sleeves. 7 sizes, 32 to 44 inches bust measure. This dressing-sack is very easily made, having the body part in one with the sleeves. The ruffled edging and the sash slipping under at the sides makes it dainty and pretty. Price, 20 cents.

1116—LADIES' NIGHTGOWN: Short One-Seam Sleeves which may be Omitted. The pattern is cut in 7 sizes from 32 to 44 inches bust measure. This is an unusually dainty design for a nightgown. The points at the shoulders tied with small ribbon bows is pretty. Use transfer 10286. Price, 20 cents.

1756—LADIES' DRESS: Back Extending Over the Shoulders; Convertible Collar or Open Neck; Long One-Seam Gathered or Short Sleeve or Long Dart-Fitted Sleeve; Four-Piece Skirt Attached to the Blouse or Worn Separately. Lower edge about 2 yards. 9 sizes from 32 to 48 bust measure. Price, 25 cents.

1748—LADIES' SLIP-ON APRON: Short Sleeves which may be Omitted; Cap. This pattern is cut in 9 sizes from 32 to 48 bust. A most unusual and becoming apron is the one illustrated here. The round neck is quite attractive. Besides being good-looking, it is practical and comfortable for housework. Price, 25 cents.

LINGERIE OF DISTINCTION

1336—LADIES' NEGLIGEE OR DRESSING-SACK. Long or Short One-Seam Flowing Sleeves; Three-Piece Gathered Skirt. 7 sizes, 32 to 44 inches bust measure. This design has an attractive collar and pointed sleeves. It is easy to make. Crêpe, albatross, cashmere and challis are suitable. Price, 20 cents.

1742—LADIES' STEP-IN UNDERGARMENT. This pattern is cut in 7 sizes from 32 to 44 bust. Where can a prettier undergarment than this be found? The outline of the yoke and the body being gathered to it is very charming. It is also a comfortable undergarment. For Scallop use transfer 10155. Price, 25 cents.

1751—LADIES' APRON: Body in One with Short Sleeve in Two Lengths, High or Open Neck. Cap. The pattern is cut in 7 sizes from 32 to 44 bust. This is another becoming apron for the neat housekeeper. The pointed collar, cuffs and trimming pieces on pockets are novel features. Price, 25 cents.

The Designer STYLES ARE REPRODUCED BY **Standard Patterns**

Blouse 1746
Jumper Skirt 1793

1789

Blouse
9811
Jumper Skirt 1779

Shirt-Blouse 1790
Skirt 1791

1769

MANY PRACTICAL NEEDS MET BY THESE DESIGNS
FEATURING PANELS AND PLAITS

1746—LADIES' GUIMPE OR BLOUSE: High, Square or V Neck. 9 sizes, 32 to 48 bust. **1793**—LADIES' TWO-PIECE SKIRT: Slightly High Waistline; Overblouse which may be Omitted; 37-Inch Length or Shorter. Lower edge about 1⅞ yards. This pattern is cut in 8 sizes from 32 to 46 inches bust measure.   Price, 25 cents each.

1789—LADIES' SLIP-ON DRESS: in Moyen-Age Style; Closed on the Shoulders; Collarless or Open Neck; Long or Three-Quarter Length One-Seam Flowing Sleeve or Long Dart-Fitted Sleeve; Overblouse which may be Omittted; Two-Piece Skirt. Lower edge about 1½ yards. This pattern is cut in 7 sizes from 32 to 44 inches bust measure.   25 cents.

9811—LADIES' BLOUSE: 5 sizes, 32 to 40 inches bust measure. **1779**—LADIES' FOUR-PIECE PLAITED SKIRT: Slightly High Waistline; Belt in One with Front and Back Gores; Overblouse which may be Omitted; 37-Inch Length or Shorter. Lower edge about 2½ yards. 7 sizes from 32 to 44 inches bust measure.   Blouse, 20 cents; skirt, 25 cents.

1790—LADIES' SHIRT BLOUSE: Convertible Collar or Open Neck or Neckband for Wear with Separate Collar. 9 sizes, 32 to 48 inches bust measure **1791**—LADIES' SKIRT: Slightly High Waistline; Two-Piece Yoke with Front in One with Skirt Front. Lower edge about 1⅝ yards. 7 sizes, 22 to 34 waist, or 35 to 48½ hip.   Price, 25 cents each.

1769—LADIES' DRESS: Collar in Two Outlines; Long Dart-Fitted or Three-Quarter Length Sleeve; Body Lining in Square or V Neck; Two-Piece Trimming Pieces which may be Omitted; 37-Inch Length or Shorter. Lower edge about 1½ yards. 7 sizes from 32 to 44 inches bust measure.   Price, 25 cents.

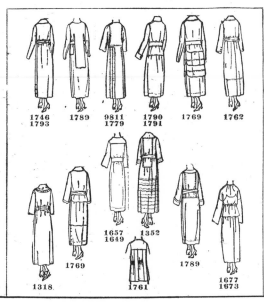

1746
1793

1789

9811
1779

1790
1791

1769

1762

1657
1649

1352

1769

1789

1318

1761

1677
1673

1352—LADIES' DRESS: to be Slipped Over the Head; Fronts Rolled to Form Revers; Long Dart-Fitted Sleeves or Short Tucked Sleeves; Two-Piece Gathered Skirt with or without the Tucks; 38-Inch Length or Shorter. Lower edge about 2 yards. The pattern is cut in 7 sizes, 32 to 44 inches bust measure.   Price, 25 cents.

1761—LADIES' NORFOLK COAT: 34 or 28 inch length at the back. Notched or shawl collar or collarless. 7 sizes, 32 to 44 inches bust. **1318**—LADIES' DRESS: to be Slipped Over the Head; Back Extending Over the Shoulders; 38-Inch Length or Shorter. Lower edge about 2½ yards. 5 sizes, 32 to 40 inches bust measure.   Price, 25 cents each.

1657—LADIES' BLOUSE: to be Slipped Over the Head and Worn Inside or Outside the Skirt; Three-Quarter Length One-Seam Sleeves or Long Sleeves. 6 sizes, 32 to 42 inches bust measure. **1649**—LADIES' TWO-PIECE STRAIGHT GATHERED SKIRT. Lower edge about 2 yards. 7 sizes, 20 to 34 inches waist or 35 to 48½ hip measure.   20 cents each.

1762—LADIES' DRESS: Back Extending Over the Shoulders; Three-Quarter Length One-Seam Flowing Sleeves or Long Dart-Fitted Sleeves; One-Piece Plaited or Gathered Straight Skirt Attached to the Blouse or Worn Separately; 37-Inch Length or Shorter. Lower edge about 1¾ yards. 9 sizes, 32 to 48 inches bust.   Price, 25 cents.

1677—LADIES' SLIP-ON BLOUSE: In Two Lengths and to be Worn Inside or Outside the Skirt; Long Shoulders. 7 sizes, 32 to 44 inches bust measure. **1673**—LADIES' ONE OR TWO-PIECED DRAPED SKIRT: Slightly High Waistline; Two Outlines at the Front. Lower edge about 1¼ yards. 7 sizes, 22 to 34 waist, or 35 to 48½ hip.   Price, 20 cents each.

Coat—1761
Dress—1318

Blouse—1657
Skirt—1649

Dress—1769

Other descriptions and illustrations are shown on page 8. [p. 146]

Dress—1352   Dress—1789   Transfer—10086   Dress—1762   Scallop—10155   Blouse—1677   Skirt—1673

1744

1785
Transfer
4216

1776

1782

1759

1752

1781

Coat 1778
Skirt 1588

SIMPLE FROCKS ON NARROW LINES

1782..Misses' and Small Women's Dress: Slip-On Blouse. For the Smocking design illustrated, use Standard transfer pattern 4478. Lower edge about 1½ yds. 4 sizes, 14 to 20 years. 25 cts.

1776—Misses and Small Women's Dress: Long Dart-Fitted Sleeve or Three-Quarter Length Sleeve. Lower edge about 1⅝ yards. 4 sizes, 14 to 20 years.   Price, 25 cents.

1744..Misses' and Small Women's Dress. For the emblems, use transfer pattern 10015. Lower edge with plaits drawn out about 2⅛ yards. 4 sizes, 14 to 20 years.   Price, 25 cents.

1778—Misses' and Small Women's Coat. 4 sizes, 14 to 20 years. **1588**—Misses' and Small Women's Skirt. Lower edge about 1½ yards. 4 sizes, 14 to 20 years. Coat 25 cents; Skirt 15 cents.

1752..Misses' and Small Women's Dress: Collarless or Open Neck; Long Dart-Fitted or Flowing Sleeves; Panel Back in Two Lengths; Separate Two-Piece Skirt. Lower edge about 1½ yards. 4 sizes, 14 to 20 years.   Price, 25 cents.

1781..Misses' and Small Women's Dress: Blouse in Regulation or Middy Style; Straight Plaited Skirt; Slightly High Waistline. Lower edge about 2½ yards. 4 sizes, 14 to 20 years. For emblem use Transfer 10015. Price, 25 cents.

1785..Misses' and Small Women's Slip-On Dress: Closed on the Shoulders; Overblouse and One-Piece Trimming Bands may be Omitted. Lower edge about 1½ yards. 4 sizes, 14 to 20 years.   Price, 25 cents.

1759..Misses' and Small Women's Dress: Back Extending Over the Shoulders; Long Dart-Fitted Sleeves or Long One-Seam Flowing Sleeves. Lower edge about 1⅝ yards. 4 sizes, 14 to 20 years.   Price, 25 cents.

1781   1778   1588   1785   1744   1776   1782   1759   1752

PRACTICAL DRESSES FOR THE MISS

1778—Misses' and Small Women's Coat: Convertible Collar; Long Two-Seam Sleeves with Slight Fulness at the Top which may be Shrunken Out; Three-Piece Gathered Skirt. 4 sizes, 14 to 20 years.   Price, 25 cents.

1744—Misses and Small Women's Dress: Blouse in Regulation or Middy Style; Lower edge with plaits drawn out about 2⅛ yards. The pattern is cut in 4 sizes, from 14 to 20 years.   Price, 25 cents.

1785—Misses' and Small Women's Slip-On Dress: Closed on the Shoulders; Collarless or Open Neck. Lower edge about 1½ yards. The pattern is cut in 4 sizes, from 14 to 20 years.   Price, 25 cents.

1341—Misses' and Small Women's Tucked Dress: to be Slipped Over the Head; Collar in Two Outlines; Two-Piece Straight Gathered Skirt. Lower edge about 1¾ yards. 4 sizes, 14 to 20 years.   Price, 25 cents.

1752—Misses' and Small Women's Dress: Separate Two-Piece Skirt. For the design illustrated, use transfer pattern 10437. Lower edge about 1½ yards. 4 sizes, 14 to 20 years. Price, 25 cts.

1759—Misses' and Small Women's Dress: Back Extending Over the Shoulders; Back Panel which may be Omitted. Lower edge about 1⅝ yards. 4 sizes, 14 to 20 years   Price, 25 cents.

1782—Misses' and Small Women's Dress: Slip-On Blouse; Two-Piece Skirt. For the smocking design use transfer pattern 4478. Lower edge about 1½ yards. 4 sizes, 14 to 20 years.   25 cts.

1776—Misses' and Small Women's Dress: Convertible Collar; Long Dart-Fitted Sleeve or Three-Quarter Length Sleeve. Lower edge about 1⅝ yards. 4 sizes, 14 to 20 years. Price, 25 cts.

ATTRACTIVE DRESSES AND COATS FOR WINTER

1763—Girls' and Juniors' Dress: High or Open Neck; Long or Short Sleeves; Overblouse which may be Omitted; Plaited or Gathered Straight Skirt. For the smocking design illustrated on figure, use Standard transfer pattern 4478. This pattern is cut in 6 sizes from 6 to 16 years. Price, 20 cents.

1771—Little Girls' Empire Dress: High or Open Neck; Long or Short Sleeves; Straight Gathered Skirt. The pattern is cut in 8 sizes from 1 to 8 years. This little Empire dress with an attractive collar is especially becoming. The sleeves and straight gathered skirt are features. It is very easy to make. Price, 20 cents.

1777—Girls' and Juniors' Dress: High or Open Neck; Long Sleeves in Two Styles at the Wrist or Short Sleeves Sewed into the Smock or Body; Plaited or Gathered Straight Skirt. For the smocking design, use Standard transfer pattern 4478. This pattern is cut in 7 sizes from 4 to 16 years. Price, 20 cents.

1760—Little Girls' Coat: Convertible Collar in Two Styles; One-Seam Raglan Sleeves. This pattern is cut in 6 sizes from 2 to 12 years. This coat with contrasting collar, cuffs and pockets is very serviceable for the cold winter days that are coming. Price, 20 cents.

1770—Girls' and Juniors' Dress: High or Open Neck; Large Collar in Two Outlines; Long or Short Sleeves; Straight Gathered Skirt with or without the Tucks. This pattern is cut in 6 sizes from 6 to 16 years. The tucks make this dress very smart. The collar is an attractive feature. Price, 20 cents.

1765—Girls' and Juniors' Slip-On Dress: Closed on the Shoulders; Collarless, Round or Square Neck; Long or Short Sleeves; Straight Gathered Skirt with or without the Tucks. This pattern is cut in 6 sizes from 6 to 16 years. An unusual design. Price, 20 cents.

1754—Girls' and Juniors' Dress: High or Open Neck; Long Dart-Fitted Sleeve or Short Sleeve; Slip-On Overblouse which may be Omitted; Plaited or Gathered Straight Skirt. The pattern is cut in 6 sizes from 6 to 16 years. This design is very becoming to a little girl. The plaited skirt is a feature. Price, 20 cents.

1772—Girls' and Juniors' Empire Coat: in Two Lengths; Convertible Collar; Two-Seam Sleeves with Slight Fulness at the Top which may be Shrunken Out. This pattern is cut in 7 sizes from 4 to 16 years. An unusually pretty coat is this. Velveteen, serge and gabardine are suitable materials for it. Price, 20 cents.

1771

1763

1777

1760

The Designer
STYLES ARE REPRODUCED BY
Standard Patterns

1770

1765

1772

1772

1754

1770   1774   1765   1209   1774   1317

Other views and descriptions are shown on page 15.

FOR THE SWEET GIRL GRADUATE

JANUARY brings to mind mid-season graduation and confirmation This time of the year all girls need pretty white dresses and outfits suited for both of these happy occasions. Dresses are very important, for they must be dainty, simple, and yet not require much work. The soft tub materials such as batiste, lawn, dimity, nainsook, dotted swiss, and voile are very pretty and any of the designs illustrated above would be excellent. Deep tucks add a great value to the plain gathered skirt. The long panel is extremely graceful and pretty especially when eyelets and buttons trim it continuing the line of the belt. Round, square and V necks are popular and both the deep and shallow openings are used. Fine frillings and edgings finish the sleeves, the trimming pieces and the panels. The bolero type of dress is always graceful, and when combined with flouncing it makes a very simple little dress. Sashes may be of ribbon, silk, cords or picot-edged organdy.

In the panels at the lower corners of this page are the little necessities and accessories which add distinction to these occasions. The net veil may be shirred into a cap-like arrangement with trimmings of silk roses and chin strap. Five rows of fine net ruffles are a pretty neck trimming and with two rows at the wrist any plain net dress would be sufficiently dressy.

For gifts there are the plain or embroidered silk stockings, pretty ribbons, long or short kid gloves and soft dainty collars. A white kid prayer-book with a white silk ribbon book-mark would make many a little girl very happy.

For the girl who is graduating there are many things such as soft fichus of point desprit with cuffs to match. A heavy satin sash with two rows of fringe is quite new and adds much to a voile or batiste dress. Both low-heeled and high-heeled kid and satin pumps are being worn. White satin garters bedecked with rosebuds make pretty gifts. Any dainty lace handkerchiefs will be appreciated by a girl at this time of the year. A party or slipper bag of soft silk lined with a bright color will be just the thing to carry one's handkerchief or slippers when going out for the evening. Such accessories and little additions as are shown here are easy to obtain in the shops and add much to the wardrobe of a girl.